Perspectives of Quality in Adult Learning

Also available from Continuum:

Analysing Teaching–Learning Interactions in Higher Education – Paul Ashwin

Consumer Experience of Higher Education – Deidre McArdle-Clinton

Developing Student Criticality in Higher Education – Brenda Johnson, Peter Ford, Rosamond Mitchell and Florence Myles

Dimensions of Expertise – Christopher Winch

Educational Doctorates and the Transformation of Knowledge – Alison Taysum

Higher Education and the Public Good – Jon Nixon

Leadership in Post Compulsory Education – Marian Iszatt-White, David Randell, Mark Rouncefield and Conner Graham

Learning Communities and Imagined Social Capital – Jocey Quinn

Lifelong Learning and Development – Julia Preece

Staff–Student Partnerships in Higher Education – Sabine Little

Vocational and Professional Capability – Gerard Lum

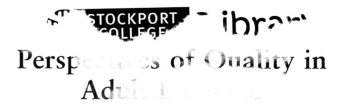
Perspectives of Quality in Adult Learning

Peter Boshier

continuum

Continuum International Publishing Group
The Tower Building, 11 York Road, London SE1 7NX
80 Maiden Lane, Suite 704, New York NY 10038

www.continuumbooks.com

© Peter Boshier 2006

First published 2006
This paperback edition published 2011

British Library Cataloguing-in-Publication Data
A catalogue record for this book is available from the British Library.

ISBN: 978-0-8264-8127-6 (hardback)
       978-1-4411-3931-3 (paperback)

Library of Congress Cataloging-in-Publication Data
A catalog record for this book is available from the Library of Congress.

Typeset by Aarontype Limited, Easton, Bristol

Contents

To Thea

Foreword

Adult education is an under-researched field in this country. Judgements about learning programmes are mostly summative, and learning that does not lead to accredited outcomes is given low priority in current policy. My study focused on adult part-time learners and their tutors, and sought to discover the meaning of quality in the adult learning process. It provides evidence of the extent to which adult students, by accepting some responsibility for the quality of their current learning and drawing constructively upon the experiences of previous learning, may be competent to be recognized as arbiters of their learning quality.

My research considers the characteristics and experiences of adults as learners and how they contribute to the interactive process of learning, and research findings present perceptions of quality from adult learners and their tutors through qualitative and quantitative data.

The strong commitment some adults give to their learning is reflected in levels of participation, and the responsibility some accept for its quality. Tutors are regarded as being the prime source of quality, with two thirds of students in this survey placing much reliance on tutors for all aspects of their learning. In contrast, one third show themselves to be highly active, participatory students, taking at least some responsibility for their learning.

There are those who will be critical of the focus of this book, because it does not accord with current government priorities of work-related, vocational and accredited learning, principally for young people, but I believe that the learning described herein is important, not only to the individual learner, but also to our society.

My findings have implications for policy-makers, practitioners and participants, more immediately in relation to requirements of the Common Inspection Framework, but also more widely for adult learning in a range of contexts, and I am very grateful to the many adult learners and tutors involved for their willingness and enthusiasm to be a part of this study.

Peter Boshier
August, 2005

List of Figures and Tables

Figures

Tables

List of Acronyms

ACACE	Advisory Council for Adult Continuing Education
AE	Adult Education
ALI	Adult Learning Inspectorate
AMA	Association of Metropolitan Authorities
CIF	Common Inspection Framework
CIT	Computing and Information Technology
CLAIT	Computer Literacy and Information Technology
CRWBL	Centre for Research on the Wider Benefits of Learning
CVCP	Committee of Vice Chancellors and Principals
DES	Department for Education and Science
DfE	Department for Education
DfEE	Department for Education and Employment
DfES	Department for Education and Skills
DTI	Department for Trade and Industry
DTP	Desk-top Publishing
FE	Further Education
FEFC	Further Education Funding Council
FTE	Full-Time Equivalent
GCSE	General Certificate of Secondary Education
HMSO	Her Majesty's Stationery Office
LEA	Local Education Authority
LSC	Learning and Skills Council
NAGCELL	Natinal Advisory Group for Continuing Education and Lifelong Learning
NATFHE	National Association of Teachers in Further and Higher Education
NFER	National Foundation for Educational Research
NIAE	National Institute of Adult Education
NIACE	National Institute of Adult Continuing Education
ODPM	Office of the Deputy Prime Minister
Ofsted	Office for Standards in Education
RARPA	Recognizing and Recording Progress and Achievement in non-accredited learning

SRHE   Society for Research into Higher Education
TEC   Training and Enterprise Council
TQM   Total Quality Management
UDACE   Unit for the Development of Adult Continuing Education
UNESCO   United Nations Educational, Scientific and Cultural
          Organization
WEA   Workers' Educational Association

Introduction

Education for adults, however defined, and for different reasons, has been high on the political agenda for many decades, but definitions have varied over that time. After the 1914–18 War, it was considered necessary to rebuild society, and adult education was seen as 'a permanent national necessity, an inseparable aspect of citizenship, and therefore should be universal and lifelong' (Ministry of Reconstruction Report 1919: 5). The Interim Report, which preceded the Final Report, recognized that

> ... the motive which impels men and women to seek education is partly the wish for fuller personal development. It arises from the desire for knowledge, for self-expression, for the satisfaction of intellectual, aesthetic and spiritual needs, and for a fuller life. It is based upon a claim for the recognition of human personality. This desire is not confined to any class of society, but is to be found among people of every social grade (Ministry of Reconstruction Interim Report 1918: 54)

Towards the end of World War II, the 1944 *Education Act* also recognized the importance of the education of adults, by placing a duty upon every local education authority

> to secure that the facilities for ... further education provided for their area include adequate facilities for recreation and social and physical training ...
> (*Education Act* 1944: Ch 31, 53i).

By 1944, the strength of the legislative language had reduced, but the further education of adults remained part of government policy, even though adult education and further education were combined as 'further education'.

By 1973, publication of the Russell Report was seen by adult educators as the beginning of a brave new world for adult learning, especially for 'non-vocational' education, and its publication was celebrated widely. Alas, as with many reports from Committees of Enquiry, Russell's many recommendations were only implemented in very small part. One major recommendation of the Russell Committee was for a National Development Council for Adult Education, which was not to be, but four years later the government agreed to set up an Advisory Council for Adult and Continuing Education (ACACE). This council published a large number of important reports and discussion documents, one of which advocated a comprehensive system of continuing education

> a conjunction of policies, funding, provision and attitudes, which effect changes in all the present educational sectors to the advantage of a rapidly growing number of adult learners ... which makes it increasingly possible for more and more adults to continue their education (ACACE 1982: vii).

The coherent system advocated by ACACE was intended to seek equal emphasis for all adult learning opportunities. As I indicate elsewhere in this book, the subsequent funding policies of the Further Education Funding Council (FEFC) and the Learning and Skills Council (LSC) have done little to reduce the divisions between either further and adult education, or full- and part-time adult learning, or between 'vocational' and 'non-vocational' education.

Adult education remains an under-researched field in this country, and current emphasis is on adult learning that is 'vocational', work-related and leads to an accredited outcome. The encouragement, provision and funding of a more liberal adult education, that Russell and ACACE referred to, comes very low in policy and funding priorities, and much provision has been cut as a result of funding reductions.

The content of this book is drawn from a PhD thesis, and my study focuses on the views of adult part-time learners and their tutors, about the meaning of quality, responsibility and participation in adult learning from their different perspectives. It provides evidence of the ways in which some adult learners consciously apply previous experiences to enhance each new learning episode, and how large numbers of learners rely upon the guidance and direction of their tutors.

Set within the political context of lifelong learning policy, the book considers the characteristics and experiences of adults as learners and their contribution to the interactive process of learning. The meaning of quality in learning is explored, and adult learners and their tutors describe what it means to them, who is responsible for it and how learners participate in their learning experiences.

The strong commitment some adults give to their learning is reflected in levels of participation, and the responsibility some accept for its quality. Tutors are regarded as being the prime source of quality, with two thirds of students in this survey placing much reliance on tutors for all aspects of their learning. In contrast, one third show themselves to be highly active, participatory students, taking at least some responsibility for their learning.

Evidence of high-quality adult education can be found in abundance, but practitioners and learners alike must do more to articulate the value of their learning, and to argue for its funding and retention.

My research findings have implications for policy makers, practitioners and participants, more immediately in relation to requirements of the Common Inspection Framework, but also more widely for adult learning in a range of contexts.

1 The Search for Quality

Education is the best economic policy we have.

(DfEE 1998: 7)

The distinction between economically useful education and mere leisure activity is false ... the essence of education is the improvement of the mind.

(*The Times* 1991)

The search for quality – an economic imperative

Quality and standards in all public services have received close political attention in recent years from successive governments, brought about, in part, by pressures from global economic markets and their effects on the domestic economy. Goods and services have been subjected to careful scrutiny in order to ensure that the highest standards are being set and maintained, and that effective use is being made of public funds. Attempts have been made to define and guarantee levels of service, standards and quality through charters, mission statements, service contracts and the like. The efficiency and effectiveness of management of public services, including education, is also closely monitored in order that standards, quality and value for money may be assured.

In the case of education, however, views differ between the need to see it as a provision that brings economic benefits to the country, and as the opportunity for each individual citizen to maximize his/her potential and to gain fulfilment, as demonstrated by the two contrasting quotations at the head of this chapter. The modern economic imperative 'needs to be matched by a democratic imperative which argues that a learning society worthy of the name ought to deliver social cohesion and social justice to all citizens as well as economic prosperity' (Coffield and Williamson 1997: 2–3), and it is insufficient to see education as no more than a means to an economic end. Individuals have different priorities for learning at different times in their lives and, for some, learning has little connection with work or with economic benefits, but is undertaken solely for the pleasure and fulfilment it brings (see Chapters 7, 8 and 9).

Quality and how it is identified in education

The need to ensure and maintain quality and high standards applies as much to education as to any other public service, and it is reasonable to argue that the quest to achieve and maintain quality in education is driven by varying, and sometime opposing, forces. Government targets to achieve certain outcomes, such as the raising of participation levels or attainment rates, have to some degree been successful but these can be countered by constraints resulting from the reduction or withdrawal of funding when targets are not subsequently met, or criticisms that increased participation levels, without additional funding, may actually reduce quality – although it is to *standards*, not quality, that such observations generally refer.

> Too often we hear that widening participation leads to lower standards.
>
> (Layer 2002: 16)

Often, references to *quality* in education are actually based on *standards* and *outcomes* – for example, examination results, demonstrations of acquired skills, measurable productivity or the effects of a value-added component in teaching and learning. In these ways educational services are evaluated and their effectiveness assessed. The practice of using outcomes as a basis of judging achievement enables useful comparisons to be made between institutions or groups of individuals, and the so-called 'league tables' published on the performance of schools, colleges and universities help parents or students to make informed choices, at least about which institutions appear to offer the best examination results. Such data, however, say little about the culture of the institution, or about the services and facilities it may offer its student body as part of a learning environment. More recently 'value-added' methods are addressing further aspects of the learning experience, and proving to provide important additional information (see Chapter 6). This approach begins with a level of prior attainment, adds course input and measures output, and has enabled more dimensions of the learning experience to be judged at local and national levels, comparisons to be made, for example, between students' rate of progress in relation to their capabilities and differences in performance within a single institution to be identified. This brief description, however, does not do justice to the extensive developments of value-added methods.

Less often are judgements made about the *process* of teaching and learning – the interactive exchange between teacher and learner that is the essence of a good educational experience – or about the quality of that process from the learner's perspective. This limitation is further highlighted in the case of learning programmes that do not lead to accredited outcomes, and for which alternative criteria for making judgements are not immediately evident. How then can the quality of learning be assessed when normal outcome-based criteria cannot be applied, or may not be relevant? My attempts to answer this question presented me with epistemological and methodological challenges. Our knowledge about adult learning is based largely on data concerning full-time students, principally those following accredited courses and using the outcome-based criteria referred to above. Very few data seem to be available regarding quality of the learning process, particularly from the individual's perspective and especially so far as it concerns part-time learners and their tutors.

It is, of course, not unreasonable that the validation of examination standards should be made by those external to a learning group, but judgements on the quality of the learning *process* can best be made by participants. My research provides an alternative approach to defining quality in adult learning by enabling the voices of individual participants in the adult learning transaction to be heard, and my findings show that some of these participants are competent to be acknowledged as arbiters of quality in their own learning. Data were obtained from a sample population of 2,035 (1,784 adult students and 251 tutors) in the east of England who have provided views on what is quality in the learning process. By focusing on adults learning on a part-time basis through a wide-ranging curriculum which includes 'vocational' and 'non-vocational', accredited and non-accredited programmes, the book offers further dimensions to our knowledge of adult learning (see Chapters 3 and 5).

Timing and relevance

The Labour Government's strategy of lifelong learning has given a higher profile to all education and training and, as suggested above, this has several drivers, of which global economic competition is probably the most powerful.

> Learning is the key to prosperity – for each of us as individuals, as well as for the nation as a whole. Investment in human capital will be the foundation of success in the knowledge-based economy of the twenty-first century.
> (DfEE 1998: 7)

One can recognize the economic pressures in such statements, but human capital should imply more than just a contribution to a *knowledge-based economy* and, I believe, more emphasis is required on the human dimensions of learning. Some education and training for adults has benefited from increased status and resources, and the focus on lifelong learning may provide the prospect of a new lease of life for the much older concept of adult education, although the signs thus far are not very encouraging (see Chapters 2, 3, 5 and 10). Prior to publication of the *Learning and Skills Act*, 2000 (DfES 2000), and during the regime of the Training and Enterprise Councils and the Further Education Funding Council, education and training for adults were seen principally as being related to the work needs of individuals and to the economic benefit of the country and were thus, essentially, to do with 'work-long' or, as Jarvis would have it, *'work-life'* learning (Jarvis 2001: 31). The *Learning and Skills Act* (see Chapter 2) reflects the government's policy that individuals shall have access to appropriate education and training, at a time when it is relevant for the individual and in a form that is suitable for his/her requirements. The Act, which established the Learning and Skills Councils as the means by which the requirements of the Act would be carried out, emphasises the importance of providing learning opportunities for adults that are relevant to their needs:

> The [Learning & Skills] Council must secure the provision of reasonable facilities for:
> (a) education (other than higher education) suitable to the requirements of persons who have attained the age of 19,
> (b) training suitable to the requirements of such persons,
> (c) organized leisure-time occupation connected with such education, and
> (d) organized leisure-time occupation connected with such training.
> (extract from DfES 2000: 2, Section 3.1)

but, in practice, work-related learning is given a much higher priority than non-accredited, so-called 'leisure' learning. The term 'leisure', although perhaps accurate in the sense that much learning is enjoyed during periods of leisure time – that is, time that is free from work requirements – can be interpreted to imply that it is learning undertaken when nothing more serious (more worthy?) is available; 'the understanding of leisure as being something which is uncreative and of little value' (Jarvis 1995a: 40). This is echoed when certain subjects are denigrated anecdotally as not being serious learning, such as flower arranging and some crafts. Given the global pressures referred to above, a priority for work-related learning is not difficult to understand, but if lifelong learning is to mean what its name suggests, then *all* learning needs to be valued for its specific contribution to the life of each citizen and to our learning society. That some learning may be less easy to measure and assess should not mean that it is ignored or denigrated. Nor does current policy (despite the wording of the *Learning and Skills Act*) acknowledge the advantages to society of citizens who are stimulated and fulfilled by learning that is relevant to *their* needs, and who, perhaps as a result of that enhancement to their lives are more independent, develop wider social circles and may require less support from social and medical services – although this last point is not easy to quantify. It may be argued, also, that these experiences contribute towards another government priority – that of active citizenship (see below). Further information of this type has already emerged and will be forthcoming, as the Centre for Research into the Wider Benefits of Learning (CRWBL) (see Chapter 2) continues to research different aspects of learning, e.g. parental perspectives, family learning and health.

Evidence of the importance of adult education to the self-esteem of learners is shown in data in Chapter 7, and echoed by the findings of Green and Preston:

> Respondents frequently refer to the effects of their current and previous learning on social aspects of their lives and provide accounts of how different forms of learning have increased social competencies, widened networks, enhanced self-esteem and helped shape identities.
>
> (Green and Preston 2000: 14)

What remains underdeveloped, therefore, is a theory regarding quality in adult learning that is not specifically work-related; which may or may not lead to an externally accredited outcome; over which the participants have more control; and the quality of which process they are themselves arbiters, if shown to be competent to be so. This, in turn, raises questions about how quality can be measured in non-accredited learning, the subject of research, for example, by the Learning and Skills Development Agency, and previously by John Daines on behalf of the Workers' Educational Association.

> As adult educators, we have long maintained that students should take responsibility for their own learning, but we have not done enough to involve them in agreeing the learning objectives of their course of study.
>
> (Daines 1994: 12)

More recently, some exciting developments have taken place to gain recognition for a system to measure progress and achievement in non-accredited learning. Recognizing and Recording Progress and Achievement in non-accredited learning (RARPA) has been developed by the

Learning and Skills Development Agency, and is rapidly gaining credibility across the sector.

This book argues that the needs of part-time learners following either accredited or non-accredited courses should be given serious consideration as well as those of full-time learners engaged in work-related education and training. Whilst presenting the views of the research participants, the book also supports the view that adult learners bring to the learning environment a wealth of experience which will contribute to, and often enhance, the quality of new learning (Jarvis 1995a). Evidence is included that shows some adult learners are very realistic judges of their learning and supports the proposition that they can be recognized as arbiters of its quality. For this reason, the book also argues for the retention and support of liberal adult education (see Chapter 3), used as it is by many adults as a gateway into further learning, both accredited and non-accredited, 'vocational' and 'non-vocational', and which is the source from which some research data in this study have been drawn.

My study was located within the government's policy context of lifelong learning, explained more fully in Chapter 2, in which adult learning of all kinds has become a dominant policy objective, and in which there is a stated desire to stimulate a demand for lifelong learning. Because of this, it is particularly relevant to look at the value of students' experience of learning and what, for them, is quality in learning. Quality, responsibility and participation in adult, part-time learning are, therefore, the focus of the book. The conceptual framework which underpins the whole study is outlined in Chapter 3, and the methodology and selected research methods are explained in Chapter 4.

Further explanation of the terms 'adult', 'adulthood' and 'adult education', with a consideration of andragogy and its relevance to the debate, may also be found in Chapter 5. The meanings of quality in everyday life are considered in Chapter 6 and compared with ways in which the term is used in the research data. Chapters 7, 8 and 9 are devoted to summaries, descriptions, synthesis, analysis and comparisons of qualitative and quantitative fieldwork data, and Chapter 10 offers conclusions, implications and indications of possible further research in this area.

It is my hope that this book adds to our knowledge of adult teaching and learning at a time when all learning for adults is receiving more attention as part of the lifelong learning agenda. It makes a contribution to the lifelong learning debate by providing evidence from adult learners, many of whom are undertaking learning that is not related to work or to national economic benefit, and regard the continuance of their learning as life-enhancing and essential to their well-being. The study ends by arguing that no government should ignore the contribution that part-time learning makes within a lifelong learning strategy, and that it should receive a greater degree of recognition and support than it attracts at present.

2 Lifelong Learning: The Current Policy Context for Adult Education

> There can be no more critical issue for the future of our economy, our social cohesion and the development of the potential of each and every one of us, than the nation's investment in lifelong learning.
>
> (Labour Party 1997: 2)

> Learning offers excitement and the opportunity for discovery. It stimulates enquiring minds and nourishes our souls. It takes us in directions we never expected; sometimes changing our lives ... [it] contributes to social cohesion and fosters a sense of belonging, responsibility and identity.
>
> (DfEE 1998: 10–11)

> Lifelong learning can enable people to play a full part in developing their talent, the potential of their family, and the capacity of the community in which they live and work. It can and must nurture a love for learning.
>
> (DfEE 1999: 3)

Introduction

As explained in Chapter 1, my study was set within the context of the government's policy of lifelong learning. This current chapter contextualizes adult education within that policy, and argues that alongside the challenging strategies being established to ensure a widening of learning opportunities for adults, so far as they relate to their work needs, other areas of learning that affect adults remain largely underdeveloped. These are to do with recognition of the other benefits of learning which are important to so many: informal and experiential learning, including the learning experiences of daily living; and learning gained through formal learning programmes which may not necessarily lead to accredited outcomes. That said, however, recent developments by the Centre for Research on the Wider Benefits of Learning (CRWBL) acknowledge that learning is to do with more than just the acquisition of qualifications, important as they are. Adult education forms part of the lifelong learning agenda and contributes to the development of our learning society – a society which, hopefully, will be so organized as to provide maximum learning opportunities for each of its members and also to value a broad range of that learning (Field and Leicester 2000). Some provisions of the *Learning and Skills Act* (DfES 2000), which have profound implications for adult learning, are explained, and particular references are made to the requirements of the Common Inspection Framework (CIF), by which the standards of education and training for adults are currently assessed, and with which some of the outcomes from this research are compared. Finally, the chapter argues for a wider recognition of adult education and the ways in which it supports the lifelong learning philosophy by acting as a gateway to further learning for many adults.

Lifelong learning – an emerging policy

Publication of the Green Paper, *The Learning Age: A Renaissance for a New Britain* (DfEE 1998) gave indications of the government's thinking across a range of learning issues and paved the way for many relevant initiatives. In his Foreword, the Secretary of State for Education and Employment wrote encouragingly of the potential for human development and growth that a more open and reflective approach to learning would offer:

> As well as securing our economic future, learning has a wider contribution. It helps make ours a civilised society, develops the spiritual side of our lives and promotes active citizenship. Learning enables people to play a full part in their community. It strengthens the family, the neighbourhood and consequently the nation. It helps us fulfil our potential and opens doors to a love of music, art and literature. That is why we value learning for its own sake as well as for the equality of opportunity it brings.   (DfEE 1998: 7)

As is often the case, however, in government education documents, the encouraging tone of the Secretary of State's foreword was not sustained by subsequent actions. The results of this wide-ranging review included a number of proposals and developments, and it was followed, in 1999, with *Learning to Succeed* – a White Paper (DfEE 1999) which set out more ambitious proposals, generally to take effect from 2001, and which formed the basis of the *Learning and Skills Act*, 2000 (see below). These documents together produced a number of key initiatives, which included Individual Learning Accounts and an Adult and Community Learning Fund. The most important initiative from these documents was the establishment of the Learning and Skills Council (LSC). As described elsewhere in this book, the Council, and its 47 local councils, is having a huge impact on the provision and funding of post-compulsory learning.

The Learning Age and *Learning to Succeed* had been preceded by *Learning for the Twenty-first Century* (1997), the first publication from the National Advisory Group for Continuing Education and Lifelong Learning (NAGCELL), which provided a wide-ranging review of lifelong learning opportunities and possibilities, but which paid closer attention to adult education, to learning in the community and in the home, and which called for the government to 'seek to construct a popular and coherent vision of a nation-wide learning culture for the many and not the few, with shared responsibilities for its achievement' (NAGCELL 1997: 24). The report referred, for example, to the need to develop collaborative arrangements and formal partnerships between providers; the need to improve information, advice and guidance for adult learning; the need to embrace new technologies whenever possible; and the continuing problems of social exclusion. The report also referred to the inadequate levels of data available on lifelong learning. The second NAGCELL document, *Creating Learning Cultures* (NAGCELL 1999), developed the theme of learning cultures and emphasized among others, the contributions made by family learning, subsequently to be placed high on the funding agenda by the Learning and Skills Council.

These documents demonstrated how the government's approach to education and training was 'shaped by its responses to globalization and its view of the role of the State in economic and social policy' (Hodgson and Spours 1999: 11). In responding to the increasing pressures of globalization, government policy has endeavoured to move on several fronts. It has encouraged greater participation in learning (e.g. Learn Direct); it has encouraged greater degrees of cooperation between providers (e.g. Lifelong Learning Partnerships); it has encouraged and promoted the importance of information technology through a range of initiatives, including with schools and small businesses; it has sought to improve the skills base of our work force; and it has promoted the importance of citizenship and of family learning. It has also, by establishing the Learning and Skills Council, endeavoured to exercise greater control over the provision, funding and accountability of education and training. This accountability is assured by inspections of learning providers carried out by a partnership of the Office for Standards in Education (Ofsted) and the Adult Learning Inspectorate (ALI), based upon a Common Inspection Framework (CIF), to which further reference is made below. Despite the rhetoric of some of the documents referred to above, however, emphasis remains on work-related, economically beneficial learning and training, which is only part (albeit an important part) of educational opportunities in a learning society.

Lifelong learning is seen by the government as a central strategy for ensuring the future prosperity of the UK, as well as for developing a more just and inclusive society.

> Our vision is to build a new culture of learning which will underpin national competitiveness and personal prosperity, encourage creativity and innovation, and help build a cohesive society   (DfEE 1999: 6).

Publication of the *Learning and Skills Act* (DfES 2000) paved the way for profound changes in the education and training of adults, and provided the framework within which the government's policy of lifelong learning is being developed. By giving learning throughout life a high profile on the political agenda, the British Government has endeavoured to revitalize thinking about all education and training, especially post-school, although if lifelong learning is to become all-embracing then the schooling of young people must be seen as an integral part of a system that is genuinely lifelong. Until the late 1980s earlier developments had produced a plethora of largely uncoordinated provision for the education and training of adults, with much wasteful overlapping and confusing provision.

> ... many of those who commented recommended a bold programme of change in national and local arrangements. They confirmed our views that current arrangements provided an insufficient focus on quality, failed to give men and women the support they need, and were too provider driven
> (DfEE 1999: 3)

The lifelong learning policy attempts to forge all education and training into a coherent, inclusive and holistic system which supports and encourages learners at whatever point they have reached in their lives. Indeed lifelong learning has become central to the political philosophy, economic strategy and social policy of the Labour Government (Hodgson and Spours 1999). But, as learning is central to economic prosperity and to the health of our society, the achievement of economic goals and social cohesion are intertwined (Jarvis 2001), and 'lifelong inclusive learning becomes meaningless rhetoric if money is not available to make such a grand project a reality' (Kennedy 1997: 9).

The effects of globalization on the economy, the rapid and hugely significant developments in technology and the associated transformation of labour markets, 'have made education and training central instruments of economic and social policy-making' (Hodgson and Spours 1999: 5):

> Education is the key to economic success, social cohesion and active citizenship. Our future national prosperity depends on the skills and abilities of our people. In a rapidly changing, technologically advanced and

increasingly competitive global economy, Britain needs a world-class system of education and training. The regular updating of skills and knowledge has become essential to maintaining and enhancing productivity and security in the workplace.   (Labour Party 1997: 2)

Although critics of New Labour may argue, with some justification, that 'lifelong learning existed long before the emergence of our current interest in it, and would continue to occur even if educators ignored it' (Cropley 1980: 1), the policy initiatives that proposed to draw together these elements and to create from them a more structured, clearly defined and coherent system, supported with funding and political will, were not implemented. Focus remains, in my view, less on the coherence of a holistic scheme and more on those aspects of learning that are driven by economic considerations. 'Lifelong learning' is an attractive slogan, but it is insufficient to use terminology without adequate description. The importance of lifelong learning (whatever it is) is recognized well beyond the boundaries of the UK. 1996 was designated as the European Year of Lifelong Learning and the European Community identified three main thrusts that its member countries were encouraged to promote:

- the advantages of lifelong learning to individuals;
- effective links between businesses and education providers;
- the European dimension of lifelong leaning.   (Tuckett 1997: 4)

These three main approaches were to be implemented through eight themes, which include:

- the value of high quality general education as preparation for lifelong learning;
- vocational training to increase the qualification base; motivating un-represented groups towards lifelong learning;
- promoting to parents the importance to their children of education and of lifelong learning.   (Tuckett 1997: 14)

The importance of lifelong learning was later reiterated by the Group of 8:

The challenge every country faces is how to become a learning society and ensure that its citizens are equipped with the knowledge, skills and qualifications they will need for the next century. Economies and societies are increasingly knowledge-based ... everyone should be encouraged and enabled to continue learning throughout their lives, not just in the years of compulsory schooling.   (Group of 8, 1999)

These expressions of encouragement and intent, as in the UK, are welcome so far as they go, but detailed implementation remains far behind theo-retical aspirations.

Lifelong learning – theory and context

So lifelong learning is not a new concept. 'Adults have always learnt, for learning is an important dimension of the human condition. They have learnt in the course of their daily lives but they have also purposively sought out knowledge and skills, and have been prompted to learn by curiosity and in response to necessity' (Commission on Adult Education 1985: Introduction). Plato, in 2000 BC, made reference to the notion of learning throughout life (Longworth 1999), and 'prior to the middle of the nineteenth century, learning was accepted without question as a life-long activity' (Houle 1984: ix), although at that time for small numbers of privileged people.

In the post-war years the need to rebuild applied not just to industry, but also to society, social values and the important elements of citizenship, which are again being revived in the early twenty-first century. Our capacity to adapt and learn 'can be almost as unconscious as breathing' (Field 2000: vii) and a shift in emphasis by the present government from 'education' to 'learning' is significant in promoting the value of all learning throughout the individual's lifetime. The new emphasis on *learning*, rather than on education or training, recognizes that learning is not limited to certain specific stages of our lives, or particular contexts. What is different about lifelong learning is the policy context in which it has now been placed – in this country by the government and, on behalf of other countries, by the International Commission on Education for the 21st Century in its report to UNESCO, which recognizes it as one of the keys to the twenty-first century. The Commission sees lifelong learning as forming 'four pillars as the foundations of learning – learning to live; learning to know; learning to do; and learning to be' (UNESCO 1999: 22–23). This philosophy aims to bring the different dimensions of the life of an ordinary citizen into one all-embracing theory that links daily living, with an understanding of how and why we learn, with the skills acquired from learning, and with a better understanding about being a citizen and a member of a learning society.

Despite current rhetoric, there are not yet sufficient signs that lifelong learning policy in the UK is moving towards the fully inclusive and all-embracing system that it professes to promote. Lifelong learning needs to break free from the constraints of formal education which makes learning exclusive, and from vocational training which is inevitably narrowly focused on current technologies. It needs to help people engage with the 'dilemmas, contradictions, doubts and enthusiasms' which are both at the centre of human lives and of human knowledge itself.

As suggested in Chapter 1, within the context of Labour's lifelong learning agenda, the emphasis on learning for adults is principally work-related, underpinning the need for citizens to be educated, trained and retrained in order to maintain employment, and for the country to be able to compete in a global economy. It is part of the 'emerging powerful paradigm' (Hodgson and Spours 1999: 8), which has become known as *The Third Way* (Giddens 1998), in which people and business are equipped 'to thrive in the competitive economic environment created by globalisation' (Blair 1999, cited in Hodgson and Spours 1999: 8). The impressive number of initiatives in the government's lifelong learning policy points towards a more wide-ranging set of learning opportunities for all citizens which will add immeasurably to the range of available learning opportunities and qualifications and, in the government's view, move towards making Britain a more competitive and educated society.

Since the principal focus of these initiatives is on work-related and work-based learning, however, a recognition of the other benefits of learning beyond the purely instrumental or vocational remains under-developed, since for many individuals, the value of their learning is not related to any vocational or work context. Many of these individuals are represented by the data in Chapter 7 and I refer below to some of the distinctive aspects of adult education which show that its philosophy and practices have much to contribute to the lifelong learning agenda.

There is a need to move beyond the level where members of a society 'are educated only to a level at which they may be exploited', to a level where individuals are 'sufficiently educated for its complexities' (Hoggart 1995: 226, cited in Williamson, 1998: 2). Lifelong learning is meant to close the gap, which exists both within and between all societies in the modern world, between the 'learning-rich'; and the 'learning-poor' (Williamson 1998: 1).

The Learning and Skills Council

As indicated above, one provision of the *Learning and Skills Act* (DfES 2000) was the creation of a Learning and Skills Council to oversee all post-compulsory education and training, other than higher education. The work of this council is supported by 47 local learning and skills councils, and inspection is carried out by a partnership of Ofsted (the Office for Standards in Education) and an Adult Learning Inspectorate (the ALI). The criteria for inspection are summarized in a Common Inspection Framework (ALI/Ofsted 2001), which assesses all aspects of learning, teaching, resourcing, management and governance of providing bodies in order to ensure that the individual learner is placed at the heart of their philosophy and practice. Creation of the LSC resulted in a higher profile being given to all adult learning. For the first time, by placing responsibility for provision, funding *and* inspection in the hands of one agency, the government has given enormous power to the LSC which can be seen as a dangerous precedent, but which could yield considerable benefits for all learning, if managed in partnership with providers and users of learning services.

The Common Inspection Framework (CIF) is designed to ensure that all aspects of providers' activity are focused on the needs of each individual learner; to ensure that providers relate the planning, delivery and assessment of courses with the management and use of resources and the creation of a holistic approach to learning provision. The terminology of the CIF is designed to enable inspectors to form judgements about the standard and quality of learning by considering, for example, not just whether students are learning, but 'the extent to which learners make significant progress towards fulfilling their goals and potential', and 'the extent to which learners develop attitudes and skills necessary to maintain lifelong learning, including the capacity to work independently and collaboratively' (ALI/Ofsted 2001: 7). Inspectors' judgements are, therefore, to do with both standards and quality. In order to make such judgements, inspectors need to speak to learners as well as to staff, and the approach taken by the CIF emphasizes the need for students to be able to articulate and demonstrate what they have learnt. In my view, preparation for these encounters should assist learners in acquiring further knowledge about the structure of their course, the teaching and assessment methods used and how tutors plan to meet their learning goals as the course progresses. Data in Chapter 7 show the extent to which many students place a heavy reliance on their tutor, following the tutor's directions without question and showing little inclination to take responsibility for their learning. These findings suggest that, without further preparation, large numbers of students may be ill-equipped to share with inspectors the nature and extent of the learning that is undoubtedly taking place (see Chapters 7, 9 and 10) and, more importantly, be less than fully aware of their learning and so underrate its extent and contribution to their lives. In contrast, some learners are very clear about what they want to learn and what they expect from their learning experience. In addition, some are able to articulate persuasively the value of their learning and why it should continue to be supported.

Lifelong learning – interpretation and practice

It is, perhaps, symptomatic of all-embracing terms such as lifelong learning that organizations and individuals will interpret its meaning according to their standpoint, giving very wide use to the term. 'In its sometimes rather uncritical use' lies the danger that it will 'lose any sense of significance' (Oliver 1996: 1). It is important, therefore, that those for whom lifelong learning is of significant value should voice their opinions as widely as possible. These include the respondents in this study, whose views are recorded in Chapters 7 and 8. It is the lack of precise meaning and its various interpretations that have attracted some of the critics of lifelong learning. Education generally may be seen as the 'servant to global capitalism' (Jarvis 2001: vii) but this modern economic imperative tells only half the story, and needs to be contextualized within a learning society that embraces and values all learning for individual and collective benefit. Lifelong learning is regarded by the government as a practical manifestation of the development of a learning society, but if this idea 'has any substance, then it clearly has powerful implications for equality and inclusion of all members of society in order to engage the hard to reach' (Field 2001: 43).

Lifelong learning is seen by some as little more than government rhetoric concerned to shift responsibility on to individuals for the future of the economy. Others see it as the most fundamental challenge to our ideas about education since the beginning of mass schooling having the potential to create a paradigm shift in the approach to adult learning (Wagner 1998) or representing a set of organizational and procedural guidelines for educational practice, aimed at fostering learning throughout life. It may be seen, not as the spontaneous learning of coping skills in daily life, but as deliberate learning (Tough 1971) having the following definitive characteristics:

- it is intentional – learners are aware that they are learning;
- it has a definite, specific goal and it is not aimed at vague generalisations such as 'developing the mind';
- this goal is the reason why the learning is undertaken (i.e. it is not motivated simply by factors like boredom);
- the learner intends to retain what has been learned for considerable period of time.   (Knapper and Cropley 1991: 20)

One of the difficulties is that vagueness of definition means that the Green Paper (*The Learning Age*) (1998), seemed to be pointing in two directions at once. 'It stresses that becoming a lifelong learner is an individual responsibility while, at the same time, recognising that lifelong learning is too important to be left to individuals on their own and requires the intervention of government' (Young 2000: 97). Data in Chapters 7, 8 and 9 show that at least a third of the sample of learners in this survey do have much to contribute to the goals of a lifelong learning society through the benefits they gain as learners. Their knowledge, experience and skills of judgement, formed as a result of previous learning, enable them to distinguish between high and low-quality learning. The data also show that many students are highly active, participative learners.

Extension of the 'active learning' and 'individual action planning' approaches to learning, a previously recurring theme in the 14–18 age groups, relates learning throughout people's lives in contexts additional to those associated with formal education and training, and acknowledges that important learning can take place 'independently of any formal provision' (Young 2000: 97–8). New governmental policies at any time legitimize changes in expenditure but may provide politicians with a pretext for action that may not be widely supported. Increases in expenditure relating to lifelong learning may be seen to deflect attention away from the need for economic and social reform and to offer a 'comforting illusion that for every complex problem there is one simple solution' (Coffield 1999: 486). To some extent it may also be argued that lifelong learning has been used by policy-makers as little more than a 'modish repackaging of rather conventional policies for post-16 education and training, with little that is new or innovative' (Field 2000: viii–ix), and that it is 'an instrumental process, not a vocational, let alone ontological purpose. It is about learning for a living, rather than learning for living' (Martin 2001: 17). For learners, lifelong learning may be a means to an end, or an end in itself. In seeking to achieve a truly learning society, lifelong learning may be seen as realizing a vision in which:

employers will be learning organisations, committed to investing in their work force as an integral feature of their business development;

individuals will recognise the personal, social and economic benefits of learning and will have taken greater control and responsibility for their own learning and development;

and there will be a high quality market in the supply of learning guidance by both providers and employers to support individuals in achieving their goals.
(TEC 1997: 2)

But to achieve these ideals there will need to be more preparation (for work) and remedial provision encompassing literacy and numeracy, as well as the key skills of:

communication, working with others, application of number, improving learning and performance, problem solving, and information technology.

(TEC 1997: 7)

One of the major characteristics of lifelong learning 'as an organizing principle for the provision of educational services is its rejection of the view that organised, systematic support for learning should be confined to childhood' (Knapper and Cropley 1991: 30), and in a system of lifelong learning there may be seen to be a set of definitive principles under which education would:

- last the whole life of each individual;
- lead to the systematic acquisition, renewal, and upgrading of knowledge, skills and attitudes, as this became necessary in response to the constantly changing conditions of modern life, with the ultimate goal of promoting self-fulfilment of each individual;
- be dependent on people's increasing ability and motivation to engage in self-directed learning activities;
- acknowledge the contribution of all available educational influences, including formal, non-formal and informal.

(Knapper and Cropley 1991: 31)

Some writers have enthusiastic views on lifelong leaning. It may be seen as contributing to a 'Shamrock life, where learning, labour and leisure each have equal shares' (Ball 1990: 11), and as a contributing factor to improving the quality of life. The genuine lifelong learner can never have sufficient of learning which 'liberates, empowers, awakens, releases, nourishes, inspires, nurtures and grows' (Longworth 1999: 11). Two writers are very confident that the case for lifelong learning is already made:

> The case for lifelong learning does not need to be strenuously argued to those who have a vision of a richer and more fulfilled future for individuals, for society and for humankind as a whole.   (Longworth and Davies 1996: 8)

They offer a definition:

> Lifelong learning is the development of human potential through a continuously supportive process which stimulates and empowers individuals to acquire all the knowledge, values, skills and understanding they will require throughout their lifetimes and to apply them with confidence, creativity and enjoyment in all roles, circumstances and environments.

(Ibid.: 22)

This Longworth and Davies passage has some resonance with David Blunkett's comments in his Foreword to *The Learning Age* (1998) (see above) but the reality thus far shows practice to be less all-embracing that these writers suggest:

One person may argue that the principal purpose is the general spiritual and intellectual uplifting of people in order to become better and more fulfilled citizens in a genuinely participative democracy. Such lofty ideals may be countered by another who suggests that lifelong learning has essentially utilitarian purposes in terms of helping to ensure a frequently trained and re-educated work force able to adapt easily to fresh economic imperatives and hence ensure the prosperity of the nation state. (Oliver 1996: 2)

It is my view that lifelong learning, in its most all-embracing manifestation and as the description itself suggests, may be seen to encompass learning virtually from cradle to grave and may reasonably be seen, therefore, to offer dimensions and advantages in addition to the economic. As Alan Tuckett points out both at a national and a European level these advantages may be seen to benefit individuals as well as to form effective links between business and education providers (Tuckett 1997). If 'lifelong learning' is to be widely interpreted to mean what it actually says, then we must develop a seamless robe of learning opportunity throughout life. Beginning with younger people, the school in a lifelong learning culture will provide 'a central core of learning' (DfES 2002: 3) and will enable the acquisition of life skills, social skills, learning skills and enabling skills. It will provide a skills-based curriculum, will have strong links with industry, other education providers and the community and will establish in young people a lifetime learning strategy (Longworth and Davies 1996). Increasing attention being given to the life skills and transferable skills, required in a lifelong learning world, means that young people must not only be taught, but must understand that they will possess, for example, the skills of handling large quantities of information, decision-making and problem-solving. This will in turn enhance their self-esteem and self-management, and will develop their communication skills and critical judgement. To develop these desirable, and mostly essential, skills and attitudinal changes to achieve 'education with character' (DfES 2002: 5) will present schools with a huge challenge and one which can only be met by close cooperation with other providers. From a structural point of view, lifelong learning 'must be conceived of as a learning system incorporating not only schools, colleges and universities, but public libraries, correspondence tuition, the mass media and work-related activities' (Williams 1978: 27). It must genuinely provide for all members of society, according to their needs at any given time, which must include an acknowledgement that for some citizens at certain times in their lives formal, qualification-based learning may not be what is wanted or needed. Data in Chapter 7 show that, at least for some students, learning is more informal, although provided in a formal or organized structure. Learning brings empowerment, and the range of skills individuals acquire are recognized as part of another government strategy, for example, to achieve neighbourhood renewal (ODPM 2002: 6).

However, lifelong learning remains a poorly defined concept that lacks a theoretical foundation. It can be seen as 'a set of fashionable notions, uncritically presented and devoid of empirical evidence' (Coffield 1997b: 3), and its meaning can be interpreted, as shown in this chapter, in several different ways. Adult education is, nevertheless, a real basis for much of the further learning undertaken by so many individuals after initial schooling, and the springboard from which many, if they wish, will progress to some kind of 'formal' learning. Thus, lifelong learning as a policy may be seen to have, in addition to economic advantages, a social, political, personal and educational meaning.

It is important to the government's strategy of implementation that lifelong learning is seen as an investment to benefit everyone, which puts people first and 'places the learner at the heart of the new system' (DfEE 1999: 4). It provides an opportunity which also brings broader benefits in that it encourages and supports active citizenship, helps communities help themselves and opens up new opportunities such as the chance to explore art, music and literature (DfEE 1998; DfEE 1999). A vision of a learning and inclusive society could offer all its citizens success and benefits as individuals, as well as contributing to the common good:

> Individuals will be part of an inclusive society and will enjoy greater employability and material success, self-betterment and personal fulfilment together with an enhanced quality of life.   (TEC 1997: 6)

Staff of the Centre for Research on the Wider Benefits of Learning (CRWBL), set up by the Department for Education and Employment and managed by a partnership between the University of London's Institute of Education and Birkbeck College, are researching the non-economic benefits that learning brings to the individual learner and to society as a whole through two overarching themes: social cohesion and quality of life (Schuller *et al.* 2001). The Centre researches attitudes, values and behaviour which influence approaches to learning, and has collected data from practitioners which show the wider benefits of further education to be:

- esteem and efficacy;
- independence of thought, problem-solving, and improved IT skills;
- social integration;
- the college as a community resource.

(Preston and Hammond 2002: Executive Summary)

In addition, there are specific socio-educational benefits to older citizens, and research has shown that those who continue to be active learners enjoy a healthier lifestyle and maintain their independence longer than those who stop learning (DfEE 1999). Current and future research by the CRWBL should aid our understanding of these phenomena, and how they can be measured. Focus on these alternative and wider benefits of learning, and my emphasis on non-accredited learning, should not be taken to imply that either accredited or non-accredited learning is more important than the other (except for the individual learner), but rather that there should be close links between all forms of learning. The importance of the links between 'vocational' or work-related learning, and learning for personal fulfilment and development – for which I argue – is recognized in some quarters:

> An adequate supply of affordable and accessible non-vocational adult education should be made available to all who aspire to it. This is an essential part of a democratic and civilized society, and a provision that needs to be made in addition to, not instead of, high-quality work-relating training.
>
> (AMA 1999: 14)

Lifelong learning and adult education

If lifelong learning is a policy which offers a framework for all aspects of learning – education and training – that involves citizens from cradle to grave, then adult education may be seen both as a form of learning which contributes to that end, and as a provision for adult learners alongside other forms of education and training which are part of the lifelong learning agenda. The recent census shows that there are already more people over 60 than under 16 in Britain (Tuckett 2002: 34) and with this ageing population there are at least four ways in which good-quality adult education, readily available, is and can be of direct benefit. Based on my own experience and evidence of data in this book, I suggest these may be:

- to enable adults to remain mentally and physically active, bringing a sense of well-being and purpose to individuals, and representing possibly significant, although unquantifiable, savings to health and social services;
- to enable adults, whose literacy and numeracy skills are inadequate to cope in a modern society, to receive tuition structured to fill the gaps in their competencies;
- to provide an accessible route for adults to return to study after a (sometimes) considerable period away from formal learning,

whether or not they have at that stage a clear learning goal in mind or intended outcomes from their studies;

- to enable adults to pursue courses of study which have a cultural, spiritual, moral or artistic dimension, thus providing immediate benefits for them, but also leading to longer-term benefits to society by the individual's improved knowledge, attitude, health and participation.

I do not intend to suggest that adult education is distinct from lifelong learning, nor am I forwarding a claim for its superiority over other aspects of adult learning. Rather, I am arguing that adult education, as I describe it, is or should be an integral part of a lifelong learning philosophy and practice, which collectively support the inclusiveness that is part of the government's policy. In my view, and in the views of learners and tutors in this survey, adult education has much to contribute to the lifelong learning strategy and the value of its contribution may better be recognized by an interpretation of lifelong learning that embraces the wider values and benefits of *all* learning. To be more precise in my arguments, I should clarify that the model of adult education on which I focus meets the following criteria:

- it is essentially learner-centred, not just in its delivery, but also in its purpose and planning; it is provided for adults primarily to meet their needs at any one time, not the needs of industry, the work force, an employer or the country (although any of these may benefit at a secondary level from individuals who are better informed, stimulated by their learning and who have gained valuable skills such as the ability to work independently);
- it is carried out in a way which is negotiated with the participants, including course content, methods, assessment and outcomes; it may, but does not necessarily, lead to an accredited outcome;
- it acknowledges the valuable experience adults bring to their learning and respects their need to know that this is recognized;
- it is provided by those who have knowledge and expertise in the education of adults, as distinct from children; it is delivered either by trained teachers of adults, or untrained but highly experienced individuals who recognize the value of prior learning, both structured and experiential;
- it is undertaken as and when adults choose to participate.

This working summary may be regarded as both formative and pedagogic, and to some degree organizational. It cannot be taken as, in any sense, a legal definition and, of course, may not be accepted by other writers, but it does accord with the experiences of my research participants, and with the practice of adult education as I have known it for over 30 years. I acknowledge that the final requirement I have listed above has to be tinged with reality and practicality, but it is an issue for many adults, whose courses may be provided in shared buildings, such as schools, that are open only during school term times.

To the above list, personally, I would add that adult education should be delivered in an environment that is conducive to adult learning, but data in Chapter 7 show that adult learners are very tolerant of the conditions in which they are taught and that the sometimes unattractive uncomfortable surroundings, and faulty or unreliable equipment with which they may be faced do not seem to deter them from undertaking their chosen courses of study. In stating these characteristics of adult education, it must be acknowledged, of course, that some of these criteria are met in other forms of adult learning, but 'adult education', as referred to in this book, requires them all to be present or applicable. Philosophically, therefore, adult education differs from other post-compulsory education in that it is student-centred, not only in its delivery (as now increasingly pertains elsewhere) but essentially in its *purpose and practice*. Adult education has no compulsory curriculum determined by work force or other requirements, although there are large areas of commonality in the curriculum for adults across the country (see Chapter 3). Since lifelong learning is what people do and not just what institutions provide (Young 2000), the curriculum should, in my view, become even wider to meet individual need more closely. Adult education is a negotiated activity, planned and executed in partnership with its participants.

Traditionally, this form of learning opportunity and this type of activity by adults has been provided by organisations such as local education authorities, the Workers' Educational Association (WEA) and community and voluntary groups, although some further education colleges have also met the criteria listed above. In some parts of the country, where the LEA does not provide a separate adult education service, all such adult learning provision is made by a local further education or tertiary college. In addition, during recent years, in part as a result of the *Learning and Skills Act*, there has been a marked increase in the provision of adult learning opportunities, especially work-based training and basic skills, by private companies and agencies.

In Britain the short-term residential adult education colleges continue to play an important role in providing education opportunities for adults, complementing the good (but depleted in some areas) services of non-residential adult learning provided by local adult education colleges and centres, and the WEA. These, generally very local, adult learning opportunities serve the needs of large numbers of adults who may be returning to structured learning after a significant break. For some the break from learning activity may stretch back to their initial schooling, whilst for others it may be of a much shorter period. The range of uses to which such learning experiences are put is enormous. For some, whose education was interrupted by national hostilities or illness, it will be compensatory learning; for others it may be a means of helping to keep up to date as children progress rapidly through their own schooling; for some the opportunity to repair inadequacy in basic skills will be welcome; for others the opportunity to take a break from the domestic scene and daily child care will provide adult intellectual stimulation; some will have a set of learning goals leading towards a qualification; some will simply enjoy the pleasure of learning away from other demands on their lives. The motivation for enrolling on a structured learning programme will vary according to individual needs, and may not always be clear, even to the individual learner (Daines *et al.* 1993; Jarvis 1995a; Lovell 1980; Rogers A. 1986; Rogers J. 1971; Sargant 1991; Stuart and Thompson 1995).

Another dimension of adult learning which should be mentioned is the work of the Open University and other university continuing education departments, such as those at London, Cambridge and Nottingham, as part of what Harold Wiltshire called the 'Great Tradition' of adult education (Wiltshire 1956). These 'Responsible Bodies' (which also included WEA branches), were created by the 1924 Board of Education and authorized to direct-grant three-year tutorial courses and a whole range of shorter courses (Fieldhouse *et al.* 1996: 48). The University of London extension courses, for example, made available across a wide geographical area and facilitated, among others, by local authority adult education colleges and centres, have enabled many adult students to attend certificate and diploma courses on a part-time basis.

For individual learners, therefore, adult education may variously provide a complete, self-contained learning menu, or may be a gateway through which they return to more structured, sometimes accredited, learning programmes. Such learning activities must surely accord with the principles and desires of a system of lifelong learning, however defined, and enable individual citizens to review and refresh their thinking, add to their stock of knowledge, extend their activities as citizens and contribute towards a truly comprehensive learning society.

Definitions of adult education differ and I have taken a particular stance to emphasize a number of points. For some writers, the term is all-embracing, reflecting more general recent use:

> Adult Education includes all systematic learning by adults which contributes to their development as individuals and as members of the community and of society apart from full-time instruction received by persons as part of their uninterrupted initial education and training. It may be formal education which takes place in institutions, e.g. training centres, schools, colleges, institutions and universities; or non-formal education, which is any other systematic form of learning, including self-directed learning.
>
> (Commission on Adult Education 1985: Introduction).

This all-embracing description of adult education is one which is often used in this country, but which can lead to confusion when the same term is used to refer to a specific form of adult learning, or learning that is available from certain providers. In my view, the above description refers to the wider 'education of adults', rather than to 'adult education'.

This chapter has outlined the context within which this book is written and the background against which research findings are compared in Chapters 9 and 10. The powerful influence of the Learning and Skills Council and its various agencies are having a profound effect on all adult learning and further references are also made to it in later chapters. Chapter 3, which follows, explains the conceptual framework for this study and the questions that were formulated to carry out my research.

3 Conceptual Framework and Research Questions

Introduction

In this chapter I describe the conceptual framework within which my research was carried out, and how my research questions were framed against the background of published literature. I explain my methodology and research methods selected, and why my findings can add to our knowledge of adult education and its processes.

In Chapter 1, I explained that the purpose in undertaking this research was to identify what constitutes quality in adult learning from the different perspectives of the participants, and to ask whether it is reasonable that adult learners can be acknowledged as arbiters of the quality of their own learning, particularly where that learning episode does not lead to an accredited outcome, and where alternative measures of progress and achievement are needed. My purpose was also to enable the voices of adult part-time students and their tutors to be heard alongside current discourse, and the all-pervading protagonists of accreditation and 'vocationalism'. Within the political context of lifelong learning, championed by the government, the purpose of learning for adults has become principally that of an instrumental means to an economic end, albeit with the highly desirable outcome of a better qualified, better skilled and more competitive work force.

In the circumstances of modern society, with global competition a daily reality, it may not be considered unreasonable for educational provision to be strongly influenced by economic pressures, since it is incumbent upon any government to support ways in which learning contributes to the economic success of a nation. I believe, however, that it is also desirable that we acknowledge and support the other values of learning – such as social, aesthetic, cultural, intellectual, spiritual, moral and ethical – for not to do so will mean that we shall become a lesser nation and, moreover, undermine the widely expressed desire to become a truly learning society in a learning age (Ball and Coffield 1999; Coffield 1997a; DfEE 1998; DfEE 1999; Hodgson 2000; Hutchins 1968; NAGCELL 1999; Ranson 1994; Small 1992).

As mentioned above, the *Learning and Skills Act* (DfES 2000) established a Learning and Skills Council, which came into being on 1 April 2001 (see Chapter 2). The Council's role is to oversee the provision of all post-16 education and training, other than higher education, and its creation has resulted in a higher profile being given to all adult learning. Much of the emphasis of the Council's activities remains, understandably, on learning related to work and skills, and the wording of the *Learning and Skills Act* suggests that the wider aspects of learning in *all* its many manifestations should receive closer attention. However, as shown above, the LSC has interpreted the Act to focus principally on work-related learning. Data in Chapter 7, and my conclusions in Chapter 10, show that adult students greatly value their learning to the extent that for some it is a life-enhancing experience, and much remains to be achieved within the LSC agenda to ensure that it supports *all* learning for adults within its philosophy and practices. The National Institute of Adult Continuing Education (NIACE) has accepted and welcomed the economic arguments for an expansion of the learning community, and endorsed National Targets for Education and Training, but has also been at pains to maintain that education makes an essential contribution to other aspects of life in a civilized society. There are many people who do not form part of the work force at any one time – young parents and other carers, for example – and many who never will, such as the elderly retired. As pointed out earlier, the 2002 census records that the balance of young and old in Britain has altered, and that we are becoming an increasingly ageing society. This makes Tony Uden's comments, although written several years ago, as relevant today as then:

> These people have as important a place in the 'learning community' as the employed and those acknowledged as unemployed. The place of education and training in the self-development of individuals and their ability to contribute to family and community life must not be separated from, and certainly not thought of as less important than, the development of people as more direct contributors to economic life.   (Uden 1994: 7)

The continuing emphasis on accrediting much learning and of prioritizing 'vocational' learning – whether compulsory or voluntary – has had a major impact on adult education services. The economic imperative to reorganize what were programmes of liberal adult learning (see Chapter 3) into credit bearing units has required the reassessment of a wide range of courses for adults – not in itself a bad thing – but personal growth in such circumstances is then 're-defined as the acquisition of fragmented units and competencies' (Wallis 1996: viii). This has produced anecdotal reports of some adult students, especially those who see themselves beyond the point of requiring further qualifications, forsaking those courses which they no longer see as relevant for them, although no precise data are available to support these claims. Conversely, others are reported as having welcomed the accreditation of their learning programme, as this seems to imply for some that their learning is more 'worthy' (my interpretation) for having gained the status of a qualification-bearing experience (see Chapter 7).

I do not make a plea in favour of one form of learning versus another, nor do I argue against the accreditation of some previously non-accredited learning outcomes. I point out that adults choose learning programmes that are of relevance to themselves *within the context of their lives and at a time relevant to their current needs*, and that those experiences, whether or not accredited, are deemed by the individual to be of value to him or her, and may not necessarily be directly associated with work, or economic benefit. It is still reasonable to suggest, despite the above acknowledgements, that current governmental discourse, which refers to meeting the needs of individuals in society, actually means *so far as it relates to their employment skills needs*. This book argues for a system that supports those individual learning needs *as they are perceived by the individual and for whatever purpose, recognizing the ability of the adult to make informed choices* and, as Chapters 9 and 10 show, the competence of some adults to make informed and valid judgements about their learning.

One of the findings from a national survey, conducted in the early 1990s, stated that evidence collected for that project refuted 'the notion that adults participate in general, un-certificated learning primarily for leisure or recreational purposes' (McGivney 1992: 15). Data in Chapter 7 of this thesis, in contrast both to that statement and to the current qualifications-as-paramount discourse, show that so far as the participants in this survey are concerned, the opposite is true. Students state that they undertake their learning for a number of reasons other than to gain qualifications, including for the simple pleasure of learning. I argue for the retention, and continued public recognition and support, of what has been known for many decades as liberal adult education, and the values and opportunities that it embraces, despite those who pronounce its demise or castigate it as avoiding 'the serious business of wealth creation' (Taylor 1996: 61), and are 'dominated by a work/achievement ethic that is obstructing our society's capacity to benefit from real human creativity and energy' (Field 1990: 53). It is from empirical research into such learning, and the value it has for so many adult learners, that my research was formulated, drawing upon data which show what it is that constitutes quality in the learning process from the perspectives of its participants.

Liberalism, freedom and values

If an argument for liberal adult education is to be made, its meaning must be clarified. The meanings of 'adult' and 'education' are explored in Chapter 5, but reference should be made here to 'liberal' and its meanings, often linked, as suggested above, with concepts of freedom. The notion of liberalism may seem to be rather outdated in our world dominated broadly by right or left politics, although attempts to find a middle way, or 'third way' (Giddens 1998) as favoured by the current UK Government, suggest moves towards a more central political ground. Even those who see themselves in the centre of political dogma mostly avoid use of the word 'liberal' (other than, of course, those individuals and organizations which specifically select that term to express their beliefs), and choose instead to describe themselves as 'centre-left' or 'centre-right'. If challenged, however, it is likely that honest politicians of any political persuasion would acknowledge that they support fundamental liberal concepts, such as freedom, as a basis for our society. Nagel suggests liberalism is 'the conjunction of two ideals … the first of which is individual liberty' and the second a 'democratic society controlled by its *citizens*' (Nagel 1982: 191, cited in Lawson 1996: 190). From this, liberty may be seen as a 'prime value and democracy is merely a mechanism which makes liberty possible' (ibid.). Current discourse on individual rights and responsibilities relates, in educational terms, to supremacy of the 'vocational' and instrumental basis for learning; and if the liberal democratic rights of the individual are to be met in terms of his/her learning there needs to be a recognition of the *value* of different types of learning, which in turn may perhaps lead to a parity of esteem and freedom of choice for all learning experiences. Not all writers share the view that a choice is presented between instrumental and liberal adult education, but state instead that it is possible to argue that 'liberal adult education is instrumental in the sense of being directed towards the fulfilment of the project of modernity' (Usher *et al.* 1997: 11) but, as I have indicated elsewhere, I see few signs that liberal adult education is currently recognized as contributing to lifelong learning, and progress towards a fully learning society. This is partly, perhaps, because of mixed reactions, suggested by Usher and Edwards, towards the relative decline of liberal adult education in recent years. For some, its potential loss is welcome 'since it helps clear the way for a more "business-like", vocationally-oriented and less marginalised adult education'. Others see liberal adult education 'as oppressively elitist and patriarchal and would not be unhappy to see its demise'. A further group, mainly located in the extra-mural departments of the old universities, see its undermining through certification 'as a significant limitation of the opportunities open to adults' (Usher and Edwards 1996: 39).

The relevance of liberal adult education within a policy of lifelong learning

Liberal adult education, with its strong emphasis on experiential learning, brings an intellectual freedom and freedom of choice, leaving the individual open to develop learning that is important within his/her set of personal values. This is freedom by the individual to undertake learning for its own sake, 'untrammelled by the pressures of certification or work preparation – education as an end in itself, yet which helps to bring about personal development, fulfil individual autonomy and need, build confidence and redress disadvantage' (ibid. 1996: 40). This means freedom of an individual to choose, with reasonable support from the State, any learning that is suitable to his/her requirements, at a time that is appropriate for him/her. I should clarify that by 'any learning' I accept the constraints in our society normally applied to (partially or wholly) funded public 'education', i.e. that it should be worthwhile and desirable, and be socially, legally and morally acceptable (Jarvis 1995b; Jarvis 1997; Lawson 1975; Peters 1967). Even freedom of choice in a democratic society must be constrained within the rules of that society. Tuition in, say, bomb-making or in any other extreme form of political terrorism would be excluded as unacceptable in these terms, except where such tuition formed part of a training for those charged with national safety or security. Thus, for Lawson, 'to be liberated suggests somewhat para-doxically that one accepts the constraints of knowledge and that the paradigm of an un-free man would be one who is so free of restraints that he has no points of reference which will enable him to choose and to make judgements' (Lawson 1975: 96).

I seek more than just freedom for the individual to choose a course of learning appropriate to him/her. I argue, in addition, for recognition of the value of experiences that the adult learner brings to current learning, and of his/her ability to make informed judgements about the quality of that learning. If adult learners are to be accepted as arbiters of the quality of their own learning then the integrity of their choice of learning programme must also be acknowledged (see Chapter 10). Wider recognition, greater levels of support and funding for all adult learning that meets the criteria referred to above are not unreasonable expectations in a modern society, even where equity and equal opportunity are not yet achieved. The economic implications of this are not, I submit, disproportionately great since, in most cases, adult part-time learners make substantial contributions towards the cost of their courses through taxes and course fees. It must also be the case, although difficult to measure, that all learning undertaken by adults (that meets the criteria referred to above) will subsequently benefit the society in which they live. By this I mean that through the benefits gained from learning, e.g. knowledge, practical skills, social skills, increased confidence, improved self-esteem and identity, an individual is better equipped to play his/her part as a citizen.

> Once a person's self-esteem has been raised, once they are valued, once they understand the importance of their contribution, then society is more enriched. (Preston and Hammond 2002: 24)

This may manifest itself, for example, in more voluntary work in the local community, perhaps specifically helping those less fortunate members of society who may not have access to the very learning experiences that have enabled the helper to offer such voluntary activity. The benefits of this learning may also relate, for example, to a need for less expenditure on some aspects of health or social services; to more active participatory citizenship by the individual in the form of a broad range of voluntary activity; and to a contribution towards the education of young people through reading schemes. It has to be acknowledged, however, that some of these examples are not easy to quantify.

Contextualizing my arguments within a personal experience

My role as a researcher is explained in Chapter 4, but as my work in the adult education sector covers 36 years, it is relevant briefly to outline that experience and to relate it to my present stance. My experience at different times as student, tutor, tutor-trainer, organizer, manager, college principal and researcher has brought me into close contact with many thousands of part-time adult learners and their tutors, and I have made personal observations of the motivation, commitment and effort shown, the challenges overcome and the successes achieved by these participants in the interactive process of adult teaching and learning. I stress 'interactive' because this is the essence of the adult learning with which I have been involved, which I have observed in institutions managed by myself and others and which has formed the basis of many discussion with other practitioners. It is also the basis of the learning experiences of my research participants. The principle of *primus inter pares,* although not a fully formulated theory, has long applied in adult education. This philosophy regards the tutor and students as equals in the teaching and learning exchange, other than to the degree of subject knowledge, of which the tutor will, of course, be expected to have a greater store. It recognizes the experiences that the adult learner will have acquired from a variety of sources. In some cases the individual's experience may include some knowledge of the subject being taught, or knowledge that is directly relevant to the subject. For example, a language student who has lived in a foreign country will have useful background knowledge about the country whose language is being studied; or a student who has fought in a war will have experiences that may be relevant to the period being considered on a history course, and which may also be well beyond the experiences of a younger tutor. In a general sense the combined experiences and knowledge of the adult learning group is likely to far exceed that of any individual tutor (except probably – but not always – of the subject they are studying), and Chapter 5 says more about this partnership between the adult student and tutor, and the extent to which students contribute to that process. Chapters 7 and 8 also provide evidence of students' contributions to the process, together with students' and tutors' views on the nature and value of those contributions.

The programmes or courses of study followed by those I have observed have ranged across the curriculum, as indicated in Appendix 1. These courses and many others, whether or not accredited, all led to agreed outcomes that had been negotiated between the learners and their tutor (see Chapter 5). It is also appropriate to include an explanation about the 'vocational' and 'non-vocational' nature of these courses. I place the terms in inverted commas because the 1992 *Further and Higher Education Act* (DES 1992), by creating the false, arbitrary division between so-called 'vocational' and 'non-vocational' courses, or so-called 'leisure' courses, produced two anomalies (Green and Lucas 1999; Hodgson 2000). Firstly, the Act created what for many is an unacceptable differentiation between two types of courses, indicating that one is more valid than the other. Schedule 2 (Courses of Further Education) of the Act lists those courses which, identified as 'approved' under the Act, subsequently became those funded by the Further Education Funding Council, itself established by the Act. These approved courses include:

- a course which prepares students to obtain a vocational qualification;
- a course which prepares students to qualify for – the General Certificate of Secondary Education, or the General Certificate of Education at Advanced Level or Advanced Supplementary Level;
- a course ... which prepares students for entry to a course of higher education;
- a course for basic literacy in English;
- a course to improve knowledge of English for those for whom English is not the language spoken at home;
- a course to teach the basic principles of mathematics;
- a course to teach independent living and communication skills to persons having learning difficulties which prepares them for entry to another course ...   (DES 1992, Chapter 13, Schedule 2: 74)

All other courses were therefore, by implication, not approved. This means that there was no recognition within the Act of the ways in which so many other 'non-approved' courses often led to one of the approved courses, except where this was specifically stated, or where such courses formed the first stage of an approved course. Neither was there recognition of the ways in which 'non-approved' courses themselves served the learning needs of individuals. Also, many 'non-vocational' courses 'actually develop important "vocational" skills and increased learning capacity' (Green and Lucas 1999: 71) and may be used later as a foundation for accredited study. This differentiation itself was, I believe, wrong in principle and showed a clear lack of awareness of the nature and purposes of many courses followed by adult learners or, more seriously, a deliberate denigration of 'liberal' learning. As John Field has asked, 'why are we so uneasy about accepting leisure as a valued public activity and supporting it through the public purse?' (Field 1990: 53). I believe this point is even more pertinent if it can be shown that such 'leisure' learning has direct benefits to society and lifelong learning policy. Learning which leads to qualifications is, of course, immensely important and I would not wish to imply otherwise. In our increasingly competitive world those who are able to gain relevant qualifications are likely to have an advantage in the employment market and in other areas of life over those who do not. My argument is with the explicit denigration of 'non-approved' 'non-vocational' learning, which was clearly regarded by the authors of the 1992 *Education Act* as learning of less importance and less worthy of funding, an approach which was perpetuated, following the Act, by the funding regime of the Further Education Funding Council. The Act reaffirmed the place of adult education in the 'Further Education' camp (placed there by the 1944 *Education Act*), whilst at the same time denying it funding under the new system because much of it was not accredited. There followed a vocabulary of negative terminology employed when referring to adult education and its participants: e.g. '*non-traditional*' students, *non-standard* entry, *external* institutions, and so on (my italics).

A second anomaly is that the very use of the terms 'vocational' and 'non-vocational' in such an all-embracing way is often illogical and meaningless. Local authorities for many years, therefore, perpetuated the suggestion that courses leading to qualifications were more important, because the fees were lower for these courses. The term 'vocational' is often used to imply learning that leads to paid work yet, as Glynis Cousin has pointed out, much of LEA non-accredited adult provision can be profoundly vocational, in that it may be concerned with many jobs, and she suggests, for example, the job of wife and mother (Cousin 1990). Courses in directly work-related skills, such as those of training bricklayers, plumbers, electricians, computer programmers or nurses are, of course, 'vocational' in that they (hopefully) would lead ultimately to employment for that skill. Many other courses, however, are less clear, and my contention is that the 'vocational' intent or otherwise should be determined by the individual, since the point at which any course may be judged as 'vocational' in nature (and therefore, crucially, in funding support) is significant. As Pring puts it, '... that is worthwhile which the individual finds desirable or value in'. So 'a liberal philosophy which espouses choice and diversity can hardly support the centralised control of what has to be learnt'. 'The divide is ... between liberal education and vocational preparation, but it need not be' (Pring 1995: 171 and 183).

> You don't have vocational and non-vocational courses, you have vocational and non-vocational students.   (Cara 1991: 25)

Recognition of the individual's right to choose his/her programme of learning is, I suggest, closely linked with a recognition of his/her ability to judge quality in, and of, that learning. Adults select courses for many reasons. They may, for example, be driven by a desire to gain a qualification, to update skills relating to their employment or to pursue an interest. But they may also make their selection, not so much on the basis of the course or its outcome, but rather for reasons to do with their personal life, e.g. loneliness, ease of transport to gain access to the institution or because of who is teaching the course. Chapter 5 gives further consideration to these points. Whatever the reasons for selecting a particular learning programme the adult learner is likely to bring a range of experiences, prejudices, expectations and a need to fit that particular course of learning into a busy demanding life. He/she is likely to have a shrewd sense of what is offered and, whilst perhaps not always recognizing the term, will in fact exercise critical judgements about the quality of the learning and the teaching she/he receives. Many adult learners may not be versed in precise technical terminology, nor be able to set out precisely what may be expected from a well-planned, well-delivered programme of teaching, but instinctively will gain a feeling about the quality of the experience. Chapter 7 provides evidence of the extent to which adult learners are aware of this capacity and how they form such judgements about quality.

But what is 'quality in learning'? I have suggested elsewhere that often 'quality' and 'standards' are confused and used interchangeably, as if they have the same meaning. To judge a course of study by the successful completion of some form of examination is to judge only:

- the ability of a student to recall and recount knowledge, or demonstrate a skill, after a given period of study and within the criteria established for that discipline; and
- the ability of the student to do so at a given time, within specific circumstances and within a short time-frame.

These are, of course, perfectly reasonable expectations if that is what is being assessed and I shall not rehearse here the debate about the extent to which knowledge, recalled in examination conditions soon after the completion of a course, will still be available to the individual after some months or years. If we are to have examination systems we must, of course, establish ways of examining the acquisition of knowledge and skills prior to the gaining of an award – such is the very basis of a major part of our education system. Other examinations may, where this is appropriate, require the student to explain and support his/her answers and to demonstrate critical judgement, as well as to recall knowledge. These examinations say nothing, however, about the *process* of learning leading to the examination, nor about its quality, nor about the culture of the providing institution. It is against the above background that my research was formulated. Adult education has been subjected to various descriptions over the centuries and the adult education 'service', as it became known, continues to provide for several hundreds of thousands of adults across the country, despite the many threats to its existence. The nature of adult education has been referred to above and is enlarged upon in Chapter 5, but it is relevant to this conceptual explanation that I say something here about what it entails and how it is practised.

Adult education within the education system

Our national system of education is often seen as a continuous thread of progressive learning opportunity, stretching from pre-school to higher education, along which individuals move as far as they are encouraged and able to, leaving and rejoining as their circumstances and desires dictate. For some, the thread is broken at the age of 16 (at least initially), whilst for the majority it leads them into further or higher education, or professional training of some kind. Adult education is seen variously as a provision, an activity or an ideal, but one which is either placed alongside the progressive thread of primary, secondary and tertiary education, or is interwoven with education, work and social activities. Figure 3.1 shows that, whilst adult education cannot be undertaken by those below the age of 16 (the school leaving age), it potentially continues to provide for individuals alongside all other aspects of their lives, for as long as they choose to be involved in it.

This simple visual representation shows adult education as a separate provision or activity which is available alongside whatever other education individuals may be involved in or, for example, at the same time as working, being unemployed or enjoying social activities. Those who participate are, of course, those who have discovered adult education and what it can offer them. As the real 'poor cousin' (Newman 1979) of the educational world, adult education often suffers from an insufficiently clear place in the logical, widely recognized progression of educational attainment from school to higher education. Also, the nature and purpose of adult

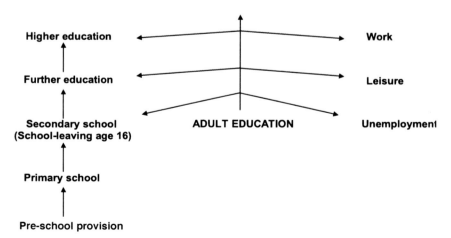

Figure 3.1: Adult education and its relation to other learning and life experiences

education is often unclear, except to those who enjoy its opportunities, pleasures and benefits. As an advocate for the removal of barriers between sectors of education I would not wish to overemphasize the separateness of adult education if that would isolate it even more, but rather to argue for recognition of its distinctive nature. Unfortunately, to seek wider recognition involves some risk of division by the use of comparisons.

Adult education can be seen as a philosophical practice which is teaching and learning that is geared to the needs of the student, places her/him at the focus of its purpose and activity, employs methods and evaluative systems which are relevant and appropriate for adults, adopts a pace that recognizes the individual learning needs and styles of adults, and moves towards outcomes that have been negotiated with the participants. Described in this way, adult education may be seen as distinct, and yet could theoretically be practised anywhere within the education system. This tends not to be so because the agenda and priorities of many educational institutions are such as not to embrace all of these requirements, and I have pointed out above that, in a political and educational climate that favours work-related education and training, adult education is given less attention, even by those who are sympathetic to its cause.

Adult learners are described as being discontinuous in their studies and their learning is episodic in character (Newman 1979), but in what are they participating? Part-time adult education, principally as provided by local education authorities or the WEA, has been for many decades provided through day, evening or weekend courses consisting usually of a number of meetings, often over the course of 30 or more weeks within any given academic year, $1-2\frac{1}{2}$ hours in length, as appropriate to the course. The majority of these courses are non-residential, but opportunities for residential adult education are many and excellent short-term residential colleges for adult education are to be found in many parts of the country. Non-residential adult education courses (see also Chapter 5) are available in adult education colleges or centres, buildings shared with schools, some further education colleges, village halls or community centres and other public places including, occasionally, rooms in public houses. They will be taught by qualified adult tutors or further education staff, schoolteachers or untrained but experienced tutors. In the case of the latter groups, training in the teaching of adults is provided to ensure that the principles of andragogy are understood and practised (see Chapter 5).

The basis of a curriculum for adult education is too extensive to describe fully here, consisting as it does of a combination of the following:

- courses requested by potential and existing students;
- courses considered by the provider as likely to attract enrolments (this decision may be based on previous successes, the successes of other providers, on a perception of current interests in society gleaned from a variety of sources, sometimes on the personal interest of staff members);
- courses established as the result of unmet demand elsewhere;
- courses designed to meet clear trends in society at different times, e.g. computing courses at different levels, foreign languages, gardening skills or women's studies;
- courses requested by local businesses, by local authorities or, in the case of the WEA, by a panel of its members.

A typical prospectus may include, among many others and in no particular order, courses in:

> Foreign languages, arts and crafts, physical activities, 'A' level and GCSE courses, office skills, English, mathematics, dance, drama, music, basic skills, humanities, business studies, information technology, domestic crafts, and 'general' education, including First Aid, homeopathy, local history, massage, gardening, cookery, return to study, navigation and women's studies.

Some of the hurdles that adult learners have to overcome – practical and psychological, social and attitudinal – have been described earlier. To obtain information on available courses, to complete the enrolment procedure, to gain access to the premises and to the classroom, to sustain attendance, to renew learning skills and to achieve whatever result they consider appropriate requires considerable effort and determination by the individual learner. Chapter 5 makes reference to the motivation which drives these students to begin and sustain a course of study against competing demands on their time, and this factor contributes much to the effective learning that is described within this book. A number of writers have referred to the rich variety of experiences, prejudices and expectations that adult learners and their tutors bring to the learning environment (Brookfield 1986; Daines *et al.* 1993; Lovell 1980; Rogers, J. 1971). The interactive exchange that takes place during learning programmes amongst this disparate group of individuals forms the essence of adult education – an exchange between equals through the medium of the subject that results in changes within all of them and other, probably immeasurable, behavioural outcomes. Furthermore, attitudinal changes, within the affective domain, will occur throughout the course, as well as development within the cognitive and psycho-motor domains (Maslow 1968). I do not claim that what is described is necessarily unique to adult education, except that some of the ingredients may not be present within a learning environment for children, and the range of children's experiences are likely to be more limited.

Why this research project was planned and developed

Over many years, in common with other adult educators, I have observed adult students learning and I have witnessed their extraordinary motivation and commitment. I have also seen the varying nature and degree of their participation in the learning process, and formed a view that those who enter more fully into the interaction of the learning exchange seem to gain more from the process. They experience, it seems, greater satisfaction, more enjoyment and a higher quality of learning from the process than do their less participative fellow students. These observations were made, of course, on a casual basis and did not then form part of structured research. Such observations were often made during necessarily brief visits to classrooms, although some more in-depth observations were possible during tutor-training teaching assessments. Before my current research it was not clear the extent to which tutors create a learning environment that encourages the more interactive participative learning exchanges I so often witnessed en passant, and Chapters 7 and 8 provide evidence to show how such an environment supports learning. This is not, of course, to suggest that the creation of such a learning environment is confined to teachers of adults, nor that it occurs with all adult learning groups. What is clear, however, in a variety of ways, is the extent to which many of the adult students in my survey are very sure about their reasons for following a course and what they expect to gain from it. These individuals are very shrewd about the teaching and learning they are experiencing. They are gaining subject knowledge, but they have in many cases a clear understanding of what they expect from their tutor, how he/she should conduct the course, how he/she should draw upon students' experiences and perceptions and how explanations should be provided whenever requested. In other words, they seem to know what a *quality* learning experience is for them.

Chapter 6 explores what may be meant by 'quality', both in education and in society generally, but it is sufficient to say here that generally, in education, 'quality' is measured by outcomes such as examination results, not processes. These outcomes are, as suggested in Chapter 1, relatively easy to measure and useful comparisons can be made between the results from schools, colleges and universities, or different groups of students. Relatively easy, that is, by setting aside the multitude of differences between individuals and groups of learners, and by focusing on the results using common criteria and measurable data. But what if, as in the case of many adult education courses, there is no previously determined accredited outcome? This book is concerned with the actual *process* of adult teaching and learning, and with attitudinal and behavioural outcomes, more than with outcomes in an accredited sense. Attitudinal outcomes will form part of the changes that will have taken place in an individual as a result of a period of formal learning and these are quite distinct from the acquisition of knowledge, tested through appropriate assessment and accreditation.

Early thoughts on the research proposal

How then could quality be determined in this process, and by whom? A great deal of work remains to be undertaken on the identification of learning outcomes in the case of adult learners whose course of study does not lead to an accredited outcome but the potential count of unanticipated learning gains may be surprising. 'Synthesising learners' achievements group by group and cohort by cohort can be an inspiring experience ... and ... a fuller picture of learning emerges' (Lavender 1999: 6). Since it is the students themselves, in partnership with their tutor, who ensure the successful outcome of their learning, why should it not be they who determine for themselves what a quality learning experience is? I began a literature search, firstly to ascertain whether such a research project had been carried out previously, and I found that this was not so. This search was then extended to ascertain what was being said about adult learning, its processes and quality (see Chapter 6).

The current change of terminology from adult education to adult learning is noted as being significant by some writers (Lawson 1996; Usher *et al.* 1997) in representing a broadening of approach and encompassing all aspects of adults learning. Earlier references were still to 'adult education', and with that title it is seen in a variety of ways. Academic writers debate the epistemological links of adult education with its source disciplines (Bright 1989) such as sociology (Armstrong 1989) or philosophy, and whether it is a separate field of study (Paterson 1989). Another suggests that in practice there is a spectrum called further education which at one end is clearly vocational (though still not unconnected with personal and social development) and at the other is personal, social cultural and non-vocational (Russell 1973). Russell asserts that adult education must be integrated with all the other sectors of the education system but at the same time remain firmly rooted in the active life of local communities: it must be readily accessible to all who need it, whatever their means or circumstances. The importance of experience and of prior learning, both experiential and structured, when referring to adult learning, is widely recognized (Evans 1994; Usher *et al.* 1997; Weil and McGill 1989).

My research was driven by a desire to gain information on the ways and extent to which prior experiences will influence the quality of current learning when students draw upon those experiences as they continue to learn. How best, then, to explore these questions and to gain useful data that would inform future provision and add to our knowledge of adult learning? In simple terms, the search was to ascertain views from students and tutors on what is quality in adult learning. When motivated to participate in the interaction of teaching and learning, the collective wealth of knowledge and experience is influenced by a range of factors, and the process will result in a range of outcomes. Early attempts to explain my proposed research diagrammatically produced Figures 3.2 and 3.3.

This very simple model saw influences on the teaching and learning process being made by the experiences that students and tutors bring to bear on the exchange.

Figure 3.3 acknowledges that as well as input from students and tutors, the process of teaching and learning has outcomes, and will be affected

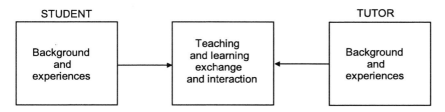

Figure 3.2: Student and tutor contributions to the teaching and learning exchange

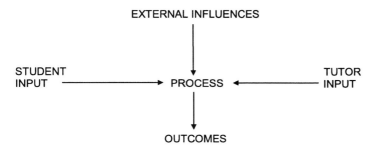

Figure 3.3: The learning process: influences and outcomes

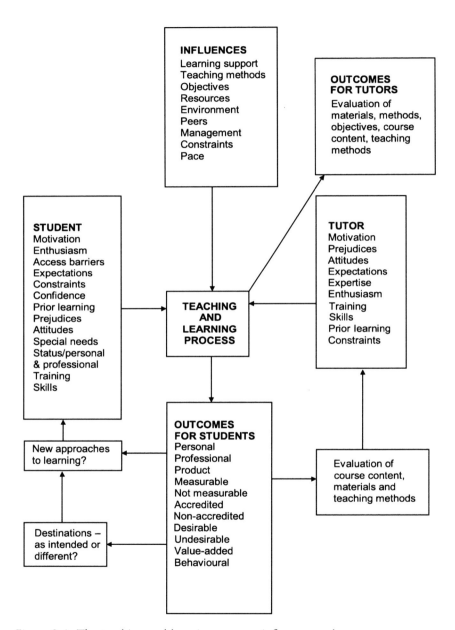

Figure 3.4: The teaching and learning process: influences and outcomes

by other external influences, such as the environment, equipment and resources. These simple diagrams, however, do not explain the wide range of knowledge and experiences brought by participants to the learning environment, nor the influences upon the learning process that are initially external to that process, nor the range of possible outcomes from the process. This wide range of factors is better represented by Figure 3.4, which suggests the numerous influences brought to bear on the process by students and tutors, all of whom bring wide-ranging knowledge, skills, experiences, expectations and prejudices, all of which will, in turn, have some influence on all participants. Outcomes and destinations will also be numerous and varied, some intended, some evolving. Experiences gained from the process will, in turn, be brought to bear on approaches to future teaching and learning. Chapter 7 shows evidence of learners' views on these influences that I subsequently gathered during my research.

Formulating research questions

Personal experience and anecdotal evidence gathered by myself and other adult educators over many years has suggested that adult learners fall broadly into two groups – those who instinctively recognize and draw upon their previous learning experiences, leading them to participate fully in the learning process; and those who seem to see each new learning experience as a new activity, unrelated to what has gone before. Data in Chapter 7 provide evidence of these two groups, and also the benefits that students believe they gain from an active participatory approach to their learning. I asked whether, since adults bring to their learning this wide range of experiences, and since so many show an ability to make shrewd judgements about their current learning and how it is delivered, it is reasonable to consider that they could be acknowledged as arbiters of the quality of their own learning. This possibility, if it gained validity, would enable judgements to be made about the quality of adult learning where no external criteria, in the form of examinations, was available. It would also cover any criticism that, even where outcome-based judgements could be made, they measure just that – the outcome, not the process. Also, as suggested above, outcome-based criteria are principally to do with stand-ards, not always with quality of the learning experience. To empower students to make these valid judgements would emphasize that the non-accredited courses they were following were initially for their benefit and, since their learning was not being measured against other criteria to enable comparisons with other students to be made, who better to judge the quality and value of the learning than participants themselves?

Adult learners are, of course, already able to make observations and judgements about their learning; some with a rich background of learning experiences to draw upon, others with less experience, but all with different reasons for learning and differing aims for the process and results of that learning. In order to argue, however, that adult learners are able to make judgements about the quality of their learning that could be regarded as valid by providing or funding agencies, one first would need to discover what the learners regarded as a quality learning experience. My research set out to do just that. Participants' views on whether or not they were experiencing quality learning and what they believe caused it, would not be sufficient, however, without further questioning about where the responsibility lay for ensuring and maintaining quality, and whether it was shared in any way by learners. My research questions that follow were formulated around these key enquiries (see copy of questionnaires, Appendices 2 and 3).

This chapter has explained the foundation for this study and identified the key questions that prompted the research (which, of course, are equally applicable to other learning in, for example, further and higher education). The chapter has argued for the importance of adult education, as described in Chapter 2, and suggests that it has an important role to play in the context of a national system of lifelong learning. Research findings in later chapters provide data to support this view and show the importance of learning to the lives of many adults.

Chapter 4, which follows, explains the methodology and research methods employed to prepare and carry out the research, which led to the findings summarized in Chapters 7, 8 and 9.

4 Methodology and Research Methods

Introduction

The conceptual framework for my research, and the research questions that formed the basis of this survey, were explained in Chapter 3. The present chapter provides an explanation of my research methodology and an appraisal of the whole process of designing and carrying out the research project. It explains my role as a researcher and the factors that influenced the research process at various stages, including my choice of research and analytical methods against the background of published literature. The survey was carried out amongst students and staff of adult community colleges in the east of England and the reason for this choice, and the advantages offered by these colleges as a rich source of adult learning opportunities, are explained.

Analysis and synthesis of the findings will be found in Chapters 7, 8 and 9.

Designing and developing a research methodology

In designing a research methodology there are aspects over which the researcher has some control but also factors that are either outside his/her control, or which exert so strong an influence that they may result in some degree of compromise. This study is such an example, and the factors which affected my research are considered below. In Chapter 3, I explained my intention to explore participants' perceptions of what, for them, is quality in adult learning. I determined at an early stage that I would design a methodology that would include some face-to-face contact with those whose opinions I intended to research. Before commencing on a detailed methodological structure, however, it was necessary to carry out a literature search to ascertain what similar areas had been researched previously, and to ensure my plans would not duplicate earlier work. Another reason for a literature search was to discover what had been written on the proposed area of research, since it would be necessary to place my research data and findings within a theoretical framework that referred to the published work of other researchers. I was aware, also, that searches of the literature would need to continue up to the time at which I concluded my research. This would ensure, so far as possible, that I would be aware of relevant works published during the period of my study. Literature searches showed that my proposed area of research had not been covered before, and also confirmed how under-researched this particular area of learning is, leading me to believe that my own work could usefully add to the epistemology of adult learning.

A methodology had to be constructed that would define my research, and a potential research population had to be identified that would give a sufficiently large sample to be valid and to enable reasonable generalizations to be drawn from the results, yet remain manageable by me as a lone researcher, both in terms of its numerical size and its geographical spread. I particularly wished to focus my research on adult learners who were following part-time courses, as I consider that this is one sector of educational provision that receives less than a reasonable share of recognition and resources. I knew from personal experience the wide range of opportunities that were available to adult learners, and I had seen how some adult students were able to grasp every opportunity as learners, taking control of their learning and accepting responsibility for its progress. I was also aware that, with a focus by successive governments on the importance of qualifications and a need to improve the level of skills in our work force, the recognition and resourcing of non-accredited learning was becoming even more problematical. Yet the importance of part-time learning, and non-accredited learning in particular is very important to a large number of adults, despite severe curtailment following the effects of the 1992 *Education Act* (see Chapter 3).

Judgements about the quality of learning are largely made from outcomes in the form of easily measurable data, such as examination results, and I wished to discover what quality meant to adult learners themselves in the *process* of learning, whatever the nature of final outcomes. I resolved, therefore, to gain information on the views of learners about what, for them, made their learning a quality experience and to compare this with the perceptions of the tutors with whom they work so closely. I also wished to seek evidence that some adults draw upon their previous learning and apply its lessons to new learning, taking responsibility for the quality of that learning.

Formulating research questions

I decided to carry out qualitative research into the perceptions of adult learners and their tutors, using quantitative data to provide a confirmatory data base. Most questions would be asked of both students and tutors but, in addition, I also wanted to gain tutors' perceptions of quality in their teaching, and quality in their students' learning, which would enable comparisons to be made between the two sets of data (see Appendices 2 and 3 for copies of questionnaires, and Chapters 7, 8 and 9 for my research findings).

It was important to my research that respondents would be able to express views using their own language. I did not wish to influence their responses by providing multiple-choice answers from which they could select the most appropriate, although this would have made data analysis much easier. To have taken this approach would have meant that respondents were presented with *my* terminology, which could have unduly influenced their responses. It would be impossible for me to avoid totally any influences on my respondents – my selection of the word 'quality' would be one example – but this was a deliberate choice, and I wished to keep other influences to a minimum. I wanted to discover what adult learners and tutors meant by 'quality' from their individual perspectives, so that when responding to my questions they were answering within the context of their own definitions and circumstances. By using more open questions that sought opinions and perceptions (i.e. that would 'supply a frame of reference for respondents' answers, but put a minimum of restraint on the answers and their expression' (Kerlinger 1970, cited in Cohen and Manion 1994: 277), the process would be seen as less threatening by respondents and should lead, circuitously, to the desired information (Tuckman 1972).

When attempting to gather data from busy students and tutors, I was aware that I would have to devise a method of doing so that balanced desirability on my part with realism. Adult learners make the most of the time they spend on courses, often having to manage learning within the framework of demanding lives, and understandably they resent undue distractions during the time they had set aside to attend courses. It was tempting to conduct a very broad-based enquiry that would encompass all those factors that students might regard as affecting their learning experience including, for example, enrolment systems, child-care facilities, information, advice and guidance and so on, but I was principally concerned with the interactive process of teaching and learning, and such a lengthy enquiry would have been discouraging to potential participants. In fact, although respondents had the opportunity to make any observations they wished on their experience as students, almost all comments related specifically to teaching and learning, or to the environment in which it took place (see Chapter 7). I was also aware of the pressures on part-time tutors who contribute, voluntarily, well in excess of the time for which they are paid, for the benefit of their students. My research, in common with many enquiries made by colleges, would be largely dependent upon the cooperation of tutors. The assistance tutors could offer, by encouraging the completion and return of forms, would be considerable, and equally any lack of encouragement could be detrimental to the whole procedure.

Ultimately, my research is about people and their views, attitudes, values and beliefs, and it became clear that it would be more effective if it included both qualitative and quantitative data to compare perceptual and factual responses for depth and scope. By giving pre-eminence to qualitative data, statistical data could be used to test hypotheses thrown up by analysis of the qualitative data (Brannen 1992). I resolved to ask questions that would elicit data within certain parameters, whilst enabling individuals to offer additional comments if they wished to do so. It would be important to ensure that I gave the same questions to all potential respondents 'in order to be confident that each question would be interpreted by each respondent in a similar manner' and that the questions would 'be as free as possible from ambiguity' (Brown and Dowling 1998: 66).

Selecting research methods

The research literature offers a rich resource of information on the relative values of research methods, and the practical implications and advantages offered by each. Attendance at various courses on research methods, and a study of the literature, had enabled me to eliminate some methods as inappropriate for my purposes. I would not use, for example, ethnography or discourse analysis, because I did not plan to dissect, phrase by phrase, the precise words employed by my respondents, but rather to find strands between their chosen language (Cohen and Manion 1994; Brown and Dowling 1998; Scott and Usher 1996). Yet I had to ensure that my empirical research was supported by 'the collection, analysis and presentation of primary data in a rigorous, systematic and methodical way' (Scott and Usher 1996: 10). My research would take place in an interpretative paradigm (Cohen and Manion 1994), because the collected data would not be a scientific mathematical certainty, but would be a synthesis of individual perceptions and descriptions. I would be concerned with individual's perceptions, as expressed through their personal constructs. A correlational approach would be most appropriate to enable me to search retrospectively for causal relationships through collected data (Brown and Dowling 1998; Bryman 1988; Marsh 1982; Scott and Usher 1996).

An advantage of using questionnaires and interviews is that it 'brings together three different methodological areas: sampling, designing, questioning and interviewing' (Fowler 1993: 4). I chose to begin distribution of questionnaires, and to gather quantitative data, in order to gain the necessary information to contact potential interviewees. Also, by completing a questionnaire, individual students would be more aware of the study and better informed when responding to my request to be interviewed.

I would be exploring differences in perceptions between my research groups and would be able to test any degree of variance from quantitative data through interviews with individual students and staff (Marsh 1982; Bryman 1988).

This approach would satisfy the requirements that:

a) systematic measurements were made over a series of cases yielding a matrix of data;
b) variables in the matrix were analysed to see if they showed any patterns;
c) the subject matter was social;
d) observations were collected at one point in time; no 'before' observations were made, no control was exercised over experimental variables, and no control groups were explicitly constructed.

(Bryman 1988: 7; Denzin 1989: 139)

Furthermore, I determined that because of the complexity of human behaviour, to adopt the use of triangulation would enable me to reach more valid conclusions from the collected data. In this case triangulation would enable me to contrast and compare the views expressed by respondents in completed questionnaires, the views from those whom I would interview and the experience of the published literature. This multi-method approach would facilitate a more holistic view of educational experiences and outcomes, as seen by the participants (Cohen and Manion 1994), and would utilize aspects of two of Denzin's types of triangulation in research: *space triangulation*, that attempts to overcome the parochialism of studies in different subcultures – in this case different colleges; and *methodological triangulation*, in that I would employ different methods on the same object of study (ibid.: 234). I would be using triangulation to make comparisons 'between perceptions, connections and descriptions' (Scott and Usher 1996: 151). I would be asking questions of my research population after the learning experiences to which they would refer had taken place. My research would, therefore, be *ex post facto* in its nature, since I was not able to observe the actual processes referred to, and planned to investigate possible cause and effect relationships (Cohen and Manion 1994; Brown and Dowling 1998).

I could not separate within their contributions how participants felt prior to that learning episode nor to what extent the episode had altered their views. I would be looking for relationships between *theoretical (concept) variables* and *empirical (indicator) variables* from the expressed views which were the culmination of the individual's experiences up to the point of my enquiry. In *ex post facto* research, control of the independent variable is not possible. Investigators must 'take things as they are and try to disentangle them' (Cohen and Manion 1994: 149). My research would involve large numbers of people and I would endeavour to record opinions and perceptions, following the experience of teaching and learning up to, and including, the point of my enquiry, but I would have no control over what had taken place prior to that point.

Questionnaire design

I was aware of the need to keep the enquiry forms as short as reasonable, not to make them look unattractive and off-putting by being over-full of text and to use a comfortable font size (many of my respondents were likely to be elderly and might have sight impairment). The forms should explain briefly what my research was about and encourage participation. They should also acknowledge that participation was voluntary and that the confidentiality of responses would be assured. Participants should feel free to express their own opinions in responding to the questions, and to add any additional comments that they might wish to make.

I would need to endeavour to see that my questions were clear, and and 'as free as possible from ambiguity'. They should be as short as possible 'free from bias' (Brown and Dowling 1998: 66–67). Brown and Dowling (1998) suggest a range of factors that can influence responses to questionnaires, and they also refer to the advantages of supervision of the distribution and completion of questionnaires. Although this was arranged during the pilot stage, it was not possible for me to supervise these aspects of my research. Had I been able to do so, it is possible that I might have achieved a higher response rate.

Interviews

Potential interviewees were selected at random from those who had returned questionnaires and had completed the optional personal identification section. A random selection was made, rather than using theoretical or selective sampling, in order to maintain the lowest possible level of influence on data acquired. As the individuals selected for interview would have previously completed a questionnaire I decided upon a semi-structured format for the interviews to enable each person to develop and elaborate on their answers as they thought fit. As Brown and Dowling point out, all interviews will have some structure, and the interviewer might work from 'a loose set of guidelines' during a conversational-style exchange (Brown and Dowling 1998: 73). In this case, my 'set of guidelines' was the questions previously asked in questionnaires. This would ensure that, as with the questionnaires themselves, all interviewees would be asked the same questions and encouraged to expand upon what they had previously written. Some individuals in interview, before answering some questions, did ask me to tell them what they had written on their questionnaire forms, and I explained that I preferred not to do so until they had answered a second time.

Locating the research

To ensure reasonable access to my research population, I gained approval from LEA officers and college principals to carry out research in nine adult community colleges in the east of England. These colleges, collectively, provide both a local service and also attract students from a much wider area, including beyond county borders.

The curriculum and services made available by the colleges offer a rich choice of learning opportunities for adults. The institutions combine a mixture of liberal adult education – a range of languages, arts, crafts, sport and physical activities, basic skills, humanities, domestic skills, dance, movement and yoga, business and office skills, computing, music and a wide range of general interest courses – accredited and non-accredited courses, cultural activities, events and exhibitions – with a further range of courses accredited through open college networks, significantly enhanced information technology facilities, and partnership schemes with a wide range of other agencies.

The role of researcher

Research literature refers to the different roles of a researcher, and emphasizes that research is not a passive activity which has no implications to those being researched, but rather is a 'mode of interrogation that drives the development of structural coherence' (Brown and Dowling 1998: 138). My research was to be of an epistemological, rather than an ontological, kind. That is, the 'realities' to be recorded would not be external to the individual, but would be transmitted through subjective interpretation of their own learning and experiences. I might be seen by my research population as a distant anonymous figure, perhaps as a part the 'authority' (certainly a few student respondents appeared to see me in this way), and I would be asking people to devote some of their time to assist me in *my* project. For some of the targeted individuals my research might be seen as intrusive, into both their learning time and their lives. My research would need the cooperation of large numbers of individuals and it would be important that, when determining practical arrangements for the distribution and collection of questionnaires and the conducting of interviews, I should ensure that, so far as possible, all concerned were clear about the focus of my research, and how it was being carried out.

The pilot stage – questionnaires and interviews

> Adults expect their status to be recognised ... they expect to be treated with respect and dignity on a course as elsewhere ... ultimately they can choose to vote with their feet if they do not find the equality adulthood that is their right.
> (Daines *et al.* 1993: 8)

Brown and Dowling warn that 'it is vital to carry out a pilot study with a sample which matches the profile of the sample for the main study' (Brown and Dowling 1998: 67), and as I planned to include ten colleges in my main research I decided to use five of them in the pilot survey. Unfortunately, the principal of one college, having agreed to take part in the pilot stage, then withdrew. I selected 44 courses at five of the remaining nine colleges, which included a representative sample of the whole curriculum on offer. Courses at this stage were chosen by selective sampling to include examples of the types of courses generally available in the colleges, and also to ensure inclusion of courses held during the day and in the evening.

By visiting each selected course, taking with me questionnaires for students and staff, I was able to avoid the difficulties of misunderstanding that can arise if enquiry forms are sent out by post (Brown and Dowling 1998). This meant, also, that I was able to clarify any obvious mis-interpretations and reduced the likelihood of this occurring in my main field research.

I conducted three interviews on the same pattern as described above, to test my methods and terminology, and to see how readily interviewees expanded upon the answers given in their questionnaires.

Main field research

At the same time as carrying out the pilot stage I had been preparing the ground for my main field research. College principals were aware in general terms of my research, particularly those whose colleges were involved in the pilot stage, but it was necessary to discuss this with them in much more detail. Since the possibility of including all students and tutors across the ten colleges was impracticable, it was necessary for decisions to be made about how my research sample was to be determined. I needed to balance the overall size of the sample with a breadth of useful data.

We agreed that, with regard to the size of the research sample, data collected from students and tutors attending on two days of the week would provide both a representative sample and a good curriculum range, as many courses were available on more than one day each week. This level of potential involvement should mean the sample would be reasonably representative of the population under survey (Cohen and Manion 1994).

Data collection and response rate

Questionnaires were distributed, as agreed, to all courses involved. Completed questionnaires were returned to me, via collection boxes provided, or by post. I indicated above that levels of return from surveys administered by post or, in this case, from a distance, can be lower than those administered face to face. The lack of opportunity to 'prompt' respondents or to offer encouragement, can mean that there may be a temptation to discard forms (Brown and Dowling 1998) or not to complete forms fully. The overall level of return, shown below, is less than I had hoped for but, considering the practicalities of the survey, the difficulties in controlling parts of it, and the pressures students and tutors are under, this was not an unreasonable level. Participation in the survey was, of course, voluntary and some students chose not to respond. There were, however, also some failings in the system for distributing the questionnaires, despite the careful preparations made by me and by college staff.

Within the returned questionnaires there were some that were 'spoilt' in one or more ways, making them of no use for analysis (see Table 4.1). Some were so incomplete as to provide little data, and certainly not comparable data across the questions; some showed signs of disruption during the completion process and one can speculate that students,

Table 4.1: Summary of numbers of questionnaires completed and analysed

Questionnaires	Students	Tutors
Number of questionnaires received	2,256	270
Number of 'spoilt' questionnaires	472	19
Number of questionnaires analysed	1,784	251
% analysed from those returned	79%	93%
% analysed of original distribution	21%	41%
% analysed of successfully distributed forms	58%	75%

having run out of time during the class, were not inclined to complete the task thereafter; and some did not include statistical data showing gender, age group or course group, removing the possibility of comparisons being made.

The final numbers of forms discounted and those sufficiently completed to allow analysis is shown in Table 4.1. It was disappointing to lose this number of incomplete forms, in addition to those not returned at all, and this re-emphasizes the advantage of a personally administered enquiry form, referred to above.

Interviews and rationale for sampling

A random sample (to avoid selection bias) of 24 potential interviewees was selected from students and tutors who had completed the questionnaires and had identified themselves, enabling contact to be made. All but two readily agreed to my request to be interviewed and most preferred their home to be the venue. I was pleased that individuals so readily agreed to my request to be interviewed despite, in some cases, personal problems in their lives. The 22 analysed interviews represented a range of subjects, as shown below.

Art History, CIT/DTP, CLAIT 1, Customer Care, History (GCSE) (2), Floristry, Italian, Keep Fit, Keyboarding, Latin, Painting – Oils, Painting – Watercolour, Parchment Craft, Pottery, Psychology (2), Reflexology, Spanish, Women's DIY, Women Returners, and Dance, Movement and Yoga

All interviews were recorded with the individual's agreement, and took 25–55 minutes. Most interviewees spoke at length about their courses, how much they enjoyed them and what benefits they had gained from them, repeating often what they had noted on their questionnaires, and adding additional remarks. Some also added comments not of direct relevance to this research, taking the opportunity to address issues about which they felt strongly, e.g. the level of tuition fees. What was underlined strongly in most interviews was the commitment that individuals felt to their courses (whether as a student or tutor), amounting for many to a passion for their studies or their teaching. The validity of data from questionnaires was strengthened by the degree to which interviewees repeated comments they had made on the forms without any prompting. Of the 24 interviews conducted (representing 1% of participating students, and 2% of tutors) 12 were fully transcribed, 3 transcribed in part, and 7 were analysed but not transcribed. Two further interviews were lost because of technical difficulties with the recording equipment and could not be deciphered.

Data analysis and coding

Chapters 7, 8 and 9 provide details of the findings from collected data, but it is appropriate here to make some observations on the approach I adopted in analysing the data, both from interviews and questionnaires. From respondents' answers during interviews (and on questionnaires), it became apparent that responses were emerging in definable groups, with individuals employing similar terminology to answer questions. Key words or phrases in all responses, qualitative and quantitative, were coded in relation to the questions asked, the gender and age group of the respondent (see Appendix 2), the subject category of the course and whether or not the course was accredited (e.g. F2BN – see p. 58). Quantitative data also indicated the questionnaire number, to assist quick retrieval of forms. From this coding response groups emerged that are shown in tables in Chapters 7, 8 and 9, and examples of qualitative data from interviews and questionnaires are given verbatim in the analysis chapters.

Evaluation of research methodology

I am very pleased with the amount and detail of data collected, but I am aware of the limitations of this approach. Principally, the reduced control I had over questionnaires once they were delivered to colleges was of concern. One result of this, and the impracticability of visiting all courses, meant that I did not meet all the tutors involved who were, of course, pivotal to the successful distribution and return of the forms, despite the fact that some chose not to participate. I have also become aware that, as a result of the current closer scrutiny of all educational services, students and tutors are increasingly confronted with surveys by, for example, funding bodies or colleges' own information systems. This, I conjecture, would have influenced individual's reactions to a further enquiry of this nature, and it is possible that, had I been able to establish closer contact with students and their tutors (as during the pilot stage), I might have been able to reduce the number of wasted or incomplete forms and increase the resulting level of data collected.

Questionnaire limitations

I believe the research methods used to conduct this research proved to be the right choice to achieve my ends, despite the acknowledged limitations. I set out to discover the views of my research population, and their wide-ranging circumstances in terms of age, curriculum, geographical location and experience as learners meant that I have been able to gather a considerable bank of data from the 2,035 individuals (1,784 learners and 251 tutors) that I believe can be extrapolated to a much wider population (see Chapter 10). To have used a scaled system for my questions would have made the task of coding and analysing data much easier for me. I could have provided sets of pre-coded statements with which respondents would have agreed or disagreed, or placed in rank order (Brown and Dowling 1998; Cohen and Manion 1994). From these, data tables could easily have been constructed indicating individuals' attitudes towards each question. I chose not to adopt this method, however, because to have done so would have influenced and restricted responses to what *I* had decided were the main interpretations of quality in learning. I preferred, as indicated previously, to discover what my respondents thought was quality in their learning, using their *own* terminology.

I have been greatly encouraged by the general reaction to this research and by the willingness shown by so many students and tutors towards what, for at least some, must have been an unwelcome interruption to their studies. I am aware of the way in which this and other such surveys can intrude upon students' learning time for which they have, for the most part, paid a not inconsiderable fee, and I particularly appreciate, therefore, the large number of students who took the time to complete their forms and thereby to provide valuable information about the quality of their learning and the range of effects upon it. Similarly, those who kindly agreed to be interviewed did so willingly, in their own time, and showed a broad degree of interest in my study and what might emerge from it. Although not quite a 'whirl of energy and enthusiasm' (Phillips and Pugh 1987: 88) the general level of interest amongst students to my research may, I believe, be linked in some degree to their appreciation of the fact that someone else was taking an interest in the learning that for them was so important. Tutors, similarly, were generally very supportive and willing to provide statements, some in great detail, about their teaching and their views of students' learning. The requests made to tutors were, as with students, intrusive on their time, both inside and outside the classroom, but generally the approach adopted was one of willingness to participate. Sufficient explanation for the rationale behind this research has been provided in earlier chapters so I shall avoid repetition, except to state that the choice of adult community colleges as the focus of my field research provided a rich source of data, with colleges located in widely differing areas, and serving a large number of very interested and supportive students and staff.

The applications of findings on a larger scale

It was important to ask myself whether I believed the findings from this survey would be significantly different had I adopted a different methodology or means of analysis. In casual discussions held since the survey with college principals, other senior college staff, students and tutors both from the participating colleges and from others in different parts of the country, I have been informed that my findings support the personal informal observations. I have no reason to believe, therefore, that my findings are in any way unrepresentative of adult colleges as a whole, nor of similar institutions across the country. Findings from my research are shown in Chapters 7 and 8, and the results are compared and contrasted in Chapter 9.

5 Adults as Learners

Introduction

> The preservation and acquisition of knowledge and the ability of individuals to fulfil their personal capacity to learn are vital signs of a free and civilised society.
> (DfE 1995b: 6)

> Learning remains the responsibility of the adult learner; as teachers we cannot learn for our students. We can, however, strive to provide sound and accessible learning opportunities for them by thoughtful planning and preparation, by well-run sessions and by careful evaluation of the whole process.
> (Daines *et al.* 1993: 131)

I make frequent reference to the terms 'adult education' and 'values' and, as an introduction to the data and research findings in later chapters, this chapter considers briefly what is meant by these and other terms. The meaning of adult education in this book was explained in Chapter 3, and in this chapter it is located within the overall framework of post-compulsory education. The concepts of 'adult' and 'adulthood' are explored, with particular emphasis on learning as an adult, and the teaching of adults from tutors' perspectives. The chapter considers what it is that adult learners bring to their learning, and what are the characteristics of being an adult learner, as distinct from a child learner. It suggests that these characteristics enable some adults to develop an increased awareness of, and to exercise a greater control over, their learning – constructively drawing upon previous experiences, and thereby enhancing the quality of their current learning. As in other chapters, the discussion is linked to research data presented in subsequent chapters.

In this and other chapters, quotations from research data show an alphanumeric reference that indicates, respectively, gender (F or M), age group (1–6: see Appendices 2 and 3), curriculum group (see Appendix 1) and whether or not the course is accredited (Yes or No – see Appendix 4). Quotations taken from interviews show the suffix, INT. (Example: F5AN:INT refers to a female, aged 51–60, who was attending a visual arts course that was not accredited, and was one of those interviewed by me.)

Adults and adulthood

As this thesis is concerned with quality in adult learning from the perspectives of adult students and their tutors, it is appropriate to consider briefly what is meant by various terms employed in different parts of this study. To provide a definitive explanation of what is an adult and what constitutes adulthood could take the form of a significant paper in its own right and such precise definitions are not required for the purpose of this book. In different parts of the world formal transition from childhood to adulthood may variously imply a certain stage of experience, or the successful completion of certain rites, or no more than the reaching of a specific point in chronological development. In the Western world we have adopted the last as the formal stage at which a young person achieves adulthood, reaches the 'age of majority' and gains, for example, the right to vote in elections. Yet before this stage is reached, presently at the age of 18 in the UK for most legal purposes, some activities generally associated with adulthood may be exercised, such as marriage, full-time employment, fighting for one's country, driving a motor vehicle and being subject to taxation. This formal status of becoming an adult at the age of 18 in the UK recognizes no more than the achievement of the required number of years of life and implies no specific maturation of physique, nor of intellect, nor of the ability to make critical judgements. In common discourse we tend to think of an adult in terms of age but further consideration evokes a wide range of concepts. The word can refer to 'a stage in the life cycle of the individual'; or to 'status, an acceptance by society that the person concerned has completed his or her novitiate and is now incorporated fully into the community'; or to 'a social sub-set: adults as distinct from children'; or 'it can include a set of ideals and values: adulthood' (Rogers 1986: 5). It is with the last of these, with connotations of experience and personal values, that this study is principally concerned. With increased attention being given today to the concept of citizenship and to adult learners being responsible for their own learning, it is these experiences, together with intellectual advancement, that can contribute to the well-being of an individual and to the development of a more useful member of society. Even when 18 years are attained, adult status is not accorded to all. Severely disabled people, for example, 'may never achieve or be allowed full adult status' (Tight 1996: 13–14). If, therefore, physical or chronological maturity are insufficient to define adulthood the idea of 'adult' is not directly connected to age, but is related to what generally happens as we grow older. Transition from child to adult is not sudden or instantaneous – linked as it is by what we often still refer to as 'teenage' or 'adolescence' – and individuals will progress to and through each stage at different times in their lives and at a different pace from one another. It may be that the key is to be found in Knowles' proposition that adulthood is reached at the point when adults perceive themselves to be essentially self-directing (Knowles 1980), and this point is explored further below, with reference to the theories of andragogy. If, then, it seems difficult to reach a generally acceptable definition of what constitutes an adult or what precisely 'adulthood' is, perhaps a more satisfactory approach may be to identify some of those characteristics inherent within the concept of adulthood. From those characteristics of adulthood which might be generally acknowledged as part of being an adult – e.g. farsightedness, self-control, established values, experience and autonomy – there emerge three clusters of ideas which are also likely to lie within any view of adulthood. These characteristics are amongst the ones most commonly advanced, although not all of us would claim that to be an adult an individual needs to possess all these traits. Alan Rogers describes the three clusters of characteristics as 'maturity', 'perspective' and 'autonomy':

> Maturity: the idea of full development and personal growth, the expansion and utilisation of all the individual's talents.
>
> Perspective: we expect an adult to be able to make sound judgements from their sense of perspective, drawn from accumulated experience, and to show a more balanced approach to life and to society.
>
> Autonomy: one of the key elements of adulthood is that of thinking more about oneself and taking responsibility for one's own deeds and development.
> (Adapted from Rogers 1986: 6–7)

Other earlier writers have offered similar examples of possible criteria for defining adulthood taking, for example, either a categorized approach (Allport 1961), or a stage of responsibility approach (Havighurst 1972) or a social role approach (Boshier 1980). These writers refer to the development of competencies and degree of responsibility which we expect to find in the maturing adult, and some evidence of these may be found in Chapter 7. The idea that adulthood can be explained through changing social roles or developmental tasks undertaken as the individual matures is adopted by other writers. In Verner's view, for example,

> An adult is a person who has come into that stage of life in which he [sic] has assumed responsibility for himself and usually for others, and who has concomitantly accepted a functionally productive role in his community.
> (Verner 1964: 29)

Ethical and moral issues influence adults both as citizens and as learners to a far greater degree than in the case of children and young people, as do the characteristics of autonomy, self-awareness, judgemental skills and responsibility. Adults are expected to exercise ethical and moral judgements, and will also exercise other judgements based on their own set of personal values (see below). Evidence of these characteristics may also be seen in research data in Chapter 7.

The characteristics of adults as learners

It was pointed out above that to give a full explanation of the interpretations and definitions of 'adulthood' is both inappropriate and beyond the scope of this book. Similarly, it suffices here to state that an adult learner for the purposes of this survey is one who has reached the statutory school leaving age of 16 (the legal age under which adult education services are not usually available) and who, essentially, is a voluntary (usually paying) participant in whatever 'formal' learning is presently being undertaken. The word 'formal' is used here to indicate some structured learning experience in or organized by an institution, as distinct from informal experiential learning which takes place throughout an adult's life before, during and after the course he/she is currently attending, and to which further attention is given below.

It would not be appropriate to offer here a full explanation of how people learn. This is a huge field and other writers have done more justice to the many facets of the subject than would be possible in this context. There are, however, certain aspects of the psychology of learning in general which are relevant to this study of adults as learners, and to which some reference should be made. Many adult learners are experienced in assessing the quality of their own learning. They bring to the learning environment wide experience of life and of learning in a variety of contexts since completion of their initial schooling. They will have learnt strategies for coping with, for example, the effects of ageing, the challenges of access to institutions and courses, the requirements of work and family and of managing their time to allow for many competing demands.

New students are not new people, however; they possess a set of values, established prejudices and attitudes in which they have a great deal of emotional investment (Rogers 1986). The extent to which individuals are aware of this will vary, and evidence of these conditions is to be found in Chapter 7, from examples given by students. Against the background of maturity described above, adults (significantly those attending adult education courses (see below), despite their personal or professional 'status' – as employees, employers, managers, parents, house-holders, etc. – are often, at least initially, very compliant and passive as students. This reflects, perhaps, the influences of schooling which, for many, was their most recent formal learning experience. Data in Chapter 7 give examples of the ways in which some adult learners adopt a very subservient attitude in the classroom. Some students will revert to what they see as a 'student role' (my terminology) and do not question the standards, processes and environment by which and in which their learning takes place.

Adult learning carries with it a connotation of activity, something external engaged in by the would-be learner for some definite end. 'The notion of activity, action, behaviour or conduct is embedded in the term participation' (Courtney 1992: 99), but 'learning' and 'participation' may not be the same thing. Yet although as adults they bring considerable experience, both of life in general and sometimes of the subject they are studying, many seem often not to recognize or value this experience or its relevance to their present studies. Data in Chapters 7 and 9 show that learners in this study fell into two distinct groups – those who recognized the value of that experience and drew upon its lessons, and those for whom each learning episode was a new experience, unconnected to what had gone before.

Mature students' experiences of schooling may have established in them concepts of what constitutes 'good' teaching and learning processes, assessment and examination procedures and classroom activities. They will, perhaps, have expectations about the environment in which their learning takes place, possibly low expectations reflecting their previous experiences, which may be linked to recollections 'not of hope' but, in some cases, 'of humiliation' (Williamson 1998: 9). In particular they may have a firm, though often erroneous, view of what is expected of them as learners, although because they have a much wider experience than younger students of life outside educational institutions it is often the case that 'their short-term memory will be more critical in evaluating new information before accepting it' (Williams 1978: 103). It has also been found that the quality of the initial return to learning experience is a factor influencing movements between types and levels of learning (McGivney 1992). As two respondents in my study commented:

> 'The more study one does the easier it becomes; learning is an art in itself.' (F4LN)

> 'It makes me highly critical – but also very appreciative of excellence in whatever form.' (F5AN)

References to the subservient approach adopted by some students, although supported by data to be found in Chapter 7 are, of course, generalizations. Whilst they are demonstrated by many adult part-time students they can also be contrasted with the significant, although smaller, number who show that they do acknowledge the value of their previous experience. These individuals illustrate ways in which prior learning can influence current learning, by the nature and extent of their active participation in the learning process (see Chapters 7, 8 and 9).

Adult learning theory and the andragogy debate

As suggested in Chapter 1, although traditionally less attention has been given to the study of adult, as distinct from child, learning it has been from the general theories on learning (with reference to children) that the nature of adult learning has developed and received separate consideration. There are many characteristics of effective learning that would apply equally to a learner of any age – a conducive environment, effective teaching, encouragement and support, awareness of success and so on – yet for some writers the nature of adult learning and adult learners (e.g. Lawson 1975 and Lovell 1980) and of the adult curriculum (e.g. Griffin 1983) deserve separate and equal consideration.

It would not be appropriate here to summarize the many theories of learning, but some must be referred to briefly, especially to the extent that they are applicable to learning as an adult, and are therefore likely to affect an adult's approach to the quality of the learning experience. Also, the work of some earlier psychologists, although at the time referring to child learning, has proved to be of such fundamental importance that it forms the basis of any study of learning. The early work of Thorndike (1928), whose theories of the stimulus and response effects on learning (the Law of Effect, 1898) were drawn upon by Skinner (1971) with his theories of operant (or instrumental) conditioning, having at their heart acts of voluntary behaviour. Skinner, as an extreme behaviourist, advocates the effects of reward and punishment and to this extent his theories can be seen to apply to learners of any age, since the notion of rewarding application and success in learning (whatever the nature of any 'reward') is likely to find agreement in most circles. However, with adult learners the negative effects of 'punishment' (perhaps more appropriately described as lack of encouragement, or as positive discouragement and criticism) are sometimes quoted as examples of poor teaching by dissatisfied students in my survey.

'The tutor tends to speak to those who are already fluent in Spanish, and ignore those who are not.' (F6LN)

The question of differences between 'teaching' and 'facilitating learning' are discussed below and data in Chapter 7 suggest that some tutors (though, it seems, not many) may show a rather distant approach, being unaware of the need to stimulate their students.

'A tutor who constantly reads word for word from his notes scarcely lectures with enthusiasm.' (F5KN)

Few psychologists ignore the progression of ageing in their writings and most make some reference to increased maturity, following on from the learning of earlier years. Piaget is one such psychologist who, although often quoted with reference to child learning, also emphasized the way in which 'new material is assimilated by the learner who modifies it to fit the previously learned material which is stored in memory. In its turn the contents of the memory store become modified by the accommodation of the new material' (Lovell 1980: 53). As suggested above, some adult educators would argue that of all the schools of learning theory, the Gestalt school is the most relevant to adult learning. Certainly, it is often demonstrated that adults learn more effectively if they see the whole task stretching out before them and can thus more easily relate the current topic to this completeness of goal. Proponents of the Gestalt school suggest that the four rules of 'Pragnanz' or 'meaningfulness' will structure the perceptual field in as simple and clear a way as possible in order to impose meaning on it. 'The four laws of similarity, proximity, closure and good continuation account for the way a learner structures his perceptual field.' The basis of the Gestalt school is, stated simply, that the whole is greater than the sum of its parts; that the 'extra element of meaningfulness that comes when we recognize five pencil strokes as the face of a well-known politician, for example, results from the four laws of perception' (ibid.: 43).

Breaking down the processes of learning into stages, types of learning and outcomes seems a logical way to investigate those processes, and observable changes in skills, cognitive patterns (knowledge and understanding), motivation and interest and ideology (fundamental beliefs) can provide valuable evidence. It is not the function of this chapter to venture into a detailed exploration of learning theory, but a further brief reference to one or two theorists is appropriate before a discussion of andragogy.

Domains of learning are used by some theorists to catalogue aspects of the adult learning process. Gagne (1972) includes motor skills, verbal information, intellectual skills, cognitive strategies and attitudes (cited in Rogers 1986: 43–4). Bloom employs domains of cognitive, affective and psycho-motor, often drawn upon in the training of adult education tutors (ibid.: 51). Both Carl Rogers (1974) and Abraham Maslow (1968) describe learning as the main process of meeting the compulsions of inner urges and drives, rather than responding to stimuli or meeting the demands of new knowledge. Carl Rogers viewed it as a series of drives towards adulthood – autonomy, responsibility and self-direction – although Alan Rogers (1986) points out that it is now clear that the precise forms of such drives are culturally bound, that they do not apply in all societies. Maslow, on the other hand, saw the need to satisfy in part or in whole a hierarchy of needs; satisfaction or control of the needs at each level being required before the individual can progress to satisfy higher-level needs The highest level which comes into operation when all other levels have been satisfied, or are controlled, is the need for 'self-actualization'. Maslow's hierarchy, frequently used in the training of teachers of adults, is expressed in Table 5.1.

Table 5.1: Maslow's hierarchy of needs

Level 1	*Physiological needs*: such as hunger, thirst, sex, sleep, relaxation and bodily integrity. These needs must be satisfied before level 2 needs can be considered.
Level 2	*Safety needs*: which call for a predictable and orderly world, safe, reliable, just and consistent. While these are not satisfied the person will be occupied in attempts to organize his/her world so as to provide the greatest possible degree of safety and security. Once these needs are satisfied the individual can look to satisfy level 3.
Level 3	*Love and belongingness needs*: which cause him/her to seek warm and friendly human relationships.
Level 4	*Self-esteem needs*: the desire for strength, achievement, adequacy, mastery and competence, for confidence in the face of the world, independence and freedom, reputation and prestige.
Level 5	*Self-actualization*: the full use and exploitation of talents, capacities and potentialities. Self-actualizers are able to submit to social regulation without losing their own integrity or personal independence; that is, they may follow a social norm without their horizons being bounded in the sense that they fail to see or consider other possibilities. They may on occasion transcend the socially prescribed way of acting. Achieving this level may mean developing to the full stature of which they are capable.

Source: Maslow 1968; cited in Tennant 1997: 12–13

Adult learners have many reasons for undertaking a course of study, some with immediate use, others for a longer-term benefit, and it is possible to reduce these into three main 'orientations' (Houle 1961). In any adult learning situation some of the student participants are 'goal-oriented'. They wish to use education to achieve some clear-cut external objective such as a certificate or promotion or to solve an immediate problem they face. For them the learning experience tends to come to an end once the objective (often separate from the learning process) has been achieved. A second group is described as 'activity-oriented'. They like the atmosphere of the adult class, they find in the circumstances of the learning a meaning for themselves independent of the content or of the announced purpose of the subject matter; it meets a range of needs that are mainly personal and/or social; these people frequently seek the continuance of the activity even though the content of the learning may well change; they pass from one course to another, searching for satisfaction in the activity itself. The third group is described as 'learning-oriented'. They desire the knowledge or skill for its own sake. They pursue the subject out of interest and will continue to pursue it even without the assistance of a formal programme of adult learning (Houle 1961, cited in Rogers 1986: 30). Adult educators, in an attempt to illustrate the differences between adult and child learning, quote the writings of Michael Knowles, who has offered many examples of these differences and his theories of andragogy are offered as evidence. His theories, whilst embraced by many adult educators as further evidence of the distinctive nature of adult education, are also criticized by a number of other authors. The concept of andragogy can be interpreted in several ways. To some it is 'an empirical descriptor of adult learning styles, to others it is a conceptual anchor from which a set of appropriately "adult" teaching behaviours can be derived, and to still others it serves as an exhortation; a prescriptive rallying cry' (Brookfield 1986: 90). Adult educators, perhaps in an attempt to gain further recognition for their work, 'commonly claim a distinctive nature of their enterprise, implying that adult education differs significantly from the rest of the educational system' (Keddie 1980: 45). Andragogy has for some time been a 'badge of identity' for many educators and trainers of adults. They have often used it to combat what they see as the use with adult learners of overly didactic modes of teaching and programme planning. Other writers are critical of the theory and, as suggested above, argue that most of the aspects referred to in relation to adult learning apply just as much to the learning of children. Knowles himself describes andragogy as 'simply another model of assumptions about learners, to be used alongside the pedagogical model of assumptions' (Knowles 1980: 43). However the extent to which andragogical approaches have been adopted by many adult educators suggest that he may have under-valued the impact made by his theories.

At the conceptual core of andragogy is the first of these characteristics. That is, the idea that the attainment of adulthood is concomitant on adults 'coming to perceive themselves as self-directing individuals, witnessed by adults' assumption of such social roles as worker, spouse, parent and citizen'. In relation to discussions of adulthood above, Knowles declares that 'the psychological definition of adulthood is the point at which individuals perceive themselves to be essentially self-directing' (ibid.: 46). These comments raise the question as to whether this stage is automatically reached by all individuals, although at different chronological points in their lives or, since some individuals attain chronological maturity with little demonstration of self-directedness, adulthood can only be said to have been reached when this ability is evident. This theory is then more complicated than the notion of adult education as the imparting of skills and knowledge to individuals who have attained a certain chronological age (a limited perspective that is discussed below with other considerations of the nature of adult education). At the heart of Knowles' theories is an ideal teacher-learner relationship

in which the andragogical teacher accepts each student as a person of worth and, respecting his feelings and ideas, seeks to build relationships of mutual trust [and] exposes his own feelings. The use of well-defined objectives, contractual agreements, and objective records of behavioural changes are all seen as essential to a successful programme of behavioural change.

(Knowles 1990: 85–6)

Not all writers on adult learning fully accept the andragogical model, at least as a theory of adult learning. This may in part be because it can be interpreted in a number of different ways:

as an initial guide to assist adult learners towards self-direction; as a process of learning appropriate for adults who have already attained the capacity to be self-directed; or as a means through which individual needs can be reconciled with institutional or organisation's demands.

(Tennant 1997: 14)

It may be that whatever interpretation is adopted by proponents of the andragogy model (and for some it has acquired the status of an established doctrine) the difficulty that remains is whether the theory is based in insufficient empirical research to justify its dominant position (Jarvis 1984). The scale of the influence of andragogy may be said to 'outstretch its substance' and is explained by the observation that it

> is not really a theory of adult learning at all, it is more a philosophical position on the aims of adult education and the relationship between the person and society; a position which ultimately places faith in the potency of the individual to transcend their social and historical situation.
>
> (Tennant 1997: 18)

Other critics question andragogy on the grounds that it selects, *a priori*, one aspect of teaching and sets it above all others. It may be that it is empirically unsound in that some of the supposed differences between adults and children are a function not of age but of the nature of the institutions. I cannot support that view, except to the extent that until recent years it was reasonable to state that types of provision for adults learning were grouped into certain kinds of institution.

Continuing efforts by many adult educators to argue for the distinctive nature of adult learning suggests that this debate will continue for some time. It is possible to identify distinct characteristics of the adult learner and of adult learning, and to show how these may in many instances differ from those of the child learner. The essential argument is whether or not the differences are fundamental, or only a matter of degree and emphasis.

There is no doubt in my mind that many differences do exist, and should be addressed in practices and methodologies. This is not say that the differences *should* exist. All the characteristics of good teaching and learning with adults referred to above should, in my view, apply equally to younger students. The key questions considered within this thesis are the extent to which these differences affect current learning and, more particularly, the extent to which adult learners recognize and draw upon these differences to assist their current learning. Debate continues on the value and relevance of andragogy as distinct from pedagogy, and despite the enthusiasm with which many adult educators cite its philosophical basis as justification for the distinctive nature of their work, the evidence presented in this chapter suggests that insufficient evidence is available to claim it as an alternative theory. Indeed, so much uncertainty was offered from so many sources that at least one writer sought to be delivered from 'the andragogy morass' (Davenport 1993: 109). What is evident also, however, is the significant number of ways in which adult learning can be distinguished from learning by children, principally because of the nature of the learner, and the next section considers further what is 'adult education'.

The experiences of adult learners

Adult-education students may range in age, as stated above, from 16 with no upper age limit, and there are examples across the country of students attending adult education courses regularly well into their 70s (Sargant *et al.* 1997). The majority in my survey are female (79 per cent, to 21 per cent male), reflecting the predominance of women that has applied in adult education over many decades, although more recently across the country the balance has altered slightly in favour of men (ibid., 1997). Of these, a large majority may be described as addictive adult students, in that they will attend courses year after year, sometimes taking one subject for up to six years (e.g. a foreign language), and then changing to a different subject. Others, however, take a series of one-year or shorter courses, pursuing perhaps well over 50 courses over their life of study. Adult students attend courses for a variety of reasons, so far as limited research suggests (e.g. Rogers 1971; Sargant 1991; Smith and Spurling 2001; Stuart and Thompson 1995) and are unlikely to share one motive for joining a course. Many choose a course either because they have some experience of the subject and wish to pursue it to a higher level, or to learn a new subject. Others may choose from the 'menu' of courses on a given day or evening, because they are unsure which course to join and have reliable transport available, perhaps with another student. Others will be motivated by challenges – keeping up with the academic progress of family members, or obtaining a qualification which will enable them to progress or work better in their employment. Others will wish to study a subject with which they have, perhaps, had a passing acquaintance over many years. Others, so far as is known, come because they are lonely or wish to escape from the domestic environment for a few hours and for whom, at least initially, the actual subject is of a lesser importance than the opportunity to meet and mix with others. This, apparently haphazard, basis for joining a course of learning does not reflect the motivation and commitment most adults demonstrate towards their learning. Adult learners have a complex interweaving of motives for learning and will have gained a whole range of experiences, according to their age, life-style, employment status, family status and prior formal and informal learning. Their attitudes to current learning will have been influenced by their prior learning, although this raises the question as to whether they recognize the value of that prior learning and to what extent it influences new learning. They may, for example, have fought in a war, raised a family, suffered bereavement, enjoyed a high profile career in industry, experienced unemployment, suffered disappointing or unsatisfactory previous learning, experienced serious illness or undertaken no structured learning for several years. There may be as many examples of these and many other human experiences as there are people on a course. Their tutor also may have enjoyed any one or more similar human experiences, and he/she will also have gained a knowledge of the subject that will form the context or medium through which they all will be learning for the duration of the course. For learning entails learning above and beyond an acquisition of knowledge, and the active interchange of ideas and views will provide a rich source of other learning for all involved.

What adult learners bring to the learning environment

The adult mind is not a *tabula rasa* on to which knowledge is to be etched by those who 'know' and, whether or not this is recognized by individual learners, adults bring to the learning environment a range of experiences, prejudices and expectations that will influence their process of learning and, I contend, to some degree the process of their fellow learners. These points are echoed by Jarvis:

> Learners do not come to education as empty containers to be filled, what Freire (1972) called 'banking education'. Education should now both seek to use the learners' expertise and build on their knowledge, which can be done through a variety of teaching techniques, including a mutual sharing of expertise amongst the learners (and the teachers) .... (Jarvis 2002: 208)

Adults learn in part through their experiences and the process and quality of their learning will be influenced by, and often directly assisted by, their life experiences and prior learning – formal, informal and experiential.

> Precisely because adult learners are members of society not 'apprentices' preparing for entry to it, they have a different status, they have the right to challenge what is offered in the light of their own experience in the world, and of their rights as citizens. (McNair 1997; cited in Elliott 1999: 38)

Many writers offer lists of characteristics of the adult learner (e.g. Brookfield 1986; Daines *et al.* 1993; and Powell 1991) and there is, not unexpectedly, often much similarity between these lists. The following list offers examples of what these writers claim summarize the *main characteristics of the adult learner.*

Typically adult learners, in comparison with younger learners:

- bring greater experience to learning;
- participate on a voluntary basis;

- have complex, and individual, objectives and circumstances, requiring individualized responses;
- participate in education intermittently throughout their lives;
- are restricted by work or domestic circumstances, in their ability to participate in learning at some distance from their workplace or home, and at certain times of the day;
- wish to have earlier learning recognized when they do participate.

(Adapted from Powell 1991: 13)

Other writers offer much longer, more comprehensive lists (e.g. James 1983, Daines *et al.* 1993) but probably the two distinguishing characteristics of adult learning most frequently advanced by theorists are the adult's autonomy of direction in the act of learning, and the use of personal experience as a learning resource (Brookfield 1986; Simpson 1980). And yet, as suggested above, there are many adults who, at least initially, seem not to be fully aware of the value of personal experience to their current learning. Data from this research in Chapter 7 offer evidence of this apparent paradox between one set of learners who portray an autonomy of direction, drawing upon their personal experiences:

'As an adult you choose to do it, so there's more interest.' (M2LN:INT)

and those who, despite their apparent maturity, show little evidence of these traits, having made a conscious choice unchallengingly to attend a course of study. They explain their role thus:

'To behave in a considerate manner to other students.' (F2CY)

'I take up as little of the tutor's time as possible.' (F4EN:INT)

'I contribute to the course by being courteous, attentive and not disrupting.' (F4PY:INT)

The adult learner is likely to have views on aspects such as the learning environment, course content and structure, tutor preparedness, teaching methodology, use and clarity of teaching and learning aids, tutor/student interaction, degree of tutor support and effectiveness, etc., as well as administrative efficiency and physical convenience. The degree of awareness of these influences on current learning will vary considerably and, as demonstrated in Chapter 7, is likely to be greater in the more experienced learner – that is, one who has been involved in institutional learning for a longer period and perhaps of a varying nature. Yet data in Chapter 7 also show that some students seem not to draw upon those previous experiences (see also Chapters 9 and 10).

Seeing learning from the learner's point of view

As referred to in Chapter 2, the *Learning and Skills Act* (DfES 2000) has brought about profound changes in education and learning. As I have mentioned earlier, the Act created a Learning and Skills Council which was empowered to oversee the provision, funding and inspection of all post-16 education and training other than higher education. The Act also created an additional inspectorate to work with Ofsted when inspecting adult learners and institutions providing learning opportunities for adults. Members of the Adult Learning Inspectorate (ALI) work in partnership with Ofsted inspectors, with either group taking a lead according to the ages of those being inspected. The published criteria for inspection by the ALI are contained within *The Common Inspection Framework* (ALI/Ofsted 2001), which requires evidence of the progress and achievement made by each individual learner, measured against stated objectives. All aspects of the providing agency are inspected, including leadership and management, and use of resources, but to focus here on teaching and learning, inspectors will make judgements by carefully considering, among others, the following:

- advice and guidance, given as necessary for the individual's needs;
- a pre-course statement of intent and purpose, a Learning Plan, which outlines the learner's wishes for learning and what he/she hopes to gain from the course;
- the tutor's course planning material, showing clear learning objectives;
- on-course assessment methods employed by the tutor to maximize the progress and achievement of each learner, and to maintain records of each individual's achievements;
- portfolio containing all relevant material in order that each student may take away from the course a full record of their work and achievements during the course, for use as they wish in future learning.

This CIF model set of criteria seems designed to meet all the needs of inspectors and enable them to make judgements about the planning and delivery of a course, and the progress made by each individual course member, as recorded by the tutor and student in partnership. The focus on progress and achievement by each individual learner is designed to ensure that each learner's separate and specific needs are catered for, as well as the collective needs of the learning group. This rigorous approach is intended to ensure that the achievement of each individual learner is measured against his/her starting point and personal progress. Records of course content, learning objectives and the individual's progress and achievement are to be retained to form part of a learning portfolio which individual students can take with them at the end of each learning episode as evidence of their learning. This seems to offer students an improved opportunity to measure and record their individual progress against previously agreed objectives, on a course that has been carefully planned, well-delivered, using relevant up-to-date material, that is regularly evaluated to ensure that it meets their individual needs. A set of circumstances with which it is reasonable to suppose no one would disagree. But, in my view, this is what should be happening in any case on good quality courses and, in my personal experience, generally has been the case in adult education for several decades. What is questionable, it seems to me, is whether the more rigorous approach required by the CIF will be relevant to all learners, and even in cases where it is, will it improve quality and standards?

As a result of recent work with staff at an adult college that is preparing for the new CIF-based inspection regime, I believe that what is needed to meet CIF criteria is to ensure that:

- students need to be clear about how their Learning Plan relates to the phased and final, assessed outcomes of their learning;
- students need to understand that the Learning Plan is designed, not to restrict their learning development and force them into a straightjacket of accreditation, but to encourage them to be clear about why they are undertaking a course of learning and where they see it taking them in terms of their future learning;
- tutors are required to maintain accurate records of each individual learner's progress and achievement from the starting point of the Learning Plan, and make copies of these records available for students to take with them at the end of their course;
- colleges, or other providers, are required to ensure that all the relevant records are kept and that all staff are aware of the requirements and their role in the revised system.

This is not to imply that the CIF offers a perfect set of criteria for judging learning, but it is the mechanism by which formal judgements currently are made and providers are aware of the LSC's powers over provision and funding (see Chapters 9 and 10). For some students, who follow non-accredited courses, a plan for future learning may not have been formulated, but by understanding better what they have learnt, and by receiving guidance on where their learning could take them, individual learners can maximize its value. As the CIF is implemented on a wider basis its impact will become clearer, but it is evident from data in Chapter 7 that some learners misunderstand the intent of the CIF, and resist what they see as irrelevant and unwanted accreditation and inspection of their course, which they may have joined just for the pleasure of learning. For some of them, quality is the absence of compulsory accreditation.

'... previous year's courses were straightjacketed by open college demands which offered no perceived advantage to us, the students – we did not even receive the completion certificate.' (M4LN)

'A flexible syllabus not encumbered by tests/credits, etc.; we can say – to some extent – what we want to learn.' (M6FN)

'More people, particularly pensioners, would attend more courses if the dreaded 'accreditation' was made optional!' (M5KN:INT)

Other writers have also found the sheer pleasure of learning expressed by adult students:

'So I thank God for the chance to return to learning. I feel like a sponge that's been squeezed dry and is now opening out through the joy of learning.'
(Coare and Thomson 1996: 5)

The processes involved in being a member of a course may be as important to the individual as the learning gained from that course. A student's commitment to the student role may be predicated on his commitment to homework and his willingness to engage in class activities; the kind of interaction possible within the class is largely determined by the style and methods of the teacher (Norris 1985). Various studies (ACACE 1982; McGivney 1992; Sargant *et al.* 1997; Sargant 1991) offer useful data describing why individuals choose particular courses, who they are, what educational needs they may recognize in themselves, the attitudes of families and friends towards their current studies, their attitude towards education generally and their awareness of future educational opportunities. Sargant *et al.*'s study (1997) offers data on student participation in past and present learning, and future intentions, portrayed by age, gender, social class, employment status, ethnic origin and regional spread. These highly informative data offer valuable comparisons across these criteria ranges, and emphasize the importance of all providers being aware that the adult learner is a highly complex individual, whose learning needs may not always be clear or well-formed, but whose motivation is likely to be high, as will be his/her commitment to learning and to the learning group.

The learning outcomes of any course of learning can be many and varied, and may be formal, informal, accredited or non-accredited, measurable or unquantifiable, intended or unintended. Many important outcomes of learning are not formally recognized or adequately described, yet could provide useful measures of student achievement and could be used as a basis for accreditation where no other exists. Learning outcomes could be used in the measurement of the effectiveness of learning processes if a collaborative approach is adopted by learners and tutors, and it is helpful to distinguish between 'outcomes' and 'outputs' in order to recognize the value of experience and prior learning, and the uses to which they may be put:

> Learning outcomes . . . should be seen as broader than outputs, and include the results of all the learning undertaken. Outcomes are concerned with what people can do as a result of the whole learning activity, whereas outputs tend to focus on what the learner knows about, or has learned from, the course content. Differentiating between outputs and outcomes is particularly important for the adult learner and for those concerned with the education of adults. Adult participants bring with them a wide range of previous experience, knowledge and learning, which they use as a basis for interpretation and understanding of new ideas. They may apply new knowledge and experience in much wider contexts and may therefore benefit from a learning programme in a range of quite different ways.   (UDACE 1989: 18–19)

The characteristics of adult learners, their motivations and expectations, the ways in which they are taught, and probably the learning environment, together with some personal factors can all have significant influences on how they learn, and it is difficult to separate these aspects one from the other. Chapter 7, however, shows that, for some students, the learning environment is less significant than one might have imagined. Some writers argue that the very nature of being an adult learner implies that he/she will learn in different ways from those of a child. Others will suggest it is easier to indicate what must be present or operating for successful adult learning to take place, rather than to suggest how adults learn in ways that would not apply to children (see the discussion of andragogy above).

For example, Daines *et al.* suggest that adults learn best when:

- they feel secure and they can try out things in safety;
- their needs are being met in ways that they can see are relevant and appropriate;
- they know what they have to do, especially where they have been involved in setting their own goals;

- they are actively involved and engaged;
- they know how well they are doing;
- they see and experience that they are welcomed and respected;
- both as adults and as individuals in their own right.

(Daines *et al.* 1993: 10)

Although all the above points could apply equally to child learners, one characteristic that is particularly relevant is the Gestalt theory, that the adult learner needs to be aware of the whole task, or whole pattern within which a particular aspect is being considered (Boydell 1976). Children seem more willing to learn slices of knowledge in isolation, but this may be simply because they lack the maturity to question how what they are studying fits into the whole task. Adults are likely to learn more effectively when the learning tasks are seen to be relevant, meaningful, interesting and useful, whereas children seem better able to reorganize knowledge into, for example, the order in which it will be examined. Often adults will 'tend to underestimate their ability to learn new material by giving too much emphasis to their school experience whilst overlooking the value of their more recent extensive informal learning experiences' (Lovell 1980: 28). For many, reared on the more traditional teaching methods, attempts to assess, with them, the value of their prior experiential learning may initially be met with resistance. Adults students are aware, of course, that previous learning has taken place but are not always easily able to relate the extent and value of that learning to their current studies. They often find it difficult to draw upon their disorganized collection of prior experiences and learning when faced with a well-structured learning opportunity in the form of a course, and may be uncertain exactly how much they already know, how this knowledge relates to what they are now expected to learn and how to recognize the connections between the two.

Some students do not appreciate and value their prior learning (see Chapter 7), perhaps because they think of learning as only that which is obtained during 'education', a term they seem to use to mean formal structured learning – probably aimed at an accredited outcome – such as they experienced during their schooling. In the current system the assessment of prior learning is restricted because qualifications are largely described in terms of outcomes, rather than of processes leading to outcomes. Other students seem to regard experiential learning (whether or not they recognize the term) as being limited to that which is not normally considered as academic – in that it is not subject-based and teacher directed – either in its content or in its location, or that such experience has no value unless it illustrates some part of a course (Kershaw 1979).

The relevance and value of prior learning experiences are not always seen in the same light:

> [because adults'] experiences are richer and more complex than younger learners this may make it difficult for them to approach a new task with an open mind. (Rogers 1971: 62)

This statement appears to conflict with others that suggest it is the adult's experience that enables him/her to draw upon prior learning when approaching a new task and assists in the differentiation of material, relating also to the writings of the Gestalt theorists. Boud *et al.* point out that 'experience is the foundation of, and the stimulus for, learning' (1993: 8) and for Usher *et al.*, this 'is at the heart of pedagogies of experiential learning' (1997: 100). This apparent paradox will be explored further in Chapter 7, drawing upon data collected from individuals who appear to display these contrasting views in their recorded observations.

Teaching adult learners

A student-centred approach to teaching and learning – not just in terms of methodology and delivery, but more significantly, as a basis for planning and rationale (for many decades the hallmark of adult education) – has become more frequently the practice in other post-compulsory education sectors. This is, perhaps, more evident in adult and higher education than in further education, where pressures by industry and businesses require the focus of teachers and managers to be always on the work-related training aspects of their endeavours. In all post-compulsory sectors, however, more attention is being given to the accreditation of prior learning, to recognition of the broad value of life-experience in the mature student and to the flexible approaches to learning from which older students can benefit. The essential difference with adult education (still used here in the liberal sense described above) is that for many years it has encouraged participation by students in decision-making about all aspects of their learning experiences, course planning, curriculum content, course delivery, teaching methodology, outcomes and assessment. The relationship between teaching and learning is explored by a number of writers. It is taken 'as axiomatic that teaching is important only in so far as it affects the outcomes of learning ... the quality of learning thus depends on the quality of the whole learning environment, of which face-to-face teaching is but one component' (Entwistle 1993: 14).

Teaching adults can present conflicting obligations which, as it involves a transaction between equals, brings the obligation to maximize the freedom of students and affects the methods as well as the content of education (Wiltshire 1980). The crucial idea in teaching and learning lies in the word 'relationship', involving patterns of interaction. If the educational process is teacher-centred the teaching and learning transaction is a process in which the teacher controls and students are given no encouragement to grow or develop (Jarvis 1995a). There is a need for teachers to recognize individual needs and differences and to 'capitalise on individual experience and expertise' (DES 1991: 8) as the complexity of classroom interaction, body language and the multiplicity of roles of student and tutor should be recognized (Hostler 1982). Teachers of adults (and of all learners) need to be sensitive to the needs of each student. A continuing challenge to tutors is the need to maintain a balance between the needs of the curriculum (where this is set externally) and the needs of the students, individually and collectively. This may at times produce 'a tension between the ethic of individualism and the spirit of collectivism' (Tennant 1997: 107). The terms 'teacher' and 'tutor' are used interchangeably by some writers and some students (see Chapter 7) but in adult education the latter term seems to enjoy most common use, perhaps because of a need to distinguish the activity from teaching in schools, and perhaps to relate the nature of the adult class more closely to the intimacy of a university tutorial group. Brookfield also is uncomfortable with continued use of the word 'teacher' and suggests as an alternative use of term '*facilitator*' (Brookfield 1986: Chapter 4). Entwistle elaborates this view by offering six supporting activities ideally to be

Table 5.2: Functions of teaching which support learning

Orienting	Setting the scene and explaining what is required
Motivating	Pointing up relevance, evoking and sustaining interest
Presenting	Introducing new knowledge within a clear, supportive structure
Clarifying	Explaining with examples and providing remedial support
Elaborating	Introducing additional material to develop and test personal understanding
Confirming	Ensuring the adequacy of the knowledge and understanding reached

Source: Entwistle 1993: 14

undertaken by the teacher: those of orienting, motivating, presenting, clarifying, elaborating and confirming (Table 5.2).

This makes an interesting comparison with the stages or phases in group life through which the group 'sorts out its authority, power and inter-personal relationships' (Tennant 1997: 118). Trainers of adult-education tutors have for long stated that the tutor is *primus inter pares* (explained earlier), and this relationship requires a student-centred approach at all times. For many tutors (see Chapter 8) it is this which provides the stimulation and enjoyment of adult teaching.

This chapter has shown that adult learners bring a complex set of experiences and expectations to the learning environment that will inform their approach to the quality of new learning experiences. Their require-ments as learners, although in many ways similar to those of younger students, are also based around a need for their maturity and experiences to be recognized in the content and methodology of their teaching. Data in Chapter 7 show that, for many adult learners, this need manifests itself in a clear understanding of learning goals and the advantages of full participation in the learning process.

6 Quality, Standards and Values in Adult Learning

Introduction

References to 'quality' and its interpretations permeate this book and it is appropriate, therefore, briefly to examine the subject of quality, its meanings and other related issues relevant to my arguments. Quality is a term that is used in a range of contexts with various meanings, and this chapter does not attempt to provide an exhaustive summary of these, nor do I claim to provide a definitive statement of what is quality. Rather, I offer examples of how the term is used in various settings, explain their relevance to the thesis, and provide a background against which findings from my research data are presented in Chapters 7, 8 and 9.

Closely linked, and often confused, with some interpretations of quality are questions of standards, and the differences between these two terms are considered and compared, specifically so far as the terms apply to education and learning. To these are added references to the 'value-added' component of learning assessment, and to the concept of 'value-for-money'. Principally, this book enables the views of participants in the adult learning process to be recorded, and this section is closely linked, therefore, with Chapters 7 and 8, in which those views are expressed through the collected data.

'Quality' and its meaning in everyday life:

> that which makes a thing what it is; its nature; a kind or degree of goodness or worth; an attribute. (Chambers Dictionary)

> a degree of excellence; relative goodness; grade. (Webster's Comprehensive Dictionary)

In everyday usage, the term 'quality' is given a range of meanings, according to the context in which it is used. Dictionaries variously define a 'quality' as the intrinsic nature of something; e.g. the qualities of lead are that it is both heavy yet flexible; the quality of a person's character is to do with their nature, disposition, spirit or temperament; the quality of a fine diamond is that it is flawless and therefore of great worth. More common usage today also relates the term to a range of issues and judgements about products, services, agencies and experiences.

When quality is used to refer to the nature or characteristic of something, or as a degree or grade of excellence, despite the frequency and variability with which the term is employed, it may be argued that 'quality' generally is used in five distinct ways:

- *quality as a defining characteristic* – e.g. a quality of a vine is that it bears grapes;
- *quality as a grade of achievement* – a norm-referenced use – e.g. vintage champagne is better quality than non-vintage;
- *quality as a high level of performance or achievement* – e.g. Shakespeare as a poet or Einstein as a scientist;
- *quality as fitness for purpose* – i.e. conforming to specification;
- *quality as value for money* – i.e. performance or durability in relation to cost.

The notion of quality as fitness for purpose is used by a number of writers (e.g. Ball 1985; De Wit 1992) and De Wit sees this as a 'cycle of continuous improvement, including the need for a strategic approach, meeting customers' expectations, and a cohesive system of inter-connected processes' (De Wit 1992: 7). The main need for explanation is probably between quality as an 'attribute', and quality as 'worth'. Often, however, the term is used without any indication of its precise meaning nor evidence of what criteria have been used to reach a judgement. Indeed, many statements on quality have been based on no more than an instinctive subjective feeling rather than any intellectual weighing of evidence. Just as we cannot adequately sum up a person's characteristics, certainly not in one word, so we find it difficult (or may not take the time) to be precise about the qualities of whatever is the focus of our attention, and what it is that prompts us to employ the word 'quality'. Its use seems to imply a feeling, a certain satisfaction, an instinctive judgement that something is, or has been, 'good'.

> Quality, like 'freedom' or 'justice', is an elusive concept. We all have an instinctive understanding of what it means but it is difficult to articulate. Quality is also a value-laden term: it is subjectively associated with that which is good and worthwhile. (Green 1994: 12)

Perhaps, because of the variety of contexts in which the term quality is adopted, its very frequency of use makes a determination of its precise meaning even more difficult. We speak of quality, for example, when referring to the durability of a product, to the style and ease of wear of a garment, to the comfort of an armchair or to the service we receive from an airline or shop. Often, but not always, in these circumstances there seems to be an implicit relationship in the mind of the speaker between quality and value for money (see below). Quality, in the sense of worth, has its origins in the hallmarking of gold and silver in past centuries when such marks became a guarantee of quality and consistency of both the materials and the craftsman – an integral element of craftsmanship. By the 1900s the term was being used with reference to quality-control by foremen and by the 1920s as part of an inspection-based quality control system. By 1980, focus on quality issues had developed into total quality management (Sallis 1995). In terms of a product, one has to decide in what aspect of the product one is looking for quality. In everyday life, when choosing a new car, for example, one's decision will probably focus around issues of reliability, performance, a known high standard, good management and customer care. One often has to choose between comfort and performance, with the final decision usually being determined by perceived value for money.

High or low quality? Quality for what? Quality for whom?

Defining quality is problematic and debatable, and consideration of these questions seems to prompt further questions (NATFHE 1992). Is the term 'quality' a self-defining superlative that automatically implies *high* quality? Sometimes, perhaps, in general usage it is, yet we also on occasions are more specific when referring to a *high*-quality product or, conversely, we describe a poor service as being of *low* quality. When we are considering quality, of what are we speaking? Whose views and values determine what is quality or what level of quality is acceptable? Is there a continuum of quality from which our selection is made? Despite this frequent imprecision, it is reasonable to suggest that when the single word 'quality' is employed, the underlying assumption is that it is to *high quality* that one is referring. We make references to 'good' and to 'better' in many contexts but the term 'quality' is used as a 'hurrah' word (Barnett 1992), used sometimes as a superlative and sometimes as a generalization to imply something 'good' and highly acceptable. We may list a number of attributes that support the use of the term 'quality', as suggested above and, in different contexts, these attributes may be seen as complementary, alternative or even competing definitions. Attempts at defining 'quality' abound, each with contextually biased language and references, and precise definitions are hard to achieve. Whether quality is absolute or relative is debatable.

> Quality can be perceived as fixed, not really variable or negotiable, something which can be 'hall-marked' and thus offer assurance to society, students, paymasters and government. In language borrowed from commerce and industry, it is a conformance to requirements or meeting specifications. ... proponents of the absolute model have at the heart of their perspective a notion of fixed thresholds above which quality can be discerned.
>
> (NATFHE 1992: 16)

This suggestion that quality offers something *above* a certain normative level implies that it can, therefore, be measured by relating it to previous levels, but in doing so we immediately begin to involve *standards* against which our measurements are to be made (see below). In the area of management, 'Total Quality Management' (TQM) systems involve an approach that involves a shift of emphasis away from controlling people through systems, to developing management styles based on sound common sense, leadership and quality (DTI 1991a: 11). In industry, other systems such as the British Standards Institution's 5750 are generally assumed to provide proof of quality (FEU 1991) but it really is to standards that they refer – the matching of a product to a technical specification. Yet the materials employed and the craftsmanship involved may be of high quality. Traditionally, quality has been linked to the idea of exceptionally high standards, but other approaches see it in terms of consistency. Quality in this sense may be summed up by the interrelated ideas of zero defects and getting things right the first time (Harvey *et al.* 1992).

The implementation of TQM systems seek 'customer delight by ensuring that the organization is customer-focused and customer-driven, with the definition of quality being that laid down by the customer' (Sallis 1990: 2). These systems develop a culture of quality within an organizsation which promotes attention to detail and which aspires to the attainment of high standards. Systems such as these from industry have been adapted for use in educational management, and institutions have developed numerous ways of gathering data about themselves which can be used to inform and compare. Initially these were data-gathering systems, such as the six prime indicators of performance suggested by the 'Joint Efficiency Study' report and offer valuable data to inform current practice and future planning:

- staff : student ratio
- non-teacher costs per full-time equivalent student (FTE)
- course costs per FTE

- completion rates/costs per completing student
- qualification rates/costs per qualifying FTE
- progression/placement rate per completing FTE.   (Powell 1991: 14)

At the time, gathering this data was seen as a useful way of making comparisons between institutions, and of making comparisons about the relative performance of individual institutions. Managers in any organization need, of course, to be as fully informed as possible and data-gathering systems remain as one valuable part of efficient, informed management decision-making. These are not exercises to enable managers to attribute blame or impose penalties, but they *are* external to the learner/tutor partnership that is at the heart of educational institutions.

Quality and standards

I pointed out earlier that the terms 'quality' and 'standards' are often confused and frequently used interchangeably. The standard of public debate about these issues is becoming widely unintelligible and generally the word standard has for many come to mean quality control and audit (Maskell 2001). The quality discourse has its genesis in the advent of industrialization, and has been inserted into education as part of the reform process in public services. The discourse has become such that references to quality are now seen by many as being a mechanical process which is based on a set of permanent truths, but Ball points out that with value and excellence both to be found in quality we are faced with further choices over where to place our focus (Ball 1985). The distinction between the two terms – quality and standards – and their meanings is relevant to my arguments because, as stated in Chapter 1, measurement of standards in learning generally relates to outcomes, and many of the data presented in Chapters 7 and 8 refer to learning programmes that do not lead to an accredited outcome. Standards relating to, for example, a GCSE or 'A' level examination are often the subject of heated debate and frequently the proponents of retaining the 'A' level as the 'gold standard' of university entrance argue that standards are not as high as in previous years, or that these examinations are easier to pass than they were. Similar arguments are heard in relation to standards at GCSE level.

It is when considering the conditions under which students are prepared for and sit public examinations that the separate question of quality can arise. Students from any two schools or colleges may achieve the same examination results and thereby achieve the same standards. But there are two limitations that must be acknowledged in this. Firstly, what has been measured at that point is the student's ability to respond to the examination questions asked, at that time, and in the circumstances of the examination. The standard achieved is not a measurement of the quality of the process leading up to the examination. The quality of that process which students separately experience may be quite different, even assuming they all prepared for their examination over the same length of time. Classroom conditions, the effectiveness and consistency of teaching staff, the availability of libraries and learning materials, the ability to study independently and the practical issues of parental support may be amongst the factors that produce a very different quality of learning in the two institutions. Some may argue that in these circumstances the learning process is less important if the intended results are achieved, but in some adult education, when an externally accredited outcome may not be available, the process becomes even more important and is often itself one of the outcomes.

Findings presented in Chapter 7 show that adult students have varying views about the importance of what, for them, constitutes a good-quality learning process. Some of the examples they provide of factors that contribute to their quality learning may be regarded by others as more to do with standards, but they are clearly of importance to the individual learners, given as their responses to questions about quality. For example, a small number of students, cited in Chapter 7, seem to indicate that they do not expect their course to be of quality because it is at a beginners' or basic level. It is most likely that these individuals are referring to the low standard (i.e. level) of their courses, as distinct from a higher or more advanced level. One hopes they do not imply, or have found that, because their courses are at a lower academic level, their learning experience is of a lower quality.

Public education systems have, in recent years, received more attention from successive governments in attempts to ensure that, for example, examination results are improved and maintained. The development of performance tables of examination results, referred to previously, provide useful comparisons, and to that extent are helpful, but could be said to imply something about the intake of a school or college rather than to offer a fair and full statement about its success and practices. Increasing attempts to improve the performance of schools, colleges and universities are designed to increase public confidence in them, to offer a more informed choice to students and parents, to increase accountability of those institutions in their expenditure of public money, thus to reassure the public that value for money, as well as high standards, is being achieved.

Quality and teaching

With more attention being given in recent years to the question of standards in education, however defined, it is inevitable that more focus will be placed also on the quality of teaching. Attempts to improve the quality of teaching continue, and some progress has been made in defining those aspects of the craft that must be present and which can be measured in some way. Prior to the establishment of the Learning and Skills Council, the Adult Learning Inspectorate and the Common Inspection Framework, the Office for Standards in Education was indicating that during its inspections the quality of teaching would be judged by:

- clear aims and objectives
- sense of purpose, pace and challenge
- organization and presentation of materials
- match of content and tasks to students' needs, interests and abilities
- forms of initial, formative and summative assessment
- records of monitoring student progress
- use of accreditation and certification.   (Ofsted 1995: 34)

The same document continues:

> The quality of teaching is good where all students have access to initial assessment. Teaching has clear goals, is challenging, well planned and paced. It is well matched to students' needs and abilities and takes account of prior learning. Teachers and students are aware of progress made. Students frequently receive feedback on their work and accurate records of learning are kept.   (Ofsted 1995: 41)

The language adopted by the CIF seeks to be more helpful in clarifying the purpose of inspection (see also Chapter 2). Its frequent use of the terms 'how well ...', and 'the extent to which ...' provides clear indications of the focus of inspections, yet avoids statements of definition. Inspectors are required, for example, to evaluate:

> How well learners learn and make progress.

> How well teaching and training meet individuals' needs and course or programme requirements.

> The extent to which learners acquire new knowledge and skills, develop ideas and increase their understanding.
> (Adapted from ALI/Ofsted 2001: Section 2)

The essential basis of the CIF requirements is the word 'evidence'. Inspectors must gain evidence in relation to each aspect of teaching, learning and management, and form judgements about how well it is performing. This could be a significant improvement on previous inspection systems as it enables the provider, student and tutor to work in partnership to measure, and subsequently improve, each and every aspect of teaching and learning, and all the support functions of the providing organization. This intention will only be achieved, however, if everyone involved shares a common agenda and set of objectives, and that inspections are carried out using criteria and methods which are relevant to the teaching and learning being examined. By looking at the effectiveness and efficiency of all aspects of a provider's work in relation to the individual learner, inspectors are to judge all areas of performance, and so identify any possible weaknesses. Chapter 7 provides learners' views on what, for them, is quality in learning, together with evidence of the wide range of their definitions.

Quality and learning

Attempting to define the quality of teaching presents many challenges, and a search for definitions of quality learning, and quality in and of the learning process is no less problematic. To this end it is helpful to try to formulate such characteristics of learning as may generally be agreed to relate to quality in learning. My interpretation of data from respondents to my survey is that high-quality, effective learning might be said to have taken place when the learner:

- is able to discover knowledge for himself/herself
- can demonstrate a long-term retention of the knowledge
- is able to perceive relations between old knowledge and new
- is able to create new knowledge
- is able to apply knowledge to solving problems
- is able communicate knowledge to others
- wants to learn more.   (see Chapter 7 for evidence of this)

Similar criteria have been employed as tools for measuring quality in adult learning with learners being assessed according to their ability to demonstrate:

- motivation and ability to respond to challenges
- development of competence as independent learners
- peer-group interaction and shared learning
- good relationships between themselves and with staff
- ability to negotiate their programmes and evaluate their achievements.

(Ofsted 1995: 29)

Student response is good when motivation, effort and participation are high. Students gain in knowledge, skills and understanding as well as the capacity to learn independently. They show commitment to their learning and achieve their desired outcomes.

Student response is poor when effort is limited, there is no demonstrable gain in knowledge, skills or understanding and students remain dependent upon tutors. They show no enthusiasm for negotiating their programmes of work or for evaluating their achievements.   (Ibid.: 39)

My own view about quality in teaching and learning is that several dimensions must be satisfied for the process to be regarded as a quality experience. Many of these have been mentioned previously so, to avoid repetition, it is sufficient here to say that quality teaching and learning will be achieved when a well-informed, well-prepared tutor, who is aware of the learning needs of each student, creates a learning environment that encourages and enables each learner to know what he/she has learnt, how he/she is being assessed, how to apply knowledge gained during the process, how to discover new knowledge, and wants to learn more because the process is enjoyable.

As I have indicated, there are many references to the characteristics of quality in a variety of contexts. Data in Chapters 7 and 8 relate quality issues specifically to part-time adult learning and in this chapter I summarize the contextual definitions offered by students and tutors engaged in the *'transactions or moral interaction'* (Jarvis 1995b: 24), and processes relating to teaching and learning with adults. I have stated on several occasions that this study seeks to gain definitions of quality in learning from participants in the learning process. As shown above, quality can be variously defined as effectiveness, efficiency, even student or client satisfaction; a view, however, not shared by Jarvis:

> Quality has at times been defined as effectiveness, efficiency and even student satisfaction. [But] ... quality simply cannot be equated to another value; quality is quality and this differs considerably from, for example, efficiency, since is it possible to be adjudged efficient even though the outcome may be poor, and so on.'   (Jarvis 1995a: 226)

Students must be involved in determining whether or not their learning is of quality, for however well-prepared, supportive and encouraging tutors are it is, after all, *'the students who do the achieving, not the teaching staff, or the senior personnel, or the institutions'* (Barnett 1992: 30). One might argue that actual definitions of quality and standards matter less than ensuring that the learner receives the highest standard of teaching in the highest possible quality learning environment. Although quality is a subjective measure and the quality of a learning experience not of itself an outcome, the process may well affect people's perceptions of what it is they take away with them from their studies and what will be its usefulness (Calder 1993).

The motivation and personal values of learners

Adult students usually bring with them a high degree of motivation, an appetite for learning and a willingness to work hard and apply themselves. They also possess valuable experience in a variety of contexts and this, if sensitively drawn upon by the teacher, can enrich the learning process.

(DES 1991: 10)

For all adult learners motivation is a significant factor in their approach to learning. As two learners in this study commented:

Suitable environment and materials, tuition to enable me to do what I want to do. (F3FN)

Because it is a stimulating alternative to watching TV in the evenings and gives me a chance to try new things. (F3PN)

Most adult students are voluntary participants and choose to attend courses, to participate in different ways, to undertake some relevant form of homework, and to submit to whatever types of assessment are applied (see Chapter 7). There may be a few who attend under a certain duress, with possibilities of promotion or salary increase being withheld until the completion of a particular programme of learning which an employer regards as essential or desirable for a job. All adult learning, and especially adult part-time learning, presents many challenges to the individual student and he/she must surmount a range of personal domestic and financial hurdles in order to access and sustain a programme of learning. Research data is very limited, but the reasons why adults join a course are, as suggested earlier, probably as numerous as there are members of the course and it is fairly straightforward to identify a few common motives, as Table 6.1 illustrates.

Adult educators can provide much anecdotal evidence of other motivations that adults admit to for attending a course, which include compensating for earlier failures or inadequacies at school; to meet other people, specifically for some with a view to finding a partner or to reduce loneliness; to keep up with, or at least to understand, their children's school curriculum; to escape from their domestic environment for brief

Table 6.1 Common motives for adult learners to join a course of study

- to follow-up an existing interest
- to learn or develop a skill
- to learn or develop ideas
- to create something
- to satisfy curiosity
- to save money
- to discover 'if I can'
- to gain the approval of others
- to obtain a qualification
- to 'access' some form of further learning opportunity
- to meet like-minded people
- to make social contact
- to gain social self-confidence
- to enhance self-esteem.

Source: Daines *et al.*, 1993: 9

periods, or just to keep active. I have found this echoed strongly in my research, as some of my respondents commented:

> To make up for my failures as a child at school. (M4LN)

> Value greatly; keeps me and my brain actively learning and growing. (F5IN)

> Very important; if I have more knowledge I can pass it on to my children. (F2AY)

> Despite family commitments it's nice to be able to attend a course once a week – just for me! (F5LN)

The motivation driving adult learners may be seen in terms of specific goals, as suggested by Harrison in the list in Table 4.2. This list is noticeably similar to Daines' in Table 6.1, although more concise.

Research has shown that these broad headings can be translated into more specific data which shows comparisons between the various

Table 6.2 Motivational goals for adult learners

- a desire for knowledge
- to meet personal development goals
- to meet occupational goals
- to meet social and community goals
- to comply with external expectations
- to find activity or diversion
- to meet economic needs
- to fulfil religious needs
- to fulfil family responsibilities
- to develop or move on.

Source: Harrison 1993, cited in Uden 1994: 13

Table 6.3 Adults' expressed motives for learning (taken from a sample of 400 enquiries about courses)

36% job changes	5% training
14% personal development	4% redundancy
8% vocational education	2% leisure interests
7% finance for study	1% retirement
6% alternatives to unemployment	1% personal factors
5% general education	

Source: McGivney 1992: 15

categories within one sample group, who were asked about their expressed motives for learning (see Table 6.3).

Uden (1996) suggests that there are three main, overlapping motives for engaging in learning – vocational, academic and personal interests and development. He cites Tight (1991) in suggesting that part-time mature learners in higher education claim to be taking courses for a mix of instrumental, self-development and subject interest reasons. Adult learners may, like their younger counterparts, have short-term and long-term objectives in mind – academic achievement, vocational motives and career prospects, as well as self-developmental reasons.

Learning and personal values

This brief section on personal values is placed here, in a chapter on learning, to link it more closely to the ways in which adults approach their learning and how, I contend, their basic human values have an affect in this context, as in other areas of their lives. Evidence to support this view is to be found in Chapter 7 and what follows provides a background against which research data from students can be considered. Human values develop in the individual as he/she matures from childhood to adulthood and are strongly influenced, at least at first, by the personal values held by those adults with whom that individual is in close contact, as a child is with parents, other relatives, teachers, etc. Some of these values will be generation-specific, others cultural-specific and some will be held over several generations and passed from adults to children through changing societies. The values may be influenced by long-held religious or political belief, or by more recent personal experience, and a longer sociological study would be able to explore these issues in more depth than is possible here. There are, however, a number of personal values which have a direct influence on adults' approach to and practice of learning and need to receive some explanation as to how they form part of this study of adult learning.

Values describe basic beliefs about what is important to an individual (Kidd 1973) and when deciding what values to adopt depends on the kind of human development we want to see (Barnett 1990; 1992). Every society has its own sets of values, expressed in the form of laws, and also includes those who do not share the values, and break the laws. Whether to do with the extreme question of capital punishment, or lesser issues concerning petty crime or the dropping of litter, sets of values are formulated and held by individuals and by the society in which they live, and we use the terms ethos or culture to characterize these shared values (Halliday 1998). A frequently used term in this context found in the research data is that of 'respect' and this term summarizes the views of students and tutors heard both empirically and within the data. Students express views, for example (based on their personal values), about the ways in which tutors present themselves, and about their relationship with students in the teaching space involving their personality and, often, sense of humour. These views will often, although not always, be strongly influenced by their experiences at school, when their relationships with teachers would have been very different and more akin to those described by Harris as 'Parent–Child' relationships (Harris 1973).

> [Some learners] may be constrained by their own early negative experiences of learning and they need the context of a highly supportive and respectful environment to be able to recognize their needs and begin to explore them. ... Learning must involve the whole person not just the intellect.
>
> (Boud *et al.* 1993a: 42)

> When learning is equated with education in people's minds, they tend to remember unpleasant experiences at school, when it might not have been fun to learn, and this can cause them to erect a barrier to further education – a barrier that every adult educator has sought to overcome.
>
> (Jarvis 1999a: 161)

Some students acknowledge the respect they receive from tutors, as learners, as customers and as partners in the learning process, e.g.

> The tutor is so knowledgeable and is so patient and understanding. (F5EN)

> Excellent tuition by a compassionate tutor. (F5DY)

> Good teacher interested and involved in course; not just a job to her. (F2JY)

> Good tutor who treats people on their ability. (F6AN)

Some students also indicate that they expect to give and receive respect from their fellow students, but others do not share this view and take a more self-centred approach.

> It's my choice how much I get out of it; it doesn't affect anybody else. (F3GN)

> I am only interested in my own success; purely for self-satisfaction. (F6AN)

Adult learners, whatever the context in which they are learning, show a considerable commitment to their learning. They are usually highly motivated and often will have to overcome considerable hurdles in order to continue and complete their studies (e.g. course fees, child care, transport costs, competing demands of work and family). Adult learners generally, whether studying full-time or part-time, achieve commendable results when compared with younger students who usually will be spending much more time on the same courses of study. In many cases adult learners will gain a pass in a GCSE or 'A' level subject, for example, after only studying for one academic year (approximately 30 weeks, meeting once each week), compared with their younger counterparts who are likely to have tuition for at least twice that time, and often much longer. These examples suggest that adult students value their learning and are highly motivated but, other than by reference to outcomes, it is not easy to obtain clarification from them what precisely is the nature of this value. For some, successful accredited certification will be the most valuable outcome especially, perhaps, if this has a direct influence on pay, promotion or gaining employment, as well as the pleasure of success. For others, the satisfactory completion of an artefact – e.g. a clay pot, a piece of embroidery, a table lamp or a piece of creative writing – will be a tangible demonstration of the value of that learning experience. For yet others, the acquisition of a skill – be it as a woodworker, dancer or computer operator – will explain the main value of the experience. In addition to these relatively easy to explain values, however, many students will speak of their learning as being of value to them for one or more from a wide spectrum of reasons (see Chapter 7).

> Because I want to do well in my career. (F2PN)

> It helps me view the world differently from lots of different skills I have learned. (F2PN)

For many students, completion of their course of study will not result in any form of certification because the purpose of the study is simply to gain knowledge or a skill, and to share the experience with other like-minded adults. Or put in another, now rather unfashionable, way – to experience learning for the sake of learning. The increased emphasis in recent years on learning being solely for the purpose of gaining or improving employment – important, of course, as this is – overlooks the huge number of adult students who, for a variety of reasons, do not wish to gain further qualifications, or do not regard their learning as having any instrumental value. As indicated above in the section on motivation, it has for long been known to adult educators that reasons for attending a course, at least in the view of those adult students willing to speak of such matters (and given that they offer an honest observation), may include any one or more of the reasons indicated, and possibly others to which the learners does not refer or of which he/she may not be fully aware. These reasons, to the extent that they apply to at least some students, may offer further clues to how and why adult students value their learning experiences.

For many adult students following liberal education courses the notion of certification and accreditation is seen as unnecessary and, for some, even as a threat to their individually focused learning. There were, anecdotally, many examples of adult students who, following the 1992 *Education Act*, left their courses or did not re-enrol when hearing of the requirements of the Further Education Funding Council (FEFC) regarding formal processes to be followed to assure funding for a particular course. References to precourse guidance, predetermined outcomes, learning agreements, on-course monitoring, successful course completion, on-course and end-of-course assessment and learning destinations were assumed by students, perhaps with recollections of school days, to imply that 'assessment' meant old-fashioned tests, which they might regard as being inappropriate for the subject they were enjoying, or as simply something they did not want. I would argue that, whilst recognizing these points, the requirements of previous and current funding regimes (i.e. the FEFC and LSC) are not different in essence from what should be happening in any well-planned, well-delivered, properly assessed liberal, adult-education course. The main difference is arguably one of terminology and an acceptance that measuring the effectiveness of any course, even though it be a non-accredited, 'non-vocational' liberal education course, is not unreasonable, provided the methods of assessment are appropriate, transparent and relevant to the course and its intentions. A good adult education tutor will ensure that all the above aspects are present in a course, whatever the intended outcome, except that the precise processes and outcomes will be negotiated rather than predetermined. The essential aspect is how these processes and their purpose are explained to resisting students and what terminology is employed when doing so.

When considering the value that any learning process may have for an individual, we must ask of what value and in what form. Answers will vary according to the individual, his/her programme of learning, the presentation of the course, its assessment and ultimate outcomes (or out-puts). Its ultimate value may, of course, be different for the learner, the institution, an employer and a funding agency. All values will be regarded by those who adopt them as being worthwhile and morally unobjection-able (Peters 1967).

> Who else (but the individual learner) can tell us whether a learning experience has qualitatively changed their life for the better?
>
> (Scarlett and Winner 1995: 61)

> The notion of value is multi-dimensional in that it has a different value for its different clients; that is students, academics, institutions, ... employers, the exchequer and society in general.   (Tight 1991: 109)

Variable use of terms such as 'value', 'quality' and 'good' by students, tutors and managers when applied to courses of learning presents difficul-ties when attempting to record and measure what adult learners and their tutors mean when referring to a 'quality course', 'quality teaching' or the value of learning. Yet whether or not the success of a course is measured by a certificated outcome, it should be to the participants that we look to discover whether the experience offered was of quality and value to each individual. The interface between quality and value is critical (NATFHE 1992), as is the link between learning and personal values. Learning, as we know, can be achieved as a solitary experience, but many would argue that learning in a group of like-minded people is a more effective and enjoyable experience. Being part of a learning group, however, brings requirements on the individuals involved that solitary learning does not, and student data in Chapter 7 show ways in which personal values influence both individuals' approach to group learning, and to their interaction with other students and the tutor. Issues of age, appearance, courtesy, tolerance, willingness to listen and offers of help will all affect the performance of a student and thus his/her learning process and out-comes. Learning now, perhaps, is moving from being a 'servant to global capitalism' (Jarvis 2001: vii), and is becoming a life-enhancing cohesive force within this age of learning that will link economic and social needs The discourse on 'learning' seems to attract attention from wider social strata than did 'education' in previous generations, and if the results include wider participation in all forms of learning, then in the period of transition from the 1992 *Education Act* to the era of the *Learning and Skills Act* will have bridged far more than the eight years that separates them. The personal values of individuals will influence their choices of learning, their attitude to a selected course of learning, their approach to fellow students and their tutor. Chapter 7 shows examples of ways in which these influences operate now and Chapter 10 gives pointers to ways in which providers may plan to cater for their students' learning needs in the future.

Learning and value for money

Sometimes, as suggested earlier, use of the term 'quality' will be implicitly or explicitly related to the concept of gaining value for money. When used in many everyday contexts this relationship can be clear. The durability of, for example, a piece of furniture in relation to the price paid, or the acquisition of an object of high monetary value obtained for lower expenditure. We need to be aware of the differences between value and excellence (Ball 1985). We may purchase a basic wooden chair cheaply and although it may last for many years, serving its function well and giving value for money, it will never be the same as a classic example from master crafts people, nor like a beautifully upholstered and far more comfortable lounger.

A student who needs to acquire a particular qualification may well relate the cost of enrolling on a course, and the eventual acquisition of that learning outcome, to the expenditure in terms of effort, costs and anticipated increased income, and determine that he/she has gained value for money. In my years as an adult educator I have known students forego immediate financial enhancement in order to gain additional qualifications that will, in time, bring greater financial reward. Similarly, tutors give up some part-time teaching, and its associated income, in order to undertake an in-service training course to become a better teacher and thus enhance the likelihood of increased future employment and earning capacity. Individual adult learners will have differing views about the cost of following learning programmes, and of the 2,035 individuals who provided data for this research, only a very small number made any reference to the cost of courses. With fewer differential fees than were available some years ago it is perhaps an indication of the value that so many adult students place upon their learning that the experience, process and outcomes seem to be of higher priority than the costs. This can only be said, of course, of those who take part. It is unknown how many students are discouraged from joining courses because of the cost or other factors, although anecdotally many examples are reported. Some students' fees are paid for by their employer and for others the expenditure is offset against anticipated enhanced status or additional income that would be generated by the attainment of a qualification. Data in Chapter 7 include references to those for whom adult learning is more than an experience or a means to an end. For some, especially for many older students, it is the social or physiological experience and involvement in an activity outside the home that are part of the value of a course. For some it is a lifeline; a means of retaining mental and physical health; a way of meeting new people or an absorbing interest – any of which are regarded as giving good value for the financial outlay.

Learning and value-added

The term 'value-added' originates in economics and latterly is used to describe goods 'whose quality and value is increased by high levels of technology and skill in the manufacturing process' (Spours 1996: 7). The concept of value-added in education entered the public domain in the early 1990s and was seen as a 'possible fairer' way of measuring and reporting student achievement than the 'raw scores' used in league tables (Hodgson and Spours 1997: 162). Measurement of a student's achievement over a period begins from a 'baseline of prior attainment' and compares therefore progress against the student's previous levels of attainment, not against other students' (DfE 1995a: 2). Value-added discourse over ten years has refined the original concepts into a multi-dimensional system having distinct but interrelated dimensions. The topic is extensive but its relevance to adult learning is clear because it does more than just measure targeted outcomes. 'Any system of measurement which values only achievement of specific external targets, will favour those who are most able or highly motivated, who are easy and cheap to teach.' Much adult learning is 'working below or outside the framework of formal qualifications' and much of their progress and achievement is less tangible (Powell 1991: 22).

There is no universally acceptable measure of value. In learning, various factors contributing towards students' attainment can be measured, using different units of measurement, many of which cannot be expressed in financial or market value terms (DfE 1995a). One of the difficulties with education and learning is that whereas supermarket customers are 'generally well-informed about the differences between products, and can make rational choices over balancing price and quality' (McNair

1997: 31), the 'product' of learning is less easy to define and may take one or more of many forms. Indeed, it may be argued that insufficient consideration is given to what is precisely the nature and purpose of education and learning in our modern society, although this question is receiving more attention than it has for some generations. By recognizing the range of factors that contribute to students' progress and attainment, value-added methodology 'has the potential to raise student and tutor expectations' and to focus on 'the central task of raising levels of achievement' by making institutions become more accountable for their performance (Hodgson and Spours 1997: 163). In some adult education where no external criteria exist to measure progress and outcomes in relation to such learning experiences, judgements about value-added have to be made by a partnership of students and tutor. Since learning experiences such as these have been designed for students and draw upon collective previous learning in their development, it cannot be unreasonable to argue that learners should arbitrate over what constitutes quality in that process, and what are the value-added elements of the experience, assessed by formative methodology. This approach 'assists in the identification of strengths and weaknesses by the interpretation of the issues raised by the added value analysis' (Ashworth and Harvey 1994: 21). A value-added strategy can offer further advantages to adult learners. Quality assurance may be seen as the 'collection and evaluation of data and the making of value judgements on the basis of that data' (Melia 2001: 11), but with a value-added approach data collected are used for educational rather than accountability purposes (Hodgson and Spours 1997) and progression is measured throughout a course, not just as a summative result.

I believe that a value-added approach to assessing learning both enables the different experiences referred to above to be recognized as making valuable contributions to the learning process, and also emphasizes that learning is about process as well as about final outcomes.

> In a system which values only formal outcomes those who progress more slowly, or who have achieved least in the past, will appear to produce a poor return on an investment of time and resources, although their needs may be equally important. For this reason, the notion of value-added is important in assessing the outcomes of an education service. This implies clearer measurement of levels of achievement at the beginning and end of a learning programme than is often carried out. Since much education for adults is working below, or outside, the framework of formal qualifications, it also implies processes for measuring less tangible achievement, and fine gradations of it. ... The key to measuring 'value-added' lies in identifying,

negotiating and recording individual student, and teacher, expectations, and establishing assessment systems which reflect these.   (Powell 1991: 22).

The term quality remains one that is not often precisely defined in its use, but one which implies either a specific attribute, or at least something that is good and desirable. Chapters 7 and 8 summarize and synthesize responses regarding the quality of teaching and learning by students and tutors.

7 Students' Perceptions of Learning and Quality in Adult Education – Research Findings

Introduction

Preceding chapters have shown the theoretical background for this study, and have explained the research methodology employed. The final four chapters report on the empirical work, summarize findings from collected data and provide comparisons, conclusions and implications.

The purpose of this research, as explained previously, was to ascertain what is quality in adult learning from the perceptions of students and their tutors. The focus was the actual *process* of teaching and learning and not final outcomes, such as examination results, which are the basis of much other research. In order to focus on the learning process, the study took place during the first term of courses represented and any references made by some respondents to accredited outcomes were, therefore, at that stage anticipatory rather than actual. By collecting data at this particular point participants' observations on the 'nature of existing conditions' (Cohen and Manion 1994: 83) were gathered, in the case of those courses leading to an accredited outcome, well before any examinations were to be held.

As explained in Chapter 4, research methods included individual interviews and a questionnaire survey, and this chapter presents findings from qualitative and quantitative data collected from students.

As explained in Chapter 5, quotations from individual respondents show an alphanumeric code, which indicates gender (F or M); age group (see questionnaires in Appendices 2 and 3); curriculum group (see Appendix 1); and whether or not the course is accredited (Y or N). Quotations taken from interviews show the suffix, INT.

The results are compared in Chapter 9 with data from adult tutors, and conclusions from the research are summarized in Chapter 10.

Findings from student data

Data were collected from 16 individual semi-structured interviews and 1,784 questionnaires, and this chapter offers analysis and synthesis of the findings. Throughout the chapter, reference is made to the questions asked of respondents and illustrative examples of qualitative data are included from their individual responses, as well as quantitative data in tabular form. Those interviewed were from five of the six age groups shown in Appendix 2, ten of the fourteen curriculum groups (see Appendix 1) and from accredited and non-accredited courses (see Appendix 4). Questionnaires were completed by learners drawn from all six age groups, from all fourteen curriculum groups and also from accredited and non-accredited courses.

Students were asked ten perceptual questions, in addition to factual questions about themselves and their courses. The perceptual questions asked were designed to elicit from students views on whether their course was one of quality, and what they considered to be quality; who they believed was responsible for the quality of their course; whether they had a part to play in ensuring a quality learning experience – and if so, how; whether they believed they had responsibility for the quality of their own learning; why they valued their learning as an adult; and how they considered previous experiences as an adult learner affected their current learning. Students were asked to explain the reasons for their answers and although some give very brief responses, many provided detailed answers. They seemed to welcome the opportunity to express their views, either because of delight and satisfaction with their learning, or in fewer cases because they saw an opportunity to articulate complaints that they had not previously raised, or which had not been satisfactorily resolved within their college. Learners in this survey were drawn from courses representing the broad curriculum to be found in adult community colleges (see Chapter 4), and Appendix 1 shows the categories into which courses were grouped to enable coding of individual responses. Throughout this chapter data are presented in tabular and textual formats, classified into response groups drawn from respondents' own terminology. Tables show the number of references in each response group, not the number of individuals, reflecting the fact that respondents sometimes made reference to more than one group. Those students who were interviewed had previously completed a questionnaire and so their responses are included within data in each table. Additional qualitative data are included in the appropriate sections, and many examples are quoted throughout the chapter. Tables show responses by age group, gender and curriculum group, enabling comparisons to be made. Summaries of the findings in Chapter 9 show that, generally, age and curriculum group are not factors that seem to influence respondents' views to any large degree. In the small number of cases where this seems to be the case the results are discussed.

Student perceptions of quality in adult learning

Most (1,713; 96 per cent) of the students whose questionnaires were analysed, or who were interviewed, stated that their course was one 'of quality'. A strong sense of enjoyment and enthusiasm for learning permeates their responses and although some did not provide explanations for their conclusions, most respondents have provided at least some explanation to support their view, and many are very detailed in their comments. Even in those cases where they had cause for some criticism of their course or tutor, learners showed a high degree of enthusiasm for their learning. The largest group of students believe that their tutor

Table 7.1: Students' responses to the question 'What is it that makes this a course of quality?'

n = 1,687 (1,286 women, 401 men)	WOMEN				MEN				TOTALS
RESPONSE GROUPS	Under 30	30–50	50 +	Total	Under 30	30–50	50 +	Total	
Group U: The tutor, lecturer or instructor and pedagogy	92 (52%)	249 (55%)	438 (67%)	779 (61%)	23 (59%)	70 (59%)	165 (68%)	258 (64%)	1,037 (61%)
Group V: Learning outcomes – examination, knowledge or skill	27 (15%)	90 (20%)	72 (11%)	189 (15%)	6 (15%)	15 (13%)	24 (10%)	45 (11%)	234 (14%)
Group W: The adult learning atmosphere – stimulating and supportive	15 (8%)	39 (9%)	57 (9%)	111 (9%)	4 (10%)	14 (12%)	20 (8%)	38 (10%)	149 (9%)
Group X: Meeting personal needs	20 (11%)	33 (7%)	42 (6%)	95 (7%)	2 (5%)	7 (6%)	12 (5%)	21 (5%)	116 (7%)
Group Y: Course content and materials	22 (12%)	35 (8%)	37 (6%)	94 (7%)	2 (5%)	10 (8%)	22 (9%)	34 (9%)	128 (8%)
Group Z: The physical environment, facilities, equipment, group size	1 (1%)	10 (2%)	7 (1%)	18 (1%)	2 (5%)	2 (2%)	1	5 (1%)	23 (1%)
Totals	177	456	653	1,286	39	118	244	401	1,687

(variously called tutor, teacher, lecturer or instructor) and his/her teaching skills are the prime cause of quality (1,037), although five other causes were also identified (see Table 7.1).

For data from Table 7.1, cross-tabulated by curriculum group, see Appendix 5, Table A5.1.

Table 7.1 shows response group U to be by far the largest of the groups, producing 61 per cent of responses, demonstrating that students over-whelmingly see their tutor as being the primary cause of quality (see also Table 7.2). The figures shown by age group reflect approximately the numbers of participants in each of those age groups, although a slightly higher proportion of male students (41 per cent) see the tutor as the prime factor in terms of quality than do female students (34 per cent). Through-out response groups V–Z the figures seen by age group or by gender show no remarkable differences, reflecting approximately the number of partici-pants in each case. Response group Z indicates the low priority given by students to the physical environment in which they study, in contrast to tutors (see Chapter 8), who consider this to be a greater influencing factor.

Response group U in Table 7.1 summarizes references by students to tutors as being the prime cause of quality, and this group of references may be further subdivided into the seven categories shown in Table 7.2.

Table 7.2: Students' perceptions of tutors' contribution to course quality (a subdivision of response group U, Table 7.1)

n = 1,037 (779 women, 258 men) Response groups (sub-groups of Group U, Table 7.1):	% of women's responses	% of men's responses	Totals = 100% Women	Men
Tutor's caring approach, patience, dedication and encouragement	28%	26%	218	68
Tutor's preparation	18%	22%	137	57
Tutor's knowledge	17%	21%	136	54
Tutor's skill and expertise	17%	19%	129	50
Tutor's experience	14%	7%	109	19
Tutor's qualifications	5%	0	38	0
Tutor's regular assessment	2%	4%	12	10
Totals			779	258

In response group U (Tables 7.1 and 7.2), by far the largest of the groups in this section, many students expressed warm appreciation of their tutor, and her/his knowledge, experience and efforts on their behalf:

'We have a very committed tutor who is knowledgeable in her subject.' (F6PN)

'My current tutor is the most interesting and patient of many.' (F3LN:INT)

'Our tutor knows his subject inside out and is able to convey his enthusiasm; and brings history to life as if through the eyes of the people who made history.' (F2LN)

The importance of tutors' preparation for each meeting of the course was also acknowledged:

'My quality of learning is dependent on the amount of preparation the tutor has put in before he comes into the class.' (F5PN)

Many students seem to place in the hands of their tutor responsibility for the entire learning experience, including control of its content and pace, as Table 7.1 and subsequent tables indicate. They variously refer to their tutor as supportive, encouraging, knowledgeable and patient, speaking of the need to listen carefully and to carry out the tutor's instructions, seldom describing their tutors as anything but helpful. The sense of being part of a pleasant social circle, as well as a learning group, is strong within the responses from some students, with the tutor taking the role of leader or facilitator.

'We have an excellent tutor who makes instructions clear and has great patience too.' (F6PN:INT)

'I have a friendly, approachable, knowledgeable tutor.' (F4KN:INT)

'Our tutor is exceptionally inspirational.' (F6EY)

Table 7.2 shows small percentages of women (2 per cent) and men (4 per cent) who regard the regular assessment of their work carried out by their tutor as being the way in which the tutor contributes to the learning quality. This is another example in the data (others of which are cited elsewhere in the book) where 'standards' and 'quality' have been used interchangeably.

Several references from students refer to the multi-faceted role of the tutor, reflecting the views of Alan Rogers who speaks of the tutor variously being the 'Planner', the 'Organizer', the 'Leader', or the 'Controller' of learning; who at different times 'Tells', 'Sells', 'Consults' or 'Joins'. He suggests the tutor may move between having a 'lion-tamer' (autocratic) approach, through an 'entertainer' (*laissez-faire*) stage, to being the 'cultivator' with a more democratic approach. Rogers reflects that tutors may be seen as aloof and egocentric, or, on the other hand, may be friendly and understanding; or they may be dull and routine, or stimulating and imaginative (Rogers 1986: 120). From my research population almost all students would fall into the categories of seeing their tutor as friendly and understanding or stimulating and imaginative, including most of those who are otherwise critical of their course or college. The tutor is regarded by many as the focus, almost perhaps in some cases the purpose, for attending a course, and anecdotal reports speak of students travelling considerable distances to work with a particular tutor. One can speculate that the student body will include some mature adults who may have considerable status and experience in their personal or professional lives, and perhaps at least some degree of knowledge of the subject being studied. Such students, however, may be included with others who will look to their tutor, at least initially, to assume responsibility for all aspects of their learning, acknowledging that the tutor is in total control.

'I think it is important that the tutor is the person who makes you learn.' (F5EN:INT)

Expressions of appreciation for tutors abound in the data, of which further examples include:

'Our tutor is very, very caring; no one is ever made to feel ridiculous.' (F5GN:INT)

'It is very hard to define a good tutor, you just know when you've got one! They make everything seem easier and pleasant. I like tutors who say, "I don't know but I'll find out for you". No one can be expected to know everything. It makes you feel valued – that your opinions are valued.' (F4KN:INT)

There are contrasting opinions, with a small number of students expressing views that show they are very much 'in control' of their own learning, and only draw upon their tutors to the extent that it is necessary. This group of very active students, and their views on quality and learning, is discussed below. When these data are considered by age group the six response groups, shown in Table 7.1, are spread across the age groups and both genders, in line with the distribution of age amongst the research population. When examined by curriculum groups (see Table 7.3 and Appendix 5, Table A5.1), data show the four largest numbers of responses citing the tutor as a primary cause of quality are from students of the following subjects, which are primarily in the non-accredited category: Visual Arts, Dance, Movement and Yoga, Languages and General Interest.

Table 7.3: Students' responses to the question 'What is it that makes this a course of quality?' Data from Table 7.1, cross-tabulated by response and curriculum groups, showing the four largest curriculum groups. (Percentages are of the total response.)

Curriculum group	A: Visual Arts (including Interior design)	G: Dance, Movement and Yoga	L: Languages (includes ESOL, BSL EFL)	P: General Interest
Response group	% of total response (see Table 7.1)	% of total response (see Table 7.1)	% of total response (see Table 7.1)	% of total response (see Table 7.1)
U: The tutor, lecturer or instructor; and pedagogy	197 (6%)	154 (9%)	260 (15%)	122 (7%)
V: Learning outcomes – examination knowledge or skill	12 (1%)	12 (1%)	42 (2%)	51 (3%)
W: Adult learning atmosphere – stimulating and supportive	18 (1%)	21 (1%)	34 (2%)	29 (2%)
X: Meeting personal needs	15 (1%)	19 (1%)	22 (1%)	23 (1%)
Y: Course content and materials	12 (1%)	1	36 (2%)	31 (2%)
Z: Physical environment, facilities, equipment, group size			9 (1%)	

For a full list of responses by curriculum group, see Appendix 5, Table A5.1

In Table 7.3 the physical environment, equipment and resources are regarded by both genders as the least significant influence on the quality of their learning (see Chapters 8 and 9 for comparisons with the views of tutors on these influencing factors). Lack of reference to the physical environment as a factor in the quality of learning is particularly noticeable in the case of curriculum group G – Dance, Movement and Yoga – for which group of students one would have thought the physical environment to be of some significance.

When viewed by gender, 61 per cent of responses from women and 64 per cent of responses from men give the tutor as the principal cause of quality. In contrast only 1 per cent of each gender cite the physical environment.

Learning outcomes
Referring again to Table 7.1, the second largest group of references identified by students as the cause of quality of their course is that which

refers to learning outcomes. These refer to a range of possible outcomes, including knowledge, skills and also specific examination results although, as explained above, the latter were at that stage anticipatory rather than actual. For students on examination courses it is reasonable to surmise that the reason they joined the course was to gain the accredited outcome that it offered, and their focus is on that eventual result.

'We focus on the exam.' (F4LY)

'We get a certificate on finishing the course.' (F5IY)

'The teacher heads the course straight to the exam.' (M2BY)

For other learners the practical benefits offered by the course are its main value:

'It can be used within my current role in Customer Relations.' (F3CY)

'It keeps my mind active, it is interesting, and I am learning new skills.' (F4DN:INT)

'It teaches me what I need to know and gives me a recognized qualification.' (F2CY:INT)

Smaller groups of references were to quality being brought about through the adult learning atmosphere (149), which students found stimulating and supportive, or because the course met personal needs (116):

'There is no pressure on me; I can put as much or as little as I want into this course, which both encourages and stimulates me.' (F5LN:INT)

'It meets my needs and expectations.' (M5AN)

'It is exactly what I want.' (F4FN)

For another small group (128) the course content and materials were regarded as the causes of quality:

'Good materials and teaching.' (F4LN)

'Good learning aids.' (F4LN)

'The facilities, i.e. darkroom.' (F2PY)

Only 23 references were to the physical environment. This contrasts with responses from tutors (see Chapter 8), and suggests that students are more tolerant of their physical surroundings if the course is enjoyable and provides what they want. Further examples of qualitative data include a range of observations by students, many of whom give their views on participation and a shared responsibility for learning:

'The quality of this course is gained by the amount of effort I put into learning.' (F2AY)

'It must be of quality or I wouldn't be still doing it.' (F6PY:INT)

The enjoyment of shared learning

Some responses spoke of other gains and benefits students obtained from their course. Many enjoy and appreciate the opportunity to share their learning with others and to exchange experiences over, for example, the completion of homework assignments and classroom activities. This commitment and interaction with fellow learners are seen as important aspects of adult learning:

'Interesting, stimulating, invigorating and the companionship of like-minded people.' (M6AN:INT)

'A sense of well-being and enjoyment with others.' (F6GN)

'We ourselves make the course by interaction.' (M5JY:INT)

Thoughtful consideration for other learners shows itself when some students, speaking of the interactive and mutually supportive nature of their courses, refer to their role in assisting new students to feel welcomed into the class:

'Each course is confidence-building and you're making friends all the time; and the social side of it getting out and meeting other adults from all walks of life; all with different backgrounds, different problems.' (F4IY)

'I find that I'm one of those that like to make people welcom.' (F6GN:INT)

There is a degree to which some students seem to consider themselves to have a secondary role almost as an assistant tutor, especially at times when the tutor is engaged in helping other students, and this seems to take two different forms. Some students would offer support simply as a gesture to new members of the group, while they continue with their own work. For others it seems to be a way both of welcoming new people into 'their' course, but also to imply to new members that a hierarchy of students is already established within the group. Anecdotal evidence suggests that for some students, who have continued perhaps for too many years in the same group with the same tutor, the acceptance of new members into their 'club' is regarded as a proposition to be resisted, but no evidence has been found of this in my data. Such an approach was, in any case, allegedly only to be found amongst a very small number of students and for most the support received from and, in turn, given to fellow learners is a welcomed and valued aspect of adult learning.

Individual students have their own views, of course, about the relative value of different learning activities. One would not be surprised to hear learners speak with enthusiasm on the subject they are following at the time and for one student the value of academic subjects is much higher than for other subjects:

> 'It is an academic subject, not craft/leisure pursuit; exercises the mind not just fills time.' (F4LN)

Some students gave subject-specific replies when responding to my questions and two foreign language students illustrate the opposing views that can be held within two similar courses, each regarded as being of quality:

> 'It's not too intense, with the onus on conversation, rather than grammar.' (M4LN:INT)

> 'It's a full course, including grammar, not just conversational.' (F5LN)

Some students in foreign language courses also express strong views regarding what they see as the advantages or disadvantages of working with tutors whom they refer to as 'native speakers' of the language. Some consider that from such a tutor they will gain the 'correct' accent, whilst for others an accent that is too 'strong' is intimidating, as is the tendency they describe for a tutor to expect too high a standard too quickly.

Learning is a life-enhancing experience
Students gain much pleasure from their learning and it has importance in their lives in different ways. For some it is more than just enjoyable, it is life-enhancing, bringing specific benefits of enjoyment, greater confidence, wider friendship and increased self-esteem:

> 'Learning gave me confidence, how to mix with others with different outlooks, how to accept ideas and opinions of others, plus express my own.' (F4IY)

> 'I am now able to judge whether the teaching is appropriate and up to scratch; I am not afraid to voice my grievances or concerns.' (F4PN:INT)

> 'It challenging one's ability to be creative.' (F5FN)

> 'It's an intellectual challenge.' (M6PN)

> 'It is life-enhancing.' (F4GN:INT)

The uses to which students put their learning seem many and various, 'but adult learners – unlike some politicians – do not make neat distinctions between learning for interest and pleasure, and education for qualifications and employment.' Their learning is often gained alongside other activities which they may or may not recognize as leading to learning, and which very often will have 'multiple and even unexpected outcomes' (Coare and Thompson, 1996:189). Further reference is made to this point in Chapter 10.

Students of all ages give examples of other advantages gained from their course. For some it is the feeling of fitness; for others it is the pleasure of being absorbed in an art or craft activity, or the practical activities of a foreign language group. Some speak of being able to pass on knowledge to their children or other family members, and others of the pleasure of human interaction, often to the extent to making lasting friendships with fellow students. It is not possible to quantify from this data those students who overcome considerable hurdles to attend their course regularly and punctually, but I know from personal experience, and have often heard from other adult education providers, of the effort students make to deal with the challenges of transport, reliable child-care, indifferent or even hostile relatives, and to find the fees in order to enjoy the learning which means so much to them. References in the data to confidence-building, to the raising of self-esteem and to the general life-enhancing nature of adult education indicate its importance in people's lives in so many ways, and this is so whether their course leads to an accredited outcome or is undertaken for the sheer pleasure of learning. This point is taken up again in Chapter 10 as it, too, has implications for government and for other policy-makers.

Criticisms of tutors and of courses

Although most student respondents regarded their course as one of quality, this view was not shared by all, with 57 of them stating that their course was not of quality. Where reasons were given they can be placed into two categories – criticisms of the tutor, and criticisms about the course. Examples of these include:

'The standard of teaching is weak, with ill-defined objectives.' (M3DN)

'The teaching element of the course is not skilled and many students are left feeling frustrated.' (F4DY)

'There is too much emphasis put onto the individual to learn from a booklet; there is no overall class teaching and everyone is at different levels, so the tutor is too stretched.' (F3DY:INT)

'The format is not suitable for a group of people with such diverse needs; the tutor tries to act as a facilitator, which is very difficult for students who do not know what they are expected to do.' (F5AN)

'The class is too big, the accommodation is cramped, and there is not enough individual teaching.' (F4LY:INT)

'Computers did not work properly or kept crashing; equipment should be up and running.' (F3DY)

'I am limited by the ability of other students.' (M4LN:INT)

Responsibility for learning quality

Although many students seemed to credit their tutors with being entirely responsible for the quality of their learning, as indicated above, when a specific question was asked, 'Who is responsible for ensuring and maintaining the quality of your course?' they responded by identifying three categories of responsibility:

- responsibility that lay within the teaching area;
- responsibility that lay outside the teaching area but within the college;
- responsibility that lay outside the college.

Responsibility within the teaching space is seen as being shared between tutor and students or, in a very small number of responses, as the students' alone. Responsibility may be within the college, or in the hands of an external agency. A summary of these responses is given in Table 7.4.

For data from Table 7.4, cross-tabulated by curriculum group, see Appendix 5, Table A5.2. Data in Table 7.4 highlight the differing perceptions of students regarding where responsibility for quality lies. The findings are important to the extent that they demonstrate the range of perceptions of students about responsibility for quality in their institution. This range of views is echoed in data from tutors (see Chapter 8), and it may explain, at least in part, why some students consider that they have some responsibility for their learning quality, whilst others see it as being in the hands of college staff. For a majority of students (60 per cent), their tutor bears primary responsibility for ensuring and maintaining the quality of their course. This group (Group R) of responses (larger than all the others groups combined, and four times larger than the second category) shows that students consider full responsibility for quality to be in the hands of their tutor, whilst the second largest group (Group S) sees responsibility as a partnership between tutor and students (15 per cent). Other groups show quality to be in the hands of different groups of college staff, or of those beyond the college, and it is striking that whilst 1,416 students (Groups $R + S + T + W + X = 87$ per cent) consider that their tutor is involved in some way, as many as 190 (12 per cent) believe that

Table 7.4: Students' responses to the question 'Who is responsible for ensuring and maintaining the quality of your course?'

n = 1,621 (1,249 women, 372 men) RESPONSE GROUPS	Under 30	30–50	50+	Totals Women	Men
R: Tutor, teacher, lecturer, instructor	100 (47%)	320 (56%)	560 (66%)	755 (60%)	225 (60%)
S: Tutor and students	45 (21%)	105 (18%)	98 (12%)	190 (15%)	58 (16%)
T: Tutor and college* (i.e. excluding the students)	18 (9%)	43 (8%)	57 (7%)	88 (7%)	27 (7%)
U: The college* only	12 (6%)	31 (5%)	66 (8%)	81 (6%)	28 (8%)
V: An external agency** only	8 (4%)	16 (4%)	13 (2%)	27 (2%)	10 (3%)
W: Tutor & external agency** (i.e. excluding students and the college)	6 (3%)	15 (3%)	18 (2%)	33 (3%)	6 (2%)
X: Tutor, students and college*	8 (4%)	14 (2%)	12 (1%)	25 (2%)	9 (2%)
Y: The students alone	6 (3%)	1 (0.2%)	8 (1%)	10 (0.8%)	5 (1%)
Z: Other groupings	8 (4%)	23 (4%)	13 (2%)	40 (3%)	4 (1%)
Totals	211	568	845	1,249	372

The terms 'college' and 'external agency' in Table 7.4 are used as follows:
* college: refers to a person or group within the college – e.g. the principal, head of department, senior tutor, curriculum coordinator or the college governors.
** external: refers to an agency external to the college – e.g. the LEA, an agency, an examining board, a professional or funding body.

neither they nor their tutors bear any responsibility for quality (Groups U + V + Z). A small group of 15 students consider responsibility to be theirs alone.

Viewed by curriculum choice, Table 7.5 (below) shows the four largest response groups, which include the majority of responses.

When considered by age group and gender, responses in Table 7.4 show a few noteworthy differences. Approximately the same percentages of

Table 7.5: The four largest response groups from Table 7.4, viewed by curriculum

RESPONSE GROUP	R: Tutor, teacher, lecturer		S: Tutor and students		T: Tutor and college		U: The college only	
CURRICULUM GROUP	**F**	**M**	**F**	**M**	**F**	**M**	**F**	**M**
A: Visual Arts	80	31	18	2	3	2	2	3
G: Dance, Movement and Yoga	132	14	22	1	9	1	7	2
L: Languages	137	70	50	23	25	12	17	6
P: General Interest	103	20	41	8	6	2	9	5

men (19 per cent) and women (20 per cent) aged 30–50 regard their tutor as primarily responsible for quality. Similarly, 34 per cent of women and 37 per cent of men in the 50+ age group give the same response. These responses relate to references later in this chapter to 'active', participatory students. Responses, when considered by gender, show a pattern that follows a general three-to-one, women to men, relationship (reflecting approximately gender differences in enrolment levels across the county's colleges), and even in two instances where the ratio of responses differ (categories W and Z), the numbers involved are very small.

For a full summary of responses by curriculum groups and gender, see Appendix 5, Table A5.2.

When data from Table 7.4 are considered by subject group the results, in common with all data in this chapter, offer no striking contrasts, with a spread across the curriculum categories that follows the numerical distribution of participants. In other words, neither gender nor curriculum are statistically significant factors in responses from this research sample.

One student relates quality to the level of enrolment, i.e. 'If a course is full, it must be good, and meets public demand', and another suggests that if the course was not of quality she would not still be attending. References to the need for improvement in, for example, classroom equipment show that students do remain on a course even where they have to use faulty or unreliable equipment, although my data does not indicate for how long this problem persisted. Difficulties presented by unreliable or faulty equipment is, within this survey, a factor that applies to premises and resources shared with day schools and not where adult colleges have their own resources. I believe this problem has worsened since schools became more independent of local authorities and ceased to be required to ensure that authority-owned property was kept fully serviced for both groups of users. Students often seem unaware of who is responsible for dealing with matters such as premises and equipment, and it is generally the tutor, as the person on the spot, who bears the brunt of learners' displeasure. This can occur wherever a course takes place.

Finally, in response to the question about who is responsible for quality, a very small number of students offered responses that fell outside the main groups. For example, one gave 'the Board of Education' as his response and may perhaps have meant the college board of governors, or a committee within the local education authority. Another student offered a comment which links a question of quality with the numerical control of enrolments:

'The numbers are presumably controlled centrally.' (F4DN)

and one student's experience suggests that he saw no indications at all of anyone taking responsibility for quality:

'As far as I can see, no one!' (F6LN)

Table 7.6: Students' responses to the question 'How do you, as a student, contribute to a quality learning experience for yourself and your fellow students'?

n = 1,606 (1,229 women, 377 men) RESPONSE GROUPS	WOMEN				MEN				TOTALS
	Under 30	30–50	50 +	Totals	Under 30	30–50	50 +	Totals	
Group A: Active participation	108 (60%)	279 (62%)	364 (61%)	751 (61%)	30 (70%)	85 (70%)	142 (67%)	257 (68%)	1,008 (63%)
Group B: Completing homework/ working outside class hours	20 (11%)	41 (9%)	54 (9%)	115 (9%)	3 (7%)	9 (7%)	25 (12%)	37 (10%)	152 (9%)
Group C: Attendance and punctuality	14 (8%)	47 (10%)	65 (11%)	126 (10%)	3 (7%)	9 (7%)	12 (6%)	24 (6%)	150 (9%)
Group D: Passive participation	24 (13%)	33 (7%)	52 (9%)	109 (9%)	5 (12%)	10 (8%)	13 (6%)	28 (7%)	139 (9%)
Group E: Social interaction and mutual support	11 (6%)	25 (6%)	35 (6%)	71 (6%)	1 (2%)	5 (4%)	8 (4%)	14 (4%)	85 (5%)
Group F: A 'detached' attitude	4 (2%)	27 (6%)	26 (4%)	57 (5%)	1 (2%)	3 (3%)	13 (6%)	17 (5%)	74 (5%)
Totals	181	452	596	1,229	43	121	213	377	1,606

The students' role in ensuring a quality learning experience

Most students in the sample (1,677) believe that they have some part to play in ensuring a quality learning experience for themselves, and some acknowledge that this can influence the learning of fellow students.

> 'I think you've got to take a little responsibility .... Just because someone's standing with the chalk in their hands or on the blackboard, doesn't mean that you're going to learn anything.' (F2DY)

> 'I think it's as much the student's responsibility to take dvantage of what is there, to turn up for the lessons, properly equipped for whatever it is you are doing, to attend every session as much as possible, and not letting everyone down.' (F4IY:INT)

> 'I think that it is about responsibility and moral acceptance that you are an integral part of the course.' (F3FN)

Students' views on how they contribute to the quality of learning fell into six categories, as shown in Table 7.6.

For data from Table 7.6, cross-tabulated by curriculum group, see Appendix 5, Table A5.3.

Active and passive learners

Data in Table 7.6 show a distinction between the active and passive nature of students' roles as learners. A large group of students (1,008 – Group A), describe their role as highly active and participatory, with references to 'discussing', 'questioning', 'contributing', 'sharing ideas', 'cooperating', 'inspiring' and a 'willingness to accept criticism'.

> 'I think we do ensure the quality of the course by questioning.' (F5GN)

> 'If you don't participate you're not going to get the full benefit.' (F4KN:INT)

> 'Well of course we won't be on the course otherwise; personally would never go on a course unless I was committed to learning.' (P002F5)

Within this response group, some gender differences are noticeable. The largest groups making reference to active participation are aged 50+, with 23 per cent of women and 28 per cent of men in this age group. By contrast, the smallest figures are from the under 30 age group, with 7 per cent of women and 8 per cent of men indicating active participation. One might have thought that active participation would more readily be referred to by younger students who are closer to school experiences, but data in this research shows evidence to support anecdotal views that many adult learners become more participative as they become more experienced learners.

Good humour and a friendly attitude are frequently linked with the proactive approach shown by students who make references in this group. Some see this level of participation as expected of them, and for others it is a part of their responsibility as learners. Active learners describe their role as a partnership with their tutor to achieve the highest quality learning and for many the encouragement of other students is a part of that process. Also notable in this group is the number of references by students not only to the completion of their homework but also to the specific preparation of material for their next class meeting. This is described in a way that suggests some individuals might be presenting the material to the class group at a future meeting, thus taking a share of the course presentation. Responses in this group show students being cooperative and more open to criticism, as well as being willing to undertake limited research into their subject. A smaller group of students (152 – Group B) show themselves to be less active, in that they complete homework tasks and occasionally undertake additional work outside the classroom, but indicate less active participation than Group A. In contrast to these two groups, a little over one fifth of students (374 – Groups C, D and E) may be described as relatively 'passive' learners. This is not to suggest that they are totally inactive, but they consider that their role is to arrive regularly and punctually for their classes, to listen attentively to the tutor and to carry out instructions and to complete any homework set. This group do not indicate that they are proactive in any way, but take their lead from the tutor and cause as little disruption to the class group as possible. Some recognize, however, the value of maintaining a positive and considerate approach to their learning by offering mutual support:

'I contribute to quality by being enthusiastic.' (M3LN:INT)

'By attendance and courtesy at all times.' (F6IN)

'By paying attention to the tutor.' (F4EN)

'I think you have your own personal responsibility to turn up on time, not to disrupt the class by being late, and to listen and do as you're told and be responsible, and not stop other people getting on and getting what they want out of the course.' (F4IY:INT)

The language used by some respondents in this group shows a very low-key approach and many of their remarks suggest echoes of school days by indicating that their role is to arrive – punctually – to show respect for the tutor, not to be disruptive, not to waste time and 'not to ask "silly" questions':

'I show commitment by attending regularly.' (F4GN)

'I take up as little of the tutor's time as possible.' (F4EN)

One may surmise that this passive group are, nevertheless, learning and show an interest in what they are doing, but they also demonstrate that they feel a lesser degree of responsibility for what is happening than do their more active fellows. The completion of 'homework' of some description is for many students (and, as will be seen in Chapters 8 and 9, for many tutors) one of the most important ways in which adult learners contribute to their learning and demonstrate some responsibility for its progress. This applies to both active and passive learners, and the undertaking of homework is often stated by students and tutors alike as a fairly normal aspect of many courses. For the passive learners, however, there is a sense of routine about homework, without any suggestion of voluntarily taking this further. 'Homework' in this context includes the undertaking of some out-of-class voluntary activity and, depending on the course, may include the completion of traditional written tasks, the reading of set material and visits to museums or art galleries. For the more active learners simple research to obtain information relating to the course and on behalf of the learning group, and the purchasing or preparation of materials to take to the next class is one way of taking responsibility for their learning.

Interaction between students and the social element of courses

Interacting with other students, helping and supporting other students and sharing with them learning and ideas are aspects of adult learning that are regarded as important and valuable, but for only a minority and only 85 of the references were to this aspect of learning. For those who contributed to this group, learning is seen as a supportive team activity from which one gains as much as one contributes. Learning in a group can be seen to enhance learning 'because it encourages the pooling of resources, builds a sense of group belonging, allows participants to express their views, helps to clarify their thinking, and so on' (Tennant 1997: 108). Some students are quite clear that the social aspects of their courses are very important to them and references to the forming of personal relationships and long-term friendships are not uncommon:

'I enjoy interaction with fellow students.' (F5PN)

'We enjoy helping and encouraging each other.' (F4DY:INT)

Lovell refers to the importance of socialization and the transitional stages through which we pass in moving from child to adult and that our attitudes as adults will affect our behaviour in differing circumstances (Lovell 1980). The question of attitudes and personal values in relation to learning are considered further in Chapter 6.

Some students refer specifically to the pleasure and value of sharing their learning experiences:

> 'We co-operate in the group and share knowledge.' (F2CY)

> 'By enjoying the class you enable others to be able to enjoy their class; why spoil everyone else's enjoyment?' (F2PN)

These 'social learners' can provide a supportive dimension to many courses and reference has been made above to the help they can provide to newcomers. A cooperative attitude within a learning group can, as in many other areas of life, assist in maintaining a positive, creative and pleasurable experience for all members of the group.

A 'detached' group of learners

A final group of students (74) (Group F, Table 7.6), in strong contrast to the active learners, shows a very detached attitude towards their course. They show no sign of participating, other than being present, but rather from the way they write can be visualized sitting on the periphery of the learning group and not feeling a part of it. They consider that they have no responsibility for the quality of their learning and their responses reflect this rather 'detached' view in contrast to so many of their fellow students. There is no indication that those in this group recognize any of the participatory mutual benefits of shared learning referred to by so many others, but rather seem to see their contribution to quality as the mechanical completion of a set of tasks, such as completing questionnaires or other evaluation forms as part of a quality-control task, and by complaining to a higher authority if dissatisfied; or simply withdrawing completely from the course.

> 'If the course is not up to standard, I request a change.' (F5AN)

> 'I complain if necessary to authority.' (F5GN)

> 'If I didn't enjoy the experience I'd change classes or leave altogether.' (F6LN)

It may be that this group is not aware that students are able to take a more active role in their learning, if they choose to do so. I have come across students who, although mature and having considerable responsibilities in their lives, such as being parents or company directors, would not consider questioning or challenging their tutor, because that is what they expect the relationship to be, as they recall from their schooling.

It has to be acknowledged, also, that there is no evidence in my data to show that these students with a 'detached' attitude are learning any less than their more vocal and overtly participative fellow students. There are those, of course, who simply do not believe that it is their job to be responsible for learning quality, and 74 students stated that quality was not their concern and considered that it was someone else's job or simply not a matter with which they should be involved:

'It's the tutor's job.' (F5PN)

'Because I'm paying to be taught.' (F6DY)

I attend the course to learn – my contribution is to attend and enjoy the course.' (F3IN)

Others simply did not wish to concern themselves with the matter:

'Because I've spent my whole life ensuring quality elsewhere and I have now retired; post-retirement adult education is mainly about a satisfying activity and meeting congenial people.' (F6AN)

'I'm too long in the tooth to worry about it.' (M6LN)

And others did not feel that they had any contribution to make:

'I know so little about the subject that I wouldn't know about quality.' (M2LN)

'In any input I make I try to ensure that it is of quality, but the actual class procedures, activities, practices, etc. are surely the concern of the class teacher.' (F6LN:INT)

'I'm just doing it for fun!' (F4GN)

These comments show a group of students who, although taking a more detached view than the active learners are, nevertheless, willing to participate, they simply do not feel responsible or that it is their concern. Adult learners expect, and gain, much from their tutors, and these data suggest that they expect their tutor to know his/her subject, to show enthusiasm for the subject and to have a sense of eagerness to teach it and to be a competent teacher.

Perhaps this is not surprising because, as Daines *et al.* have suggested, adult students also:

- at first, prefer to be taught in an old-fashioned way and may be taken aback by suggestions to participate actively;
- expect value for money;

- expect to be made to work;
- expect to be told how they are doing as individuals and as a group;
- expect to enjoy their learning;
- expect their status as adults to be recognised.

(Daines *et al.* 1993: 7–8)

Value of the adult learning experience

Adult students value their learning and many recognize the affects their previous learning can have on current studies. One aspect of my research, as indicated at the beginning of this chapter, was to discover the extent to which students recognize and draw upon the value of their prior learning experiences. Two questions put to students on these aspects of their learning were placed towards the end of my questionnaire in anticipation that earlier questions would stimulate further thoughts about their previous experiences in relation to current learning.

The value students place on their learning is described by them in three different ways – broad benefits gained from the learning, a second chance or new opportunity, and specific benefits from, or purpose for, the learning. Table 7.7 shows the levels of response in these categories.

For data from Table 7.7 cross-tabulated by curriculum group, see Appendix 5, Table A5.4.

Students who responded to the question shown in Table 7.7 described how they valued their learning and for most (1,455) it was for the broad experience and benefits it afforded them.

Table 7.7: Students' responses to the question 'How and why do you value your learning as an adult?'

n = 1,648 (1,271 women, 377 men)	WOMEN				MEN				TOTALS
RESPONSE GROUPS	Under 30	30–50	50+	Totals	Under 30	30–50	50+	Totals	
Group A: Broad benefits of learning	152 (84%)	391 (86%)	574 (90%)	1,117 (88%)	26 (70%)	98 (92%)	214 (92%)	338 (90%)	1,455 (88%)
Group B: Second chance or new opportunity	13 (7%)	38 (8%)	55 (9%)	106 (8%)	6 (16%)	6 (6%)	10 (4%)	22 (6%)	128 (8%)
Group C: Specific purpose or benefit	15 (8%)	24 (5%)	9 (1%)	48 (4%)	5 (14%)	3 (3%)	9 (4%)	17 (5%)	65 (4%)
Totals	180	453	638	1,271	37	107	233	377	1,648

'To become a better informed adult.' (M6KN)

'It's more of a choice as opposed to a chore!' (F2LN)

'Without adult learning you become a vegetable.' (F3EN)

They saw it as challenging and motivating, yet relaxing. For some older students it helps to offset what they referred to as 'stagnation', brings about a general sense of well-being and achievement and provides a basis for personal and intellectual growth. For others the physical nature of their course provided a different sense of physiological well-being as well as 'keeping mind and body active'.

A second chance or new opportunity represented by adult learning that was not available in earlier years, or which they did not take advantage of, was for 128 the main value:

'Because it's a chance I didn't have as a child.' (F5GN)

'Because it has become a matter of my own choice; I also bring a different perspective as an adult than previously at school.' (F2PN)

'Unlike school, this is my choice.' (F3LN:INT)

'I wish I had started years ago as I find it quite hard now and I don't like to give up!' (M4LN:INT)

'Being treated like an adult [is a] different learning experience than secondary education.' (M3DN)

Table 7.7 also shows that the second chance/new opportunity group is, relatively, more important for women than for men, in that the ratio moves from the usual 3 : 1 to 5 : 1 in this case. Many of those responding in this way acknowledged that they had not taken advantage of opportunities at school or in their younger adult life, although for some older students the chances were not there because their schooling had been disrupted by domestic economic pressures or national conflict. Occasionally respondents admit frankly that they had not worked hard at school and had not taken up all that was on offer to them at the time. They were, therefore, even more determined to make the most of their learning as an adult. Specific benefits from prior learning, such as the gaining of knowledge and skills, or the increase of confidence and self-esteem, are referred to in 65 references, and it is evident that large numbers of students feel a distinct improvement in the way they feel about themselves, even when other benefits are not also identified:

'It improves my knowledge and gives me a skill I didn't previously have.' (F2JY)

'I value learning new skills and subjects as an adult because I am a single parent and it will help me gain new skills when I need to find a job.' (F2PY:INT)

'I improve my English every day; it's very good to learn English because it's an international language.' (F2LY)

'Keeping up to date with IT; making it possible to help my teenage daughters with their use of computers.' (F4DY)

'It enhances my quality of life.' (F6GN:INT)

'Teaches me what I need to know and gives me a recognized qualification.' (F2CY)

These students have become better able to make judgements about current courses in relation to their earlier experiences, and also have developed an ability to assess their own needs and thus to select new learning activity in a more informed way.

'Adult learning helps my mind to overcome everyday issues.' (F6JY:INT)

'The discipline of learning is good for mental well-being.' (F5LN)

Lovell points to the ways in which adults modify their values in the light of socialization and experience, 'the process by which an individual comes to accept the attitudes, values and norms of the social groups of which he is a member' (Lovell 1980: 165). Many adult learners refer to the way in which 'their first try at adult education has awakened a hunger for learning, which may be fired by the thrill of mental and physical stimulation and new skills, or by the companionship and pleasure of learning with a group' (Coare and Thomson 1996: 152).

When considering the data in Table 7.7 by age group, although responses referring to the broader benefits of learning are shown across all age groups, those to do with second chance or new opportunity, are mostly by women. References to specific benefits are made by both genders across the age groups. When considered by curriculum choice, the data in Table 7.7, the four largest groups of responses are from students following courses in Languages (21 per cent), General Interest (13 per cent), Dance, Movement and Yoga (11 per cent) and Visual Arts (9 per cent), for whom the value of learning is from the broad benefits it brings. A full summary of theses groups may be found in Appendix 5, Table A5.4.

The effects of previous learning

When referring to the affects previous learning has on current studies, those students who gave examples (1,004 references) indicate a range of benefits gained and lessons learnt from the prior learning (see Table 7.8).

Table 7.8: Students' responses to the question 'How do you think your previous experiences as an adult learner affect your current learning?'

n = 1,004 (749 women, 255 men)	WOMEN				MEN				TOTALS
RESPONSE GROUPS	Under 30	30–50	50+	Totals	Under 30	30–50	50+	Totals	
Group A: It gives broad experience and benefits	19 (42%)	167 (63%)	296 (67%)	482 (64%)	21 (91%)	42 (59%)	83 (52%)	146 (57%)	628 (63%)
Group B: It provides a foundation for further learning; it is progressive	13 (29%)	75 (29%)	102 (23%)	160 (25%)	1 (4%)	12 (17%)	56 (35%)	69 (27%)	259 (26%)
Group C: It offers practical outcomes and benefits	13 (29%)	21 (8%)	43 (10%)	77 (10%)	1 (4%)	17 (24%)	22 (14%)	40 (16%)	117 (12%)
Totals	45	263	441	749	23	71	161	255	1,004

For data from Table 7.8, cross-tabulated by curriculum group, see Appendix 5, Table A5.5.

It should be noted that, in addition to the 1,004 responses shown in Table 7.8, 346 references (258 women and 88 men) stated that previous experiences did not affect current learning, or were not applicable. Non-respondents to this question may also have seen previous learning experiences as having no value or relevance, but this is speculative. When responding to the question about effects of previous learning, 160 respondents saw no connection between their prior and current learning. Some of these, however, interpreted the question as referring to subjects rather than to learning in general so those who had studied, for example, French on a previous occasion saw no connection with the Local History course they were following now. The majority of respondents acknowledged that prior learning did affect new learning and of the 1,004 examples, 628 referred to the broad experience and general benefits they gained from the experience, including self-discipline, concentration and awareness of what to expect from future learning. Learning was seen as a cumulative experience that helped them to become more skilled effective learners:

'Encourage me to attend new courses.' (F5IN)

'More confidence in my abilities and intellectual capacity.' (F6KN)

'I have learned to work as a member of a team.' (M6MN:INT)

'It's like scales falling from your eyes and you see the wider picture.' (F4KN)

For others (259), previous learning, as well as adding to their general experiences as learners, had laid the foundations for further learning, whilst for 117 specific benefits were gained, such as:

'Better management of time; setting and aiming for realistic and realisable targets.' (M6LN)

'[Enabled me to be able to] adjust quickly; to accept criticism, i.e. constructive criticism.' (F6IN)

'I am learning how to learn and remember.' (F4LN:INT)

'Gave me confidence, how to mix with others with different outlooks, how to accept ideas and opinions of others, plus express my own.' (F4IY)

The students in this survey were divided into those who saw their learning as a series of discrete episodes of unconnected, although enjoyable experiences; and those for whom the links between all learning were clear. This latter group saw lessons being learnt and applied in subsequent studies and were able, for example, to make more informed judgements over their choice of courses and of tutors (see below and Chapter 9).

Recognition of the effects of previous learning was given by students in all age groups, and when considered by subject groups, language students, for example, refer to the advantages of laying foundations, as well as to the broader benefits of their learning. Not surprisingly, closer links are recognized between previous and current learning by those students whose activity might be seen as a more obviously cumulative progressive one – e.g. languages, art and crafts.

Gender comparisons

As indicated above, the overall female/male ratio of participants in this survey is 3 women to 1 man, which broadly reflects the participation rates in adult education. Tables show that in most categories of response the same 3:1 ratio is reflected, and they also show the few instances where this rate is different in responses to certain questions. For example, Table 7.1 shows that four times the proportion of women as men believe that their course is of quality because it meets personal needs. Another example in Table 7.4 shows that 33 women compared with 6 men believe that responsibility for the quality of learning lies with the tutor and an external agency, excluding both the students and the college. In all tables, however, the figures are quite small and afford no significant insight.

Gender differences are a little more evident over matters such as social interaction and peer support. Five times as many women students as men regard these as ways in which they contribute to the quality of learning, with the same proportions offering views on the importance of attendance and punctuality (Table 7.6).

Five to one is again the ratio by which women and men value their learning because it offers a second chance or new opportunity (Table 7.7). Relatively speaking, as indicated above, certain issues seem less important to all men in this survey than they do to women, but the numbers involved in each case are really too small to draw any firm conclusions. The majority of students and tutors in this survey are women and that alone would affect the balance of responses. Generally, other than the few exceptions cited, the response comparison rates between genders show levels that reflect their proportionate numbers in the survey.

Age comparisons

Responses viewed by age group similarly show few examples of large differences between the views of individuals, although one may see that of those aged over 50, 40 per cent of women and 33 per cent of men cite the value of broad experiences from previous learning. The same age group, however, place less emphasis on previous experiences as a foundation for further learning (14 per cent of women and 22 per cent of men), and even less on specific practical outcomes and benefits (6 per cent of women and 9 per cent of men).

When responses are considered by age group, gender and curriculum (see Table 7.9) the largest group of student respondents are those following language courses (434), and it would not be surprising, therefore, that they contribute a larger proportion of responses in each case. This group is followed by History and General Interest (348), Crafts and Domestic Skills (270), Dance, Movement and Yoga (234), Computing, Mathematics, Business and Office Skills (212) and Visual Arts and Music (185). The smallest group of respondents – Basic Skills and English – represents only a total of 101 students in this survey. See also Appendix 5, Table A5.6, for additional information.

Table 7.9 shows that those who represent the largest response groups in most curriculum sets are women aged 50+. In contrast to this, however, the number of women aged 30–50 in Curriculum sets 2 and 5 are unusually large for this sample.

Tables 7.7, 7.8 and 7.9 also show that females in this sample over 50 years of age are, statistically, more represented on Crafts, Dance and Language courses and that men over 50 are statistically less represented in

Table 7.9: Numbers of students in curriculum sets, showing age groups and gender

n = 1,784 (1,364 women, 420 men)	UNDER 30		30–50		50+		TOTALS	
CURRICULUM SETS	F	M	F	M	F	M	F	M
Curriculum set 1: Languages	47 (24%)	12 (31%)	115 (23%)	40 (33%)	122 (18%)	98 (38%)	284 (21%)	150 (37%)
Curriculum set 2: History and General Interest	57 (29%)	5 (13%)	132 (26%)	19 (16%)	99 (15%)	36 (14%)	288 (21%)	60 (14%)
Curriculum set 3: Crafts and Domestic Skills	21 (11%)	0	53 (11%)	14 (12%)	150 (22%)	32 (12%)	224 (17%)	46 (10%)
Curriculum set 4: Dance, Movement and Yoga	8 (4%)	1 (3%)	54 (11%)	5 (4%)	150 (22%)	16 (6%)	212 (16%)	22 (5%)
Curriculum set 5: Computing, Mathematics, Business and Office Studies	32 (16%)	16 (41%)	85 (17%)	24 (20%)	26 (4%)	29 (11%)	143 (10%)	69 (16%)
Curriculum set 6: Visual Arts and Music	12 (6%)	1 (3%)	33 (7%)	5 (4%)	93 (14%)	41 (16%)	138 (10%)	47 (11%)
Curriculum set 7: Basic Skills and English	18 (9%)	4 (10%)	28 (6%)	13 (11%)	29 (4%)	9 (3%)	75 (6%)	26 (6%)
Totals	195	39	500	120	669	261	1,364	420

Basic Skills and Dance. One might reasonably expect men to be less involved in Dance courses, but many men attend Basic Skills courses, and the History and General Interest Set covers a wide range. One would have expected, therefore, a larger representation from men in these two curriculum areas. Gender ratios show some variation in Table 7.9, with Curriculum set 4 showing a ratio of men to women of approximately 1:10, and Curriculum sets 2 and 3 each showing ratios of approximately 1:5.

Key findings from Chapter 7

This brief summary is of the key findings from Chapter 7, which are compared in Chapter 9 with findings from tutor data.

Adult learners gain much from their courses and greatly enjoy the learning process. They hold their tutors in high regard and are very appreciative of tutors' efforts on their behalf. The time spent by tutors keeping up-to-date with their subject, undergoing professional development and preparing for lessons is recognized and highly appreciated by students.

Many adult learners believe they contribute to the quality of their learning in a variety of ways, and some consider that they share responsibility for it. Many of the participants in this survey, approximately two thirds, show themselves to be active participatory learners who take some responsibility for the quality of their own learning, however the nature of their participation varies widely and it is likely the there is some variation between indications of intent and actual degrees of responsibility.

Students value their learning for its broad and specific benefits. From it they gain knowledge, skills and physiological benefits; it also increases their confidence and raises their self-esteem. They acknowledge, in many cases, the practical benefits provided by their previous learning experiences, and can put them to use in new learning.

Adult learning is a life-enhancing experience and highly valued by those who take part in it. It is an important part of their daily lives, providing in some cases companionship and support.

Data tables indicate responses by age group, and generally the differences between the age groups are not significant. Most levels of response between men and women reflect the gender percentage differences of participants. Differences, when considered by curriculum group, show little of note, and responses to the various questions generally reflect the numerical differences in the size of participating curriculum groups.

The analysis of data from students in this chapter shows the importance of learning to the lives of respondents, and has provided a context within which their views have been expressed on several aspects of the learning. Chapter 8, which follows, offers a similar analysis of findings from tutor data, and the outcomes from Chapters 7 and 8 are compared and contrasted in Chapter 9.

8 Tutors' Perceptions of Learning and Quality in Adult Education – Research Findings

Introduction

This chapter presents the findings from 4 face-to-face, semi-structured interviews and 251 semi-structured tutor questionnaires, in a similar way to Chapter 7. Data tables refer, in each case, to the number of responses given in each response group.

The tutors

Tutors in adult education are recruited from a wide range of backgrounds. They come into adult education from school teaching, further or higher education, industry or the voluntary sector. Many still combine the teaching of adults with other teaching or jobs outside education, and a large number are retired from full-time employment. The curriculum offered in the nine adult community colleges included in this survey is very wide, as explained in Chapter 6, and although precise numbers are not available, large numbers of adult tutors teach several courses each year and work in a number of different locations. They accumulate, therefore, a wide experience of adult teaching and learning as well an impressive length of service.

The curriculum available in the adult community colleges includes both accredited and non-accredited courses of varying length, and most colleges now include an extensive summer school, making adult learning opportunities available throughout most of the year.

Findings from data supplied by tutors

As the number of participating tutors is much smaller than the number of students, tables in this chapter show results by two age groups – under 50 and over 50. As in Chapter 7, quotations from tutors include an alpha-numeric reference which shows gender (F or M), age group 1–6 (see questionnaire in Appendix 3); curriculum group (see Appendix 1). Quotations taken from interviews show the suffix, INT.

Tutors' perceptions on learning and quality

Tutors believe their courses are of quality (249; 99 per cent). This statement is, perhaps, not surprising but tutors provide convincing evidence to support their views. Only two tutors stated that their course was not of quality and their explanations are discussed below. Table 8.1 shows tutors' views on what it is that makes their course one of quality that is within their control as tutor.

For data from Table 8.1 cross-tabulated by curriculum group, see Appendix 5, Table A5.7.

Courses are of quality because of factors that are both within and outside the control of tutors, and they provide examples of each. Table 8.1 summarizes evidence provided by tutors, using their own language, of influences on quality that are within their control. The table shows that tutors believe that they are the principal cause of quality on the courses

Table 8.1: Tutors' responses to the question 'What is it that makes this a course of quality – within your control as tutor?'

n = 244 (184 women, 60 men) RESPONSE GROUPS	WOMEN			MEN			TOTALS
	Under 50	50 and over	Totals	Under 50	50 and over	Totals	
Group A: Me – my preparation, skills, qualifications, pedagogy, being up-to-date	73 (72%)	70 (84%)	143 (78%)	18 (82%)	27 (71%)	45 (75%)	188 (77%)
Group B: The course content, materials and structure	14 (14%)	7 (8%)	21 (11%)	2 (9%)	10 (26%)	12 (20%)	33 (14%)
Group C: Assessment, outcomes, examination	10 (10%)	5 (6%)	15 (8%)	2 (9%)	0	2 (3%)	17 (7%)
Group D: Student interaction and social aspects	3 (3%)	1 (1%)	4 (2%)	0	0	0	4 (2%)
Group E: Detached approach: completion of evaluation forms	1 (1%)	0	1 (1%)	0	1 (33%)	1 (2%)	2 (1%)
Totals	101	83	134	22	38	60	244

and in their students' learning experience (188). They claim that it is the skills and knowledge they bring, together with their qualifications and a willingness to remain up-to-date in their subject that contribute significantly to course quality.

Tutors believe in themselves and in the value of what they do:

> 'I am highly qualified, very experienced, motivated, willing to alter teaching methods and materials.' (M5PN)

> 'There's no point in teaching if you don't think you've got some
> *good things*.' (F5LN:INT)

Most tutors state that their purpose is to facilitate high quality learning by their students:

> 'It's a course of quality because I provide the possibility for any student at whatever level to know the highest level of practice.' (M6AN)

> 'I keep up to date in the subject, and expect high standards from students within their capacity.' (F5EY:INT)

> 'I prepare carefully; I get to know the class members and consider their individual needs; provide a pleasant and safe environment.' (F6GN)

Tutors make careful preparations for their teaching and ensure that course structures relate to the learning needs of all students:

> 'Personalised learning programmes, formulated by students and myself; careful planning of lessons.' (F4LN)

> 'I provide teaching that is relevant to my students' needs and am open, approachable, patient, friendly and reliable.' (M5BN:INT)

Tutors believe in creating for their students through 'meticulous planning and preparation' a supportive, non-threatening and enjoyable learning environment 'that aims high for student satisfaction and achievement'.

> 'Creating a friendly, non-competitive atmosphere; encouraging useable informative knowledge.' (F4GN)

> 'By explaining techniques in a simple and understandable way.' (F5EN:INT)

> 'Students are consulted and given choices and learning is continuously assessed; the course is planned to provide opportunity for progression of ability.' (F5GN:INT)

These views accord with those of students (see Chapter 8) and tutors are aware of the way in which many students credit them with total responsibility for all that occurs during their course.

A second, much smaller group of references were to the course content, structure and the materials they use for teaching (33). That this number is so relatively small is particularly noticeable, because in this section tutors are referring to matters of quality that are within their control, and so includes those tutors who prepare their own course material, as distinct from those who are teaching accredited courses and are required to follow a set syllabus.

> 'Choice of course materials; well-planned scheme of work and lesson plans to ensure all relevant topics are covered; regular marking and feedback.' (F4CY)

One would have expected this group to have received more references, to demonstrate the confidence tutors have in their own course material, reflecting the confidence they portray in all other aspects of their work. A further smaller set of responses are to the importance of careful and regular assessment in maintaining learning quality:

> 'I monitor them along the way. I am always there to help them with any difficulties.' (F5MN:INT)

> 'By constant one-to-one assessment, my own attention to new techniques, and adapting to each student's learning needs.' (F5IN)

Some tutors evidently regard assessment as important, but far fewer than the number who believe that quality relates to their own input, as indicated above. This raises a question about the extent to which tutors see their role as teaching, as distinct from facilitating learning – or put another way – whether they see the main issues of quality relate to their teaching, rather than to their students' learning. This point is discussed further below and in Chapters 9 and 10. It is noticeable, also, that in this category the gender response comparison rate is 8:1 compared to the norm of 3:1 – the widest differential in this chapter on tutor data. This shows that, proportionately, women regard this aspect as more important than men. When referring to assessment, it is noticeable that large numbers of tutors use the term 'constant' assessment, indicating that close attention is given to this essential element of their role, but more probably and more realistically they mean 'frequent' assessment. This does, of course, emphasize that for those tutors who have referred to assessment as a factor in ensuring quality, it is one of much significance.

Social aspects

In contrast to some students' views, tutors generally do not consider the social aspects of their course to be of significance (4), although some suggest they create a friendly atmosphere for students which encourages mutual support:

> 'They enjoy the class and the company of other students.' (F5LN)

> 'They produce a portfolio of work and support one another.' (F5DY:INT)

The support gained from being part of a learning group is more strongly recognized by students in this research sample population than by tutors (see Chapters 7 and 9) and the value these tutors seem to place upon it does not accord with anecdotal reports from senior staff of colleges who refer to very effective group support for many different adult learners through a range of extra-course activities, including educational outings and social events. The value of this social experience to the quality of learning is, however, recognized by others:

> People who attend regular education classes often emphasise the positive contribution of the group experience. Though joining a new group can be an unnerving initiation, it can also provide camaraderie and support, and inspiration from diverse life experiences.
>
> (Coare and Thomson 1996: 176)

> The students being of mixed ages works well as this means there are a lot of different points of view which can only help make the course more interesting and varied, especially in the discussions we have.
>
> (An adult learner cited in Coare and Thomson, 1996: 178)

Being aware of the learning needs of each student

The importance of knowing each student's learning needs is recognized by most tutors and much effort is put into ensuring that this knowledge is obtained and frequently updated:

> 'Know students' personal goals and ambitions; try to help individuals achieve these; give much varied opportunity to hold interest.' (F3FN)

> 'Each student finishes with work done to the best of their ability, and work that they are proud of.' (F6EN:INT)

> Adults deserve a learning environment which recognizes their particular needs – for comfort, quiet, the company of other adults, space, stimulation and learning materials that respect their maturity.
>
> (Purdey and Gale 1988: 99)

Tutors in this sample do not state it explicitly, but one senses from their comments they are aware of the potential changes that learning brings about in learners of any age, and a strong feeling of care for their learning group and each individual within it is evident. As Daines points out, learning outcomes have the potential to bring about changes in an adult learner in two distinct ways:

> Firstly, the subject based learning outcomes: knowledge, understanding and skills, the ability to apply such knowledge and understanding (and skills) in different situations and the (mainly) intellectual 'processing skills' that are acquired through using and applying knowledge.

> Secondly, personal learning outcomes, such as motivation, initiative and self-evaluation, and interpersonal skills such as negotiation, collaboration and teamwork.   (Adapted from Daines, *et al*. 1993: 94)

Almost all of the elements mentioned in Daines' remarks are referred to by tutors, and also by students (see Chapter 7).

Some tutors describe the ways in which they make themselves available to their students outside course meeting times and, although this may not be possible or even desirable in all cases, it is clear that for these tutors the feeling of responsibility that they have for their students' learning progress is carried well beyond the classroom. Whatever the degree of help offered by tutors to students beyond the confines of the teaching space, students are clearly very appreciative of the caring approach shown by their tutors, as shown above.

Table 8.1 also refers to a 'detached' approach spoken of by two tutors who regard students' completion of evaluation forms as making the course one of quality. For these tutors the retrospective completion of evaluation forms, as part of a quality assurance system, sometimes only on an annual basis, seems to be seen by them as sufficient to gain satisfactory feedback from their students. These views are in such contrast to those expressed by the majority of tutors that they are particularly noticeable, and have perhaps some link with the group of students who show a 'distant' approach to their contribution to course quality (see Chapter 7). Of the two tutors who stated that their courses were not of quality, one seems to have had in mind standards because he refers to the serious physical disabilities of his students who cannot attain high levels of skill in their subject. The other, inexplicably, having stated that her course was *not* one of quality, gave as her reason, 'A level English is a public examination'. One can only speculate that what the tutor really meant to say was that, as her course led to a public examination, its quality was not in question.

When considered by age and curriculum, data in Table 8.1 show, for example, confidence amongst equal numbers of female tutors under and over the age of 50 that it is they who are the principal cause of quality. Amongst the male tutors, this view is held more by those aged over 50.

Stronger contrasts are shown between the ages of tutors in Response groups B and C, where there is a 50 per cent difference between the views of women who are under or over 50 regarding course content or student assessment, and greater difference between men in the two age groups over course content. The numbers in this latter example are, however, relatively small and do not offer much insight.

Aspects of quality outside the control of tutors

As indicated above, as well as those aspects of quality that they could control, tutors were asked about aspects of quality that they regarded as being outside their control as tutors and Table 8.2 summarizes their responses.

For data from Table 8.2, cross-tabulated by curriculum group, see Appendix 5, Table A5.8.

The professional support, encouragement and opportunities for training provided by their college is for tutors the biggest influencing factor on quality outside their control (57), as shown in Table 8.2. Part-time tutors operate in many venues that are often satellite premises some distance

Table 8.2: Tutors' responses to the question 'What is it that makes this a course of quality – within the control of others?'

n = 194 (147 women, 47 men)	WOMEN			MEN			TOTALS
RESPONSE GROUPS	Under 50	50 and over	Totals	Under 50	50 and over	Totals	
Group A: Professional support, college systems and training opportunities	29 (34%)	16 (26%)	45 (31%)	3 (20%)	9 (28%)	12 (26%)	57 (29%)
Group B: Students' attendance, their effort and homework	24 (28%)	11 (18%)	35 (24%)	5 (33%)	11 (34%)	16 (34%)	51 (26%)
Group C: Equipment and facilities, teaching and learning environment	23 (27%)	20 (33%)	43 (29%)	1 (7%)	5 (16%)	6 (13)%	49 (25%)
Group D: Accredited course, examination boards, curriculum	10 (12%)	14 (23%)	24 (16%)	6 (40%)	7 (22%)	13 (28%)	37 (19%)
Totals	86	61	147	15	32	47	194

from college main buildings (some colleges operate in up to 40 separate locations), and tutors need the support of administrative systems, professional guidance and opportunities to train and update their skills:

'I receive support and encouragement from senior staff.' (F6GN)

'Monitoring by senior tutors within college; regular training via college; updating by senior staff.' (F5LN)

'Support from the Principal, other tutors and the administrative staff are essential to maintain equipment and room conditions, enabling me to supply a quality course to the student.' (M5FN:INT)

Because of the physical isolation of some college venues, tutors may not often receive a visit from senior college staff or administrators, especially if their course happens to be the only one held at that particular location. This means that for personal contact with other staff they must visit the main college building, which can be several miles away, and often inconvenient. In addition to the complications of administration that these arrangements can bring about, it is likely that feelings of isolation could be a factor influencing part-time tutors. The disadvantages of arrangements such as these can be balanced by the advantages to students of being able to attend a course closer to where they live. Students in these circumstances, however, cannot take advantage of the interaction with a wider student body that is made possible in larger college premises.

Students' comments (see Chapter 7) include references to the ways that they, in such circumstances, assist the tutor in preparing the teaching room, which may very recently have been used for some other purpose. This is typically the case in premises shared with schools or, for example, in multi-purpose village halls.

Students contribute to quality by their attitude, attendance and punctuality

Students' attendance, punctuality, effort and completion of homework contribute almost as much to learning quality, that is outside the control of tutors (51 references), as does their first category of professional support from colleges (57 references). In the view of many tutors, the principal contribution and responsibility placed upon their students is to attend all meetings of the course punctually with enthusiasm to learn, and to undertake any tasks that are set for out-of-class work at home. Tutors (and students) regard punctual attendance at all course meetings as a basic and fundamental requirement and duty placed upon students for reasons of courtesy and practicality:

'By regular attendance; by their own efforts in class (i.e. listening/paying attention to instructions/checking their work/correcting marked faults, etc.); by asking questions.' (F4CY)

'Students contribute by their attitude, and their interest in information given; they do out-of-class homework and accept that the course is for learning, not solely producing.' (F3FN:INT)

'Students contribute to quality by developing good study habits, by attending regularly, by keeping up with the work, and by reading widely; in short – by involving themselves.' (M4KY:INT)

A few tutors refer to the effects of college selection of students which can determine those who enrol for any given course – a further aspect beyond their control. This may be in the case of an accredited course, where previous success at a lower level is regarded as a prerequisite; or it can be the result of guidance of a student into an alternative course more suited to their ability or the stage they have reached, as in the case, for example of foreign languages. 'Homework' can take many different forms, according to the nature of the course. In addition to traditional work on exercises or projects associated with an extension of the subject classwork, some tutors encourage students to undertake some basic research into their subject, from visiting museums or art galleries to view items related to their studies, to more detailed research, for example, into family history through parish records:

'By researching their own projects.' (F5EN)

'They do unasked-for homework and go to exhibitions, etc., and share the experience with the class.' (F5AN)

'They are encouraged to prepare all week for the limited oral time we all actually get together, thus optimising their performance.' (M2LN:INT)

The attitudes that students develop towards their studies play an important role in the development of their learning, tutors believe. They refer to various aspects of students' attention to their studies, and include attendance, study discipline, motivation, interest, commitment, cooperation, respect and support for each other.

For many tutors, students' attitudes to learning have a strong influence over the success of their learning. Encouraging students to feel involved in all aspects of their courses and persuading them to join in as much as possible produces positive results:

'Participation is devising their programmes of work by using their life experiences in the learning process, and by ensuring they feel a responsibility towards achieving their aims.' (F4LN:INT)

'Conduct; participation; homework; asking questions; feed-back; completing evaluation forms; exercising choice – by class vote – or alternative activities.' (M3LY)

Resources and the physical teaching space

For students and tutors alike, provision by the college of an adequate teaching and learning space, appropriately equipped, is an important influence on learning quality, although this aspect is regarded as more important by tutors (49):

'Provision of adequate space, heating and equipment; clean practice area.' (F4GN)

'Good venue; good support from management; reliable, well-maintained computer equipment.' (F4DN)

'The surroundings, the environment, warmth, and lack of noise or interruption.' (F5GN:INT)

Tutors can do much to improve the learning environment, even where the allocated space is outside their control. The learning space may be minimal, rather than ideal and purpose-built and, without undue additional work, tutors often can adapt the layout of a room, placing furniture in such a way that facilitates better eye contact between all involved, and when students realize the advantages of this improved interaction they often will assist in room preparation before a class meeting. Adult education courses, because of the extent to which they are held in shared premises, often will not have use of a room in which they can leave materials set out on tables or noticeboards, and the preparation of the room for an adult education course may involve, as well as the moving of furniture, significant time spent on retrieving items from store cupboards and setting out displays in order to make the most effective use of the class time.

The influence of examining and accrediting bodies

A final group of references by tutors to factors beyond their control that affect learning quality (Table 8.2) is to the strong influence exerted by examining bodies and the curriculum they impose on accredited courses (37). Tutors of such courses must follow the published syllabus within a tight time schedule, but in making reference to these aspects some tutors confuse quality and standards:

'A wide-ranging syllabus devised by City and Guilds ...' (F5EY)

'... examining boards maintain standards.' (F3PY)

For those courses that follow an examination syllabus the influence and constraints of the examination board are, of course, strong and leave little room for manoeuvre, requiring both tutor and students to work at a pace that will enable the necessary work to be covered in the time available. This leaves little opportunity for students to take a lead in parts of the course, which might be possible in other non-accredited courses, and results in a more tightly controlled, rigorous learning environment to be set by the tutor. This is not to imply any criticism of such a regime for, as the tutor referred to above suggests, it is the fact that her course leads to a public examination that makes it one of quality.

Adult education courses generally will operate so that the necessary work to be undertaken in preparation for a GCSE or A level examination will take place over about 30 weeks. This gives approximately 75 hours tuition time, together with the work students undertake outside class meetings. This is considerably less than younger students at school have to prepare for the same examination and means that the tightly controlled timetable referred to above is essential if the whole syllabus is to be covered in time.

When data in Table 8.2 are viewed from gender and age perspectives, the result is a more evenly spread set of figures between the response groups. Almost the same number of female tutors cite professional support, students' effort and the learning environment as the three most relevant factors affecting quality that are outside their control. Male tutors show a similar pattern, although their numbers are fewer. Both men and women tutors place issues to do with accreditation and examinations as less important in this context, and such courses represent only a quarter of courses in this survey.

Responsibility for quality

Tutors, in common with students in this survey, were asked, 'Who is responsible for ensuring and maintaining the quality of your course?' and Table 8.3 shows a summary of their responses.

For data from Table 8.3, cross-tabulated by curriculum group, see Appendix 5, Table A5.9.

Table 8.3 shows that the majority of tutors consider they have primary responsibility for quality, but also acknowledge that students have some responsibility for the quality of their own learning. Responsibility for ensuring and maintaining the quality of their course is believed by tutors to rest principally with them (119) or in a partnership of the tutor and the college (64). In common with students, tutors consider that overall responsibility lies generally within the college (241 – Groups A–E)

Table 8.3: Tutors' responses to the question 'Who is responsible for ensuring and maintaining the quality of your course?'

n = 247 (187 women, 60 men)	WOMEN			MEN			TOTALS
RESPONSE GROUPS	Under 50	50 and over	Totals	Under 50	50 and over	Totals	
A: Tutor or lecturer	38 (38%)	51 (59%)	89 (48%)	11 (55%)	19 (48%)	30 (50%)	119 (48%)
B: The tutor and the college* (i.e. excluding students)	36 (36%)	16 (18%)	52 (28%)	4 (20%)	8 (20%)	12 (20%)	64 (26%)
C: The college* only	12 (12%)	5 (6%)	17 (9%)	4 (20%)	9 (22%)	13 (22%)	30 (12%)
D: Tutor, students and college*	8 (8%)	7 (8%)	15 (8%)	1 (5%)	3 (8%)	4 (7%)	19 (8%)
E: Tutor and students	3 (3%)	5 (6%)	8 (4%)	0	1 (2%)	1 (2%)	9 (4%)
F: Tutor, college* and external agency** (i.e. excluding students)	3 (3%)	3 (3%)	6 (3%)	0	0	0	6 (2%)
Totals	100	87	187	20	40	60	247

Note: In Table 8.3 the terms 'college' and 'external agency' are used as follows:
* College refers to a person or group within the college – e.g. the principal, head of department, senior tutor, curriculum coordinator or the college governors.
* External refers to an agency external to the college – e.g. the LEA, an agency, examining board or a professional or funding body.

although six comments include reference to the influence of external agencies. The comments of four tutors are of particular interest beyond the groups shown in Table 8.3, who state that their students have no responsibility for the quality of their learning. For two, the reason given was the severe disability of their students, who could not be expected to take such responsibility. These tutors seem to have in mind some norm-referenced notion of quality which, because of disabilities, they consider their students would not understand. I would wish to explore further with these tutors what aspects of their students' learning experience they regard as determining quality. The criteria would, possibly, be different in many ways from those of able-bodied students, but they may not be (Riddell, Baron and Wilson 2001). There seems to be here further confusion between quality and standards. For another tutor, the reason his students have no responsibility is because the course in question is only a short introductory one and so the matter is not relevant. This point reflects the views of a small number of students reported in Chapter 7. A fourth tutor confused a question about students' learning with a comment on his teaching, stating:

'The quality of teaching is my responsibility.' (F4GN)

In Chapter 9, I discuss the issue of tutors focusing on *their* teaching, rather than their *students'* learning. Here a few observations by tutors raise again the question of whether there is a view that basic level, introductory or beginners' courses operate at a lower level of quality than other courses at a higher level. I do not believe that such a view is widely held but it does reflect the view of successive governments, who give such emphasis to qualifications and accredited courses, thereby implying that courses leading to a qualification are of a higher quality and more valid.

Only one issue of gender response difference is evident from Table 8.3. Group E, which suggests that tutors and students are jointly responsible for quality, shows a much higher than usual ratio difference of 8 women to 1 man, but the numbers are too small to warrant much attention. The figures, small as they are, do show, however, that proportionately, women tutors are more willing to concede that quality is a matter of partnership between tutors and students.

Data in Table 8.3, when considered by gender, show that the degrees of difference in the views between men and women, under or over 50 years of age, increase between response groups A–C. This shows that there is a greater degree of agreement, for example, between the two age groups over tutors having prime responsibility for quality, than over the question of responsibility residing outside the classroom. This echoes the views of students, as shown in Chapter 7.

Students' contribution to quality

As stated above, nearly all tutors believe that students have some responsibility for the quality of their own learning (238) and suggest that they do so in four separate ways (see Table 8.4).

For data from Table 8.4, cross-tabulated by curriculum groups, see Appendix 5, Table A5.10.

The views of tutors on how students contribute to quality are more evenly spread than in responses to other questions. Table 8.4 shows that, certainly in the case of response groups A and B, the differences between these two groups, and between the two age groups, are not particularly

Table 8.4: Tutors' responses to the question 'How can, and do, students contribute to the quality of their learning experience?'

n = 238 (180 women, 58 men)	WOMEN			MEN			TOTALS
RESPONSE GROUPS	Under 50	50 and over	Totals	Under 50	50 and over	Totals	
Group A: 'Active' participation	29 (32%)	41 (47%)	70 (39%)	11 (52%)	17 (46%)	28 (48%)	98 (41%)
Group B: Completing 'homework' and bringing materials	37 (40%)	20 (23%)	57 (32%)	6 (29%)	13 (35%)	19 (33%)	76 (32%)
Group C: Attendance and punctuality	19 (21%)	14 (16%)	33 (18%)	1 (5%)	2 (5%)	3 (5%)	36 (15%)
Group D: 'Passive' participation	7 (8%)	13 (15%)	20 (11%)	3 (14%)	5 (14%)	8 (14%)	28 (12%)
Totals	92	88	180	21	37	58	238

marked. Attendance and punctuality and passive participation, although accounting, respectively, for the views of 36 and 28 tutors, are seen as lesser contributions. What is more striking is that 76 tutors indicate that the contribution students make towards the quality of learning is to complete their homework.

The most common and effective way in which students contribute to learning quality is by being active participatory learners (98). Tutors describe such students as being fully involved in and out of the classroom in most aspects of the course. These students question, discuss, make suggestions, challenge, complete homework activities, support and encourage other students and sometimes take responsibility for the delivery of parts of some lessons:

'By regular attendance; by their own efforts in class (i.e. listening, paying attention to instructions, checking their work, correcting marked faults, by asking questions.' (F4CY)

'By tackling as many sides of the subject as they can, they can set their projects at a very high level if they like and I encourage them to do this.' (M5FN:INT)

'Conduct participation; homework; asking questions; feedback; completing evaluation forms; exercising choice – by class vote – or alternative activities.' (M3LY)

This group is contrasted by passive learners, described as those who attend and show an interest in their course, but who are much less proactive and less involved (28). These students show no willingness to take a lead in classes and they seldom question or challenge the tutor; they are much less likely to be overtly supportive to other students and tend to sit and be respectfully quiet. There is no suggestion, however, that these students are learning less than their more active counterparts, despite appearances. The difficulty would be in measuring and comparing the extent of learning in the two groups.

For about a third of tutors (76), the completion of homework is the most important student contribution to course quality. Thus includes both the completion of set tasks, but also can involve voluntary activities such as researching the subject and obtaining useful material to bring to subsequent course meetings. In the case of accredited courses, the homework element is a vital part of ensuring that syllabus content is covered within a limited time before examination dates, and students recognize this necessity (see Chapter 7).

Students who arrive regularly and punctually are, for some tutors, the only expectation that they have of learners' contribution to quality (36). These tutors consider that it is their own role to prepare for and deliver each class meeting, and students are required just to be there, and to carry out whatever activities and tasks are assigned. Table 8.4 shows that, although tutors generally concede that students have a part to play towards the attainment and maintenance of learning quality, over half of them (140 – groups B, C and D) consider that to attend the course, undertake class activities and complete homework is the extent of students' contribution. The indication is that most of these staff consider that no further action or involvement is required of students and that it is the tutor's job to take most of the responsibility for learning quality and progress.

When considering the requirements of the Common Inspection Framework (CIF) the views indicated above suggest that some students and tutors will require careful preparation prior to inspection if high grades are to be achieved. The CIF requires students to be clear about their individual learning needs, and aware of, and fully involved in, the ways in which their tutor plans to meet those needs. From the views expressed in this survey, it seems to me that approximately two thirds of students and tutors in my sample would be found wanting by the Adult Learning Inspectors, and this point is developed in Chapters 9 and 10, together with a discussion of whether the stated requirements of the CIF seem to meet the needs of adult-education participants.

Table 8.5: Tutors' responses to the question 'What does quality mean to you in your teaching?'

n = 242 (183 women, 59 men)	WOMEN			MEN			TOTALS
RESPONSE GROUPS	Under 50	50 and over	Totals	Under 50	50 and over	Totals	
Group A: My performance as tutor; my knowledge, skills, preparation and assessment, with clear objectives	70 (71%)	61 (73%)	131 (72%)	11 (58%)	26 (65%)	37 (63%)	168 (69%)
Group B: Students – high standards, attendance, learning progress, results, enjoyment	27 (27%)	23 (27%)	50 (27%)	7 (37%)	14 (35%)	21 (36%)	71 (29%)
Group C: Facilities and equipment	2 (2%)	0	2 (1%)	1 (5%)	0	1 (2%)	3 (1%)
Totals	99	84	183	19	40	59	242

The meaning of quality to tutors in their teaching

In a change of focus on questioning from learning to teaching, tutors were asked about the meaning for them of quality in their teaching, and responses refer to both teaching and learning (see Table 8.5).

For data from Table 8.5, cross-tabulated by curriculum group, see Appendix 5, Table A5.11.

Tutors' views of quality in their teaching

For tutors, quality in their teaching means three things (Table 8.5): their general performance, including their knowledge, skills, preparation and assessment of students' work (168); it means good attendance, good progress and high standards of learning by students, with good results and enjoyment (71); and it means facilities and equipment (3). Meticulous preparation, based on knowledge of students' needs, is regarded as a prerequisite by tutors of a successful course:

'Quality is ensuring my teaching meets the needs of each individual student and making the learning experience both pleasant and productive.' (F4BN:INT)

'My qualified, motivated, experienced teaching; willingness to alter teaching methods and materials.' (M5PN)

'Quality is meticulous preparation, making sure my material is relevant, and shaping teaching methods to the needs of students.' (F5LY:INT)

'Choice of course materials; well-planned scheme of work and lesson plans to ensure all relevant topics are covered; regular marking and feedback.' (F4CY)

This need for detailed preparation is noted by Daines *et al.*:

> It is evident to any teacher of adults that actual face-to-face work is only part of the business of teaching. Planning and preparation are as necessary prerequisites for a teaching/learning event as are assessment and evaluation after it.   (Daines *et al.* 1993: 17)

Most tutors acknowledge that they must prepare adequately for each lesson and, in order to provide for each individual student's learning needs they must remain flexible and adapt their teaching appropriately (see below). The meticulous nature of this preparation is acknowledged by students (see Chapter 7) and takes a variety of forms. The majority of tutors in this survey (186) teach non-accredited courses (see Appendix 4) and so, unlike most of their colleagues who teach accredited courses and for whom a syllabus may be specified, they write their own syllabi, prepare their own schemes of work and lesson plans, adapting these as required. The extent and nature of the work required varies according to the subject they are involved with. It was seen in Chapter 7 that the amount of work students undertake outside the classroom also varies according to the nature of their course. Most undertake some form of homework, but for some courses the majority of activity takes place during lessons, with students practising the activity as their homework. Students' attendance, their effort as learners, their progress and achievements are, according to 71 tutor references (Group B), an important contribution to what they regard as the quality of their teaching (Table 8.5). The balance tutors suggest between their performance and the performance of their students account together for most of what they regard as quality in their teaching. Only 3 (Group C) references are to facilities and equipment; yet at other times tutors regard the circumstances in which they teach – physical space, equipment and materials – as influences on course quality.

Further evidence emerging from Table 8.5 is of note. The low priority shown in Group C, for facilities and equipment, does not accord with the higher emphasis placed on these same factors in Table 8.2. One may speculate that tutors, having given further thought to this, concluded that their performance was the strongest influence on quality, not least because it is within their control. When considered by curriculum, tutors of

General Interest (15 per cent), Languages (11 per cent), Dance, Movement and Yoga (9 per cent), Computing and Mathematics (7 per cent), and Visual Arts (6 per cent) courses show the highest numbers in response Group A (see Appendix 5, Table A5.8).

How tutors ensure quality for all their students

Tutors make frequent references to the learning needs of individual students, in accordance with the requirements of the Learning and Skills Council which places the learner's needs at the heart of all teaching (see Chapters 2 and 9). Tutors in this survey were asked how they ensure quality learning for all their students and Table 8.6 shows how their responses fell into the three categories of preparation, knowing their students' needs and assessment.

For data from Table 8.6, cross-tabulated by curriculum group, see Appendix 5, Table A5.12.

Responding tutors acknowledge that they must consider the needs of each member of their course group, and believe that they address those needs by the rigour of their preparation to deliver the course (170). Frequent references were made to the needs of individual learners, and tutors showed that, generally, they see their work as focusing on individuals rather than groups. Tutors note the importance of keeping up-to-date with their subject, but there is little evidence as to how they do this, other than those who speak of attending up-dating courses offered by their subject-based professional organizations. One third of tutors, when referring to the support they receive from their college, identify the importance

Table 8.6: Tutors' responses to the question 'How do you, as a tutor, ensure a quality learning experience for all your students?'

n = 247 (184 women, 63 men)	WOMEN			MEN			TOTALS
RESPONSE GROUPS	Under 50	50 and over	Totals	Under 50	50 and over	Totals	
Group A: Preparation, keeping up-to-date, pedagogy	61 (62%)	61 (71%)	122 (66%)	17 (74%)	31 (78)%	48 (76%)	170 (69%)
Group B: Knowing students' needs, individually focused teaching	25 (26%)	18 (21%)	43 (23%)	2 (9%)	9 (23%)	11 (17%)	54 (22%)
Group C: Regular assessment	12 (12%)	7 (8%)	19 (10%)	4 (17%)	0	4 (6%)	23 (9%)
Totals	98	86	184	23	40	63	247

of professional training, and imply that it offers opportunity to update their skills as teachers, rather than increase their subject knowledge.

Despite acknowledgement by tutors that the needs of individual learners are important, there is still an emphasis by so many tutors on their teaching, rather than on their students' learning. The importance of planning to meet the individual needs of each student was recognized by 54 tutor references. This planning, and one-to-one teaching in the classroom, ensured that each learner was catered for, although the practicalities of much individual teaching are not clear from this data. One can speculate that on most courses it must be very limited because of the number of enrolled students on each course and the need to encompass them all during each lesson by balancing individual with whole-group teaching.

Assessment plays a part in ensuring a quality learning experience for students, but only 23 references were made to it. It is also statistically less important for male tutors. Generally, tutors make much reference to assessment, but it features as a lower ranking than preparation for teaching, and knowing their students' needs, although I think that a part of ascertaining their students' needs must include some assessment of previous learning, work they have completed and what they know in order to determine future activity. This may be a case of some tutors, as well as some students, regarding the term 'assessment' to mean only a formal examination of some kind.

Table 8.6 shows that in responses to this question there is much similarity between the two age groups of both women and men. What is more marked, as indicated above, is the 69 per cent of references to course preparation and the importance of keeping up to date with one's subject knowledge, as distinct from the 22 per cent who stress the need to know one's students. In curriculum terms, this is most marked amongst tutors of General Interest courses (13 per cent), Languages (13 per cent) and Dance and Movement (10 per cent) (see Appendix 5, Table A5.12).

When endeavouring to meet the learning needs of each student and the group as a whole, tutors speak of adapting their work in the light of recognized need, as shown in Table 8.7.

For data from Table 8.7, cross-tabulated by curriculum group, see Appendix 5, Table A5.13.

The most striking point about Table 8.7 is the emphasis given by tutors to group, rather than on individual, teaching. This does not accord with the requirements of current education policy that focus should be on the progress and achievement of each individual learner. One might, perhaps, expect a group approach to teaching more readily to be adopted by tutors of dance and movement courses, and they are certainly amongst the five

Table 8.7: Tutors' responses to the question 'How do you adapt your teaching to ensure that your students' needs for a quality learning experience are met?'

n = 233 (179 women, 54 men)	WOMEN			MEN			TOTALS
RESPONSE GROUPS	Under 50	50 and over	Totals	Under 50	50 and over	Totals	
Group A: Reassess and listen, alter pace, change content, replan, ensure flexibility	83 (87%)	71 (85%)	154 (86%)	14 (78%)	30 (83%)	44 (81%)	198 (85%)
Group B: Cater for individual needs	12 (13%)	13 (15%)	25 (14%)	4 (22%)	6 (17%)	10 (19%)	35 (15%)
Totals	95	84	179	18	36	54	233

highest instances of this, but what is more striking is that reference to group teaching is most highly found amongst those responsible for courses in general interest (17 per cent) and languages (16 per cent). This point is considered further in Chapter 10, and Appendix 5, Table A5.13, gives relevant figures for all curriculum groups.

Tutors adapt their course work, their teaching methods and the pace of their delivery as a result of assessments, and in order to meet the learning needs of individual students or the various class groups they teach:

> 'I structure the evening so there is time to help students individually or in small groups.' (M4PY:INT)

> 'I aim to tailor my methods of teaching and delivery to suit all the various classes I teach; favouring student-centred learning as I do, make frequent alterations to my material .... .' (M3KN)

> 'I continue to be a reflective practitioner; finding new ways to present material and aid learning .... .' (F4PY)

Some teachers speak of restructuring their course material regularly and one can speculate that this would be limited, especially in the case of accredited courses, but also on other courses, when a balance needs to be maintained between working to a clear course structure in which all can have confidence, and yet ensuring that as the course progresses effective assessment of each individual's progress can be met by an active response to address any perceived changing needs. Tutors speak of 'remaining flexible' and take some pride in the ability to do so and thereby to respond to all eventualities.

It would be reasonable to surmise that as students develop their learning activities and become more involved – moving from being passive to becoming more active learners – the effects on the learning group and on tutors must be evident. Tutors were asked what these effects were on them, in the form of challenges or benefits.

The benefits and challenges of active, participatory students

The active and passive nature of students' involvement in their learning has been referred to above and in Chapter 7, and in considering the effects of more proactive and demanding students, tutors were asked about any perceived benefits and challenges to them (see Table 8.8).

For data from Table 8.8, cross-tabulated by curriculum group, see Appendix 5, Table A5.14.

Generally, tutors welcomed the development of adult learners along the continuum from passive to active, but a high proportion (80) acknowledged that it creates additional work for them and their students become more demanding. For some staff the results are challenging but not, it seems, unwelcome:

'They voice their opinions about the course content delivery, which sometimes requires my teaching methods to change.' (F4LN:INT)

Table 8.8: Tutors' responses to the question 'What benefits or challenges for you, as tutor, are evident when students become more involved in the quality of their own learning?'

n = 236 (182 women, 54 men)	WOMEN			MEN			TOTALS
RESPONSE GROUPS	Under 50	50 and over	Totals	Under 50	50 and over	Totals	
Group A: Makes my job and course more motivating, interesting and stimulating	36 (36%)	32 (39%)	68 (37%)	10 (59%)	19 (51%)	29 (54%)	97 (41%)
Group B: More work for me, challenges me	34 (34%)	31 (37%)	65 (36%)	3 (18%)	12 (32%)	15 (28%)	80 (34%)
Group C: More student progress, more confidence	29 (29%)	20 (24%)	49 (27%)	4 (24%)	6 (16%)	10 (19%)	59 (25%)
Totals	99	83	182	17	37	54	236

'I have to respond to changing ideas and demands for further opportunities within and outside education.' (M4AN:INT)

'Students may become more demanding and have higher expectations.' (M4PY:INT)

Amongst female tutors, almost equal numbers of those both under and over 50 state that active learners create more work for them, but that it is at the same time stimulating. Amongst the male tutors there are some differences between the two age groups, with a higher percentage of those aged over 50 opting for the same two responses as the females. The largest group of tutors (12 women and 6 men) who find active learners to be more stimulating, teach general interest courses, with language tutors showing a similar response (11 women and 5 men). Full details of all curriculum groups can be found in Appendix 5, Table 5.14.

Other tutors are clearer about how they welcome the benefits from more proactive students (97) which bring new dimensions to their teaching:

'Very demanding on tutors but I'm pleased that students take their own responsibility for learning outcomes.' (F5CY)

'When students are taking some responsibility for their own learning, quality is continually being assessed, both by students and myself.' (F4PN:INT)

'Together we explore new avenues – we learn together.' (F5AN)

A third group of references were to do with the fact that tutors considered their students to benefit from a move towards more active participation (59). This came in the form of more progress in learning, and more confidence as learners. This, in turn, makes them more active and challenging. On balance, tutors welcomed a move by students to become more active, even though it brought them more work, more challenges and required more effort on their part. The stimulation and motivation it brought tutors more than made up for the additional demands on them.

Key findings from tutor data

A majority of tutors believe they are the prime cause of quality in their courses, but suggest that other causes include the content of their courses and learning outcomes. Contributions to quality that are not in their control are seen as the professional and administrative support they receive from their colleges, students' effort through attendance and homework, the physical teaching and learning environment (including equipment and facilities) and the requirements of examining bodies.

The majority of tutors believe that their students have some responsibility for the quality of their own learning, but most consider that this primarily rests with them. Students make a contribution to course quality by the extent to which they involve themselves in the course, by attending regularly and by undertaking some form of work outside the course meetings.

Quality for tutors means firstly their own performance, and secondly their students' achievements. They profess to spend much time preparing for their classes and planning to meet the needs of individual students and to facilitate their maximum benefit from the learning. They adapt their teaching and course material to meet the needs of all students, reassessing frequently to maintain this level of attention to individuals' needs

Tutors echo the views of students in identifying active and passive learners (although they do not use these terms), and they welcome the challenges active learners present them, resulting in more progressive learning, better results and additional learning for the tutor in partnership with his/her students. They enjoy, and feel they benefit from, the active learner who is more demanding of them and whose additional needs require more work in preparation and assessment.

Comparisons of responses by curriculum group, age or gender, as in the case of students, show no significant differences to responses in each category.

This chapter has summarized responses from tutors to a range of questions about quality in their teaching and in their students' learning. Chapter 9, which follows, compares and contrasts the findings from Chapter 7 and this chapter, and identifies areas of agreement and divergence between the views of students and their tutors.

9 Research Findings: Comparisons and Contrasts

Introduction

This chapter compares and contrasts the findings from student and tutor data presented in Chapters 7 and 8. These two preceding chapters provide evidence of what is quality for students and tutors, the extent to which they agree over causes of quality in learning and where they place responsibility for it. Some data, shown in Chapters 7 and 8 and referred to below, have implications for policy and practice at national and local levels, and these are referred to in Chapter 10, in which conclusions from this research are set out.

Quality courses

Almost all students and tutors agree that their courses are of quality (96 per cent of students and 99 per cent of tutors). Most of these respondents gave reasons for their opinion, and those who did not nevertheless stated positively that their courses were of quality. For those students who do not consider their courses to be of quality (57), the reasons given are to do with criticisms either of the course and its accommodation, or of the tutor. Tutors also refer to the need for adequate accommodation and good facilities that can otherwise detract from course quality, although for students this was not such an important issue.

The causes of quality

Over half of students (58 per cent) believe that quality in learning means their tutor. There is strong agreement that tutors' experience, qualifications, knowledge, skills, meticulous preparation of course work, careful and frequent assessment of learning and their general care for their students are the ingredients of quality learning, of which students are very appreciative.

Tutors are equally clear (75 per cent) that it is their performance and attention to the points listed above that makes learning a quality experience for their students. Tutors believe that it is their role to ensure that quality learning takes place and they cite many examples of ways in which they seek to ensure this. The focus, however, is more on their teaching than on their students' learning and this point, which has several implications, is discussed further in Chapter 10.

Table 9.1 summarizes the similarities and differences between students and tutors on reasons why they considered their courses to be of quality.

The figures in Table 9.1 refer to the number of references made to each category shown and it is noticeable that, whereas students gave only one example of what they regarded as quality, many tutors referred to more than one, hence the proportionately larger number of references by tutors.

Table 9.1: Comparison of students' and tutors' responses to the question 'What makes this a course of quality?' (Tutors' responses include factors that they consider are both within and outside their control.)

Student references	Students n = 1,687	% of student responses	Tutors (n = 436)	% of tutor responses	Tutor references
The tutor, teacher, lecturer and general pedagogy	1,037	61%	188	43%	My qualifications, knowledge, experience, constructive criticism, preparation and being up-to-date
Learning outcomes – examinations, knowledge and skills	234	14%	17	4%	Assessment, outcomes and examinations
The adult learning atmosphere – stimulating and supportive	149	9%	4	1%	Students' interaction and social aspects
Course content and materials	128	8%	33	8%	Course content, materials and structure
Meeting personal needs	116	7%			
The physical environment, facilities, group size	23	1%	49	11%	Physical environment, equipment and facilities
			57	13%	Professional support and training opportunities
			51	12%	Students' attendance and effort
			37	8%	Examination boards, accredited course
Totals	1,687	100%	436	100%	

The table shows that there are areas over which both groups have strong agreement (e.g. that tutors are the prime cause of quality) and areas where the causal priority is quite different between the two groups (e.g. over the physical environment). These similarities and differences are strong, even allowing for differences in sample size of the two groups. Students place the tutor well above other causes of quality, to the extent that the figure shown in this category far exceeds the total of all their other causal categories. Reasons cited by both groups as to why the tutor is placed as the primary cause of quality show many similarities between the groups and include, as indicated earlier, tutors' skills and experience, preparation and their attempts to provide support and encouragement for their students.

Learning outcomes (e.g. examinations, knowledge, skills) as reasons for quality feature in responses from both groups, and whilst students rank these in second place, for tutors this aspect of learning is placed in a lower position, after course content, materials and structure. This emphasizes a point discussed below, and in Chapter 10, about the pre-eminence tutors give to teaching, rather than to learning; stressing *their* performance over that of their students, as learners. A further aspect of differences in criteria for quality is that of the learning atmosphere and student interaction. For 9 per cent of students in this aspect of the survey, the human learning environment, which they find stimulating and supportive, is an important aspect of their learning, but tutors make almost no reference to this, although they do refer, *en passant*, to student interaction. Similarly, students consider their courses to be of quality because they meet personal needs, however they are described. Whilst this dimension of learning received mention from tutors as something they try to do, it did not feature in their responses as an achievement that they could claim was a cause of quality.

In Table 9.1, the final four categories referred to by tutors are quite striking. For a quarter of them, the physical learning environment (to which only 1 per cent of students made reference) is an important dimension of teaching and learning (11 per cent), as are the professional support and opportunities they received from their colleges (13 per cent), attendance and the effort put in by students (12 per cent), and the influences of examination boards (8 per cent). One might reasonably argue that students need not be aware of matters of professional support for tutors, nor perhaps of the details of how examination boards have a strong influence on providers and courses – especially those students attending non-accredited courses. But one would have thought that the physical environment in which the course takes place, and the way in which it is equipped, affects everyone in the learning group. As indicated in Chapter 10, adult learners are very tolerant of the conditions in which they learn, provided they can join the course they want and receive what they regard as good teaching. When asked about how they contribute to the quality of their own learning, students suggested a number of ways, including attendance and the effort they make as learners. These contributions did not seem to come immediately to mind when the same individuals were asked earlier about what made their course one of quality, but their later explanations were clear. Nearly all students acknowledge that they have some contribution to make towards the quality and success of their course. The differences lie in the nature and extent of those contributions (see below).

Responsibility for quality

Students and tutors agree that the tutor has principal responsibility for ensuring and maintaining the quality of their course, and tables in Chapters 7 and 8 show the range of groups into which they, severally, suggested responsibility was divided. A comparison of the largest of these groupings, however, shows that there are areas of disagreement between learners and teachers over the role they play in that regard. Table 9.2 shows the principal groupings into which respondents placed responsibility for quality.

Table 9.2: Comparison of students' and tutors' responses to the question 'Who is responsible for ensuring and maintaining the quality of your course?' The categories included are only those referring only to students, tutors and the college (see Tables 7.4 – groups R, S, T, U, X and Y; and Table 8.3 – groups A, B, C, D and E).

Response group	Students n = 1,501 (1,149 women, 352 men)	% of student response	Tutors n = 241 (181 women, 60 men)	% of tutor response
The tutor, teacher, lecturer or instructor	980	65%	119	49%
Tutor and students	248	17%	9	4%
Tutor and college	115	8%	64	27%
The college only	109	7%	30	12%
Tutor, students and college	34	2%	19	8%
The students only	15	1%	0	
Totals	1,501	100%	241	100%

Table 9.2 shows how the same groupings were used by both students and tutors, although the weighting given to each group by them differs. Both groups concur that the tutor carries the main responsibility. Where the two groups differ is over the extent to which responsibility is shared, such as with other college staff. For students, their role in partnership with their tutors is given a greater weighting than it is in the view of tutors, who believe that other college staff play a bigger part in securing quality, either with or without them. For neither group, students nor tutors, does a three-way partnership between themselves and other college staff rate very highly at all. Tutors (27 per cent) consider that they, in partnership with other college staff, are responsible for quality to a greater degree than is believed by students. Some members from each group (7 per cent of students and 12 per cent of tutors) believe that other college staff are responsible for quality, but this contrasts strongly with the view of most tutors.

Ways in which students contribute to the quality of their own learning
Both parties agree that students have a part to play in contributing towards a quality learning experience, and both acknowledge that issues such as attendance and the completion of homework are important factors, although the weighting given to these aspects differs noticeably between the two groups. Table 9.3 shows a comparative summary of main categories supplied by both groups.

Table 9.3: Comparison of students' and tutors' views on how students contribute to a quality learning experience (see Tables 7.6 and 8.4.)

Response group	Students n = 1,606 (1,229 women, 377 men)	% of student responses	Tutors n = 238 (180 women, 58 men)	% of tutor responses
Participative, active learners	1,008	63%	98	41%
The completion of homework	152	9%	76	32%
Attendance and punctuality	150	9%	36	15%
Passive participation	137	9%	28	12%
Social interaction	85	5%	0	
A 'detached' attitude	74	5%	0	
Totals	1,606	100%	238	100%

Table 9.3 shows that the same four categories were selected by both students and tutors to describe students' contributions to quality, although students also identified another smaller category – social interaction (5 per cent) and 74 of them (5 per cent) showed a 'detached' attitude, which was discussed in Chapter 7. Table 9.3 also reveals that students and tutors consider adult learners fall into two distinct groups – 'active' and 'passive'. These (my own) terms are relative, because all learners are active to some degree, but the distinction in these data is quite marked, as explained in Chapters 7 and 8, and has implications in a number of ways for learners, tutors, providers and policy-makers (see Chapter 10). Chapters 7 and 8 explored the meanings of 'active' and 'passive' in this context and I shall not repeat them here, but I return to these distinctions later in this chapter when discussing the ways in which students draw upon the lessons of their different learning experiences.

Further similarities between tutors and students, the two groups shown in Table 9.3, are the references to attendance and punctuality, and the completion of some form of homework. These two aspects of students' involvement are seen by both groups as important, but tutors consider both aspects as more significant in terms of learner contribution to quality than do students. As explained in Chapter 8, some tutors regard the successful carrying out of either or both functions (attendance and homework) as sufficient contribution to expect from students. They see the rest of the course as a matter for the tutor. This point is returned to in Chapter 10 as it has implications for the requirements of the Common Inspection Framework. Students and tutors refer variously to the importance of punctual attendance at all course meetings. Their explanations include the necessity for students to complete their course and not to miss lessons, and refer to courtesy shown to other group members and the tutor by not arriving late or otherwise causing disruption to the class. Similarly, the completion of homework in some form is regarded as very significant by both groups. For tutors, it is the basic essential minimum of student participation, and for students it is seen as a normal routine part of their learning, and one way of contributing to the progress and success of their course. As explained in Chapter 7, 'homework' is a general term used to describe any out-of-class activity related to the course.

Social interaction and the support of fellow students, important for some learners (5 per cent), is not regarded by tutors as a significant factor in adult learning. Students' references indicate that to work with motivated or experienced fellow learners is a contributing factor to the quality of their learning. The mutual sharing and support they enjoy is beneficial and in some cases creates the foundation for lasting friendships. Considering how strongly this aspect is shown in the responses of the 5 per cent of students one might have expected more students to have referred to it, and tutors to have included it in their remarks, even with a lower ranking. This point is taken up again in Chapter 10.

The relevance and value of previous learning

Three quarters of students see a direct relevance for their previous learning and consider that it has a positive use in their current learning; but a quarter regard previous learning as having no connection and as being of no particular use in relation to what they are currently studying. Of those who acknowledge a value and relevance for previous learning, many speak of specific skills they have acquired – such as study skills, judgement, what to look for in a good tutor, how to work within a learning group – and regard each learning episode as part of a valuable cumulative process. The numbers of students who recognize the value of their previous learning relate to some extent to the group of active learners referred to previously. Approximately three quarters of the student sample acknowledge the positive ways in which previous learning can bring benefits of some kind, and two thirds go on to describe ways in which they use those experiences to participate actively in their learning and take some responsibility for its quality.

There seem to be emerging issues of confidence and responsibility in the minds of many learners. Despite the extent to which the lessons of previous learning are acknowledged, many of these individuals nevertheless show their role to be more passive when describing their activity and approach to learning. Also, whilst 56 per cent of all students responding recognize the value of previous learning (Table 7.8), and 63 per cent cite active participatory learning as the way in which they contribute to course quality (Table 7.6), 79 per cent accept that they have some degree of responsibility for the quality of their learning (Table 7.4 – response groups R, S, X and Y). These anomalies can probably be explained both by issues of confidence and by perceptions of the comparative roles played by students and tutors in the learning process. I conjecture that, for some, because of a lack of confidence as learners, the undoubted lessons of previous learning cannot be translated into active participation in the classroom. For others, a long-held perception of the relative roles and responsibilities of learners and teachers (i.e. memories from school days) discourages them from drawing more actively upon their previous successes as learners. This point is taken up again in Chapter 10.

Comparisons of responses by age, gender and curriculum groups have shown that generally, with a few exceptions which were cited, these factors do not have a strong influence on participants' responses.

This chapter has summarized the similarities and differences between students and tutors over a number of matters concerning quality in teaching and learning. Differences are quite marked in some cases, reflecting strong individual views but the differences of age, gender or curriculum do not reveal any strong influences. Three aspects do show up strongly, however, from the data: students' enjoyment and the value they place on their learning; the degree of appreciation that students have for their tutors' efforts; and the view shared by both groups that the principal cause and responsibility for quality rests with tutors.

The final chapter in this thesis, Chapter 10, draws conclusions from the research data, and especially from the summaries in Chapters 7, 8 and 9, and refers back to earlier parts of the thesis and to the published literature. It indicates ways in which the research findings can be applied to professional practice, and shows how some findings have implications for future policy in lifelong learning at local and national levels.

10 Conclusions, Implications and Future research

Introduction

Earlier chapters have described my research methodology and research findings, and how adult education is contextualized within the government's current policy of lifelong learning. This chapter draws conclusions from these findings, explains their implications for policy and practice at local and national levels and suggests future research that could develop the work of this study.

Research seldom provides final solutions; at most it can claim to throw light on problems to a limited degree and at a certain time. This research has been in a relatively neglected area of education, and one that is not well understood by governments. The findings make a contribution to our knowledge of adult learning and my conclusions have implications for adult learners, tutors, providers and policy-makers. I believe that developments proposed in this chapter will, if implemented, be of benefit to those interested and involved in adult education, and those who acknowledge its contribution to the continuing formation of a learning society. Most importantly, they will benefit the individual learner who is at the heart of this research and of current lifelong learning policy.

Conclusions from my research findings

Conclusions from research data are set out in sections headed by the relevant research questions (see Chapter 1), and percentages given are drawn from tables in Chapters 7 and 8 and Appendix 5.

'What is quality in adult learning?'
To reiterate, this study set out to discover what quality in adult learning is, seeking opinions from partners in the interactive learning process – adult learners and their tutors. It also asked who is responsible for learning quality, and whether some students may be competent to be recognized as arbiters of the quality of their own learning. The study has not been on a

national scale, nor can it claim to be all inclusive, but it does claim to provide conclusions from collected data that can reasonably be extrapolated to have implications on a wider scale. 'Quality' has many meanings in learning, as data in Chapters 7 and 8 indicate, and in life generally, as discussed in Chapter 6. It is reasonable to deduce from these research data that quality, so far as it relates to learning, is at its highest when many of the aspects suggested by my research participants are present. That is, when the human interactive process between individuals who enjoy a common interest is most effective; when course content is well planned and delivered by tutors; when course syllabi and schemes of work are clear and well structured; when students know what they want to learn, and what they have learnt; when the individual needs of each member of the learning group are met; when students share with tutors the planning, delivery and assessment of the course as it progresses; and when learning progress and achievement are understood, relevantly assessed and celebrated by all.

Students' perspectives on quality

As stated in Chapter 9, most adult students (96 per cent) believe their courses to be of quality, and believe that they share some responsibility for ensuring and maintaining that quality. A majority (61 per cent) also believe that the single most important factor that assures the quality of courses is their tutor, through her/his knowledge, skills, qualifications, preparation and delivery of the course, and through her/his efforts to keep up to date with subject knowledge and professional development (Tables 7.1 and A5.1). Adult students greatly value their learning and hold their tutors in high esteem, appreciating tutors' efforts on their behalf and the profes- sional approach tutors take towards their work. The language used by some students, however, suggests that the influences of initial schooling are still very strong, and in these cases learners show an almost childlike appreciation for the attention and care they receive from their tutors. I refer below to the emphasis given by many tutors to their *teaching*, rather than to their students' *learning*, and this rather paternal and some-times patronising attitude links with my earlier comments on students, who had referred to their tutor taking full control of all aspect of the course.

As shown previously, learning is put to many different uses. It 'fills gaps', 'provides an interesting hobby', 'enables achievement and satisfac- tion', offers a 'second chance', 'enhances the quality of life' and 'opens up new horizons' – it is 'like scales falling from your eyes'. Few students are unmoved by the effects of their learning. For 88 per cent of students surveyed it brings broad benefits, and for a few (4 per cent) it has an additional specific purpose (Tables 7.7 and A5.4). In some courses, noticeably foreign languages (the largest group in this survey – see Table 7.9), students hold firm views regarding the structure and content of their courses (see Chapter 7, and section below on the curriculum). They express contrasting but strongly held views on, for example, the desirability of being taught by nationals from the countries concerned, or on the grammar/conversational balance of a course syllabus.

Learners speak of gaining high degrees of confidence and awareness and, for the most part, maintain a generally open-minded, receptive approach to their learning. From their enthusiastic comments one gains a sense that these students enjoy a high quality of active learning. The physical learning environment is not regarded by students, however, as a significant factor that affects their learning and this is in contrast to the views of tutors, as indicated below. There are students, also, for whom there seems to be a lack of congruence between the ways in which they value the lessons of their previous learning, and the extent to which they draw upon them in new learning (see below). However articulated, it is evident from data that the periods in their lives during which they attend adult education courses mean a great deal to adult learners.

Tutors' perspectives on quality

Nearly all tutors believe that their courses are of quality and that they are the principal cause (77 per cent). This accords with students' views on the efforts of their tutors. To a lesser extent, tutors consider that quality is brought about either by the course content, materials and structure (14 per cent) or by assessment and outcomes (7 per cent) (Tables 8.1 and A5.7). Four other factors outside their control are cited by just under one fifth of tutors as influences on the quality of their courses: the professional support and training they receive from their colleges (29 per cent); the efforts by students to attend and complete homework (26 per cent); the teaching and learning environment and its equipment (25 per cent); and external agencies through prescribed syllabi and assessment systems (19 per cent) (Tables 8.2 and A5.8).

Tutors show a high degree of caring for their students and believe that they have a duty to undertake meticulous preparation for their classes. They claim to make strenuous efforts to ensure that attention is focused on the individual learning needs of each student. Tutors also gain much satisfaction from their work. They enjoy seeing their students make progress and state that by frequent assessment they endeavour to ensure that this progress is maximized. When students become more confident and more proactive learners, tutors acknowledge that the additional work this may cause is offset by the benefits to them, as well as to their students, of higher levels of achievement and the stimulation of mutual learning (see below). In carrying out their work, nearly one third of tutors rely on professional support from their colleges, and just over one quarter claim that the efforts that students put into their studies are the second most important cause of course quality that is outside their control. Yet the more powerful impression one gains from data is that of the paternal approach by tutors referred to above, and this point is explored further below. The physical environment in which tutors work, and the extent to which it is adequately equipped, has a significant affect on how well they can perform, according to 25 per cent of respondents (Tables 8.2 and A5.8), yet by students this factor is given a much lower priority (1 per cent) (Tables 7.1 and A5.1).

In their teaching, tutors believe quality means their performance in preparation and delivery (69 per cent). This factor is far greater than the second which they cite, that of students' high standards and learning progress (29 per cent) (Tables 8.5 and A5.11). They endeavour to ensure a quality learning experience for their students by keeping up to date with their subject (69 per cent) and by knowing the needs of each individual learner (22 per cent), although formal assessment is considered a lesser factor in ensuring a quality experience (9 per cent) (Tables 8.6 and A5.12). When ensuring quality learning for all their students, tutors do so by reassessing and listening, altering their teaching pace and replanning to ensure flexibility, changing course content (85 per cent), whilst trying to cater specifically for individual needs (15 per cent) (Tables 8.7 and A5.13).

Who is responsible for establishing and maintaining learning quality?
Do students consider themselves responsible for the quality of their own learning?
Do tutors believe that students are responsible for the quality of their learning?

A minority of students (17 per cent) (see Table 7.4) acknowledge that they have some responsibility for the quality of their learning, and a very small number (1 per cent) believe that they alone are responsible. For the majority of students (93 per cent) responsibility for the quality of their learning resides somewhere in their college and, for 60 per cent of them, it rests principally with their tutor (Tables 7.6 and A5.4). John Daines *et al.* (1993) suggest that adult educators try to enable their students to become self-directed learners, increasingly taking responsibility for their own learning, and moving towards the goal of Maslow's self-actualization (see

Chapters 2 and 4). This point, although not easy to quantify, is echoed in the requirements of the CIF (see below), but is not entirely supported by data in this study because of the paternalistic attitude shown by many tutors towards their students, and the passive acceptance of the tutor's role by many students (see below). One may speculate that many students prefer an easy undemanding time as learners, and regard their course as a place where they come to relax from demanding lives, and to enjoy their learning. Others, in contrast, demonstrate a highly active role as learners and take some responsibility for their learning. Research data show the contrasts between approaches to learning by adult students in the language they employ to describe their learning. This language suggests, as pointed out in earlier chapters, that perhaps they see distinctions between learning and leisure, or between active and passive learning. They may distinguish between hard and easy learning experiences, with some being more challenging than others. The responsibility for learning that some acknowledge is contrasted by others who seem to take a more consumer approach to learning, apparently being content to receive whatever is on offer. Whether or not all this matters, if students are apparently gaining what they want from their courses, is discussed below. In addition, some students equate terms such as assessment, accreditation and standards to the tests and examinations they remember from school days and, according to the kind of course they are following, believe them to be irrelevant and unwanted.

Tutors believe that either they are responsible for course quality (48 per cent), or that it is a responsibility they share in some way with other college staff (26 per cent) (see Table 8.3). Unlike some students (14 per cent) (Table 7.4, Group S and Table A5.2), very few tutors see responsibility as being a partnership between them and their students (4 per cent) (Tables 8.3 and A5.9). They show a high degree of confidence in their abilities and although some see adult learning as a partnership with their students, they also believe that it is their responsibility to retain the lead and to set the overall direction of the course (Tables 8.3 and A5.9). They acknowledge that students have a part to play in their learning process and that they share some of the responsibility for ensuring and maintaining the quality of courses, although 56 per cent of tutor references suggest that student contribution is confined to punctual attendance and the completion of homework (Table 8.4, Groups B and C, and Table A5.10). This can be interpreted as students being infantilized by their tutors, who take too much responsibility for students' progress. This paternalistic attitude by tutors is likely to be seen in critical terms by inspectors with reference to the Common Inspection Framework (see

Chapter 2), because tutors would be seen as not doing enough to facilitate their students' learning and students are not being encouraged to develop independence as learners and become self-directed (see Section 1 of the CIF – ALI and Ofsted: 2001).

Tutors may take what I have described as a paternal approach to their students for several reasons. Some students and tutors regard it as the tutor's job to take the lead – he/she is (usually) in a paid position and, of course, has the subject knowledge. For some students, as indicated above, this is what they expect teachers to do, as their school days have shown them. For tutors it is probably easier to take a paternalistic approach, working on the assumption that, from their experience, they know what is best for their students. The main question here is, does all this matter? My own view is, yes, it does, if we wish to assist students to become independent, critically aware learners.

Active and passive learners
Learners can be classified into two broad categories in their approach to learning – 'active' or 'passive' (my terms) and, in varying degrees, these play some part in their own learning progress and its quality. Active learners, who represent about two thirds of those in this sample (Tables 7.6 and A5.3), welcome opportunities to take a lead in some classes, seeing their learning process as a partnership with their tutors. They show themselves to be highly active, participative, critical learners who take responsibility for their actions and their learning, and assist their fellow students as well. This suggests a link with Revans' 'action learning set, who support each other in their learning' (Revans 1983:11), and with Houle's 'activity-oriented learners' (Houle 1961, cited in Jarvis 1995a: 51). The ways in which these active students describe their involvement suggests that they regard this level of participation as normal and beneficial to them, and it contrasts strongly with the ways in which less active learners describe their role. This may also seem to be in contrast to the earlier statement – that the majority of students regard their tutors as having control of the course and being responsible for quality – and it seems that after further reflection this group of students was able to explain more about their active involvement as learners.

The relatively 'passive' group of learners (about one third) suggest they do little more than attend punctually and carry out the course requirements as requested, although they give examples of showing a serious attitude towards the work, sometimes helping their peers and completing homework assignments. This group seems to believe it is not their role to be any more active as learners, because their tutor, who knows best, will lead them in the right direction. It has to be acknowledged that it is not easy to be clear about the extent to which those in this group are learning effectively. One can speculate from their language and less participatory approach that they seem to be gaining much less from learning than their more active peers, but the evidence is not conclusive. One may also speculate whether people as learners are instinctively lazy, and that it is simply easier to allow someone else to take responsibility for all that is happening on a course. Further research on this particular aspect of students' participation might reveal more detailed data about the extent to which apparently 'passive' recipients are learning in comparison with their overtly more active and vocal peers.

Linking these comments to observations on what constitutes learning quality, which were summarized in Chapter 7, it would seem that not all students recognize the extent and importance of the positive contributions they make to their learning process. Data in Chapter 8 also show that this may be said of most tutors in this sample. Yet, when responding to later questions, about two thirds of students were able to identify ways in which they make some contribution to their learning through a variety of means (see Chapter 7). I have suggested earlier that these data may support a speculative observation, that many adult learners remain strongly influenced by their school days in many ways, including what they seem to see as an appropriate relationship with their tutors that reflects Harris' 'Adult/ Child' relationship (Harris 1973). Some students stated that they missed out at school and it may be that they have simply not gained sufficient independence as learners. If this is so, it has implications for both compulsory and non-compulsory education about the way individual learners are encouraged and taught about learning, as distinct from knowledge. Also, if this is so, then one may continue to speculate that, although some students see themselves initially in a relatively subservient role, they later come to realize the important contribution they make to their learning, to the point in some cases of taking at least some responsibility for it. Data in Chapter 7 would support his proposition. The view, shown by some students, that the partnership with their tutors is not an equal one is echoed in the attitude shown by many tutors (as reported in earlier chapters) that it is they who control the course, and that their students need only attend and complete homework where this is appropriate.

Adults tend to underestimate their ability to learn new material by giving too much emphasis to their school experience whilst overlooking the value of their more recent extensive informal learning experiences.

(Lovell 1980: 28)

Some tutors are clear that they enjoy and find stimulating the involvement of more participative learners (41 per cent), even though this may present them with more work and challenges (34 per cent). Some also gain pleasure from the increased confidence and progress they observe in their more participative students (25 per cent) (Tables 8.8 and A5.14).

One further group of students should be mentioned here. These have been referred to in Table 7.6 as showing a 'detached' approach to their learning. These students (5 per cent) are those whose responses to research questions were couched in terms that were in strong contrast to the language used by the majority of their peers. They showed no signs of regarding themselves as part of the learning group (although, of course, they were enrolled members of the course), but rather spoke of 'complaining to authority' if they were not satisfied, or 'requesting a change' if the course was 'not up to standard'. They suggested that if they did not enjoy the experience they would 'change classes or leave altogether'. This group seemed not to recognize the possibility of a learning partnership with their tutors and fellow students – something that even many of the most passive learners seemed to acknowledge – but created an image that they were on the periphery of the group and had no feeling of responsibility for how their course was progressing. In describing this group of learners, there is a danger of sounding judgmental. Each learner is, of course, entitled to take whatever approach to their learning they wish, but it is tempting to speculate that these individuals were gaining less from the learning experience than they might have done because of their detached attitude to the learning group and its activities.

Whatever the motivating factor(s) for enrolling on a course of study, there remains the separate issue of student retention on courses. What may be described as a motivation to stay, as distinct from the motivation to join, is an area that needs further research and one that has become more significant to providers in recent years because of its direct link to funding formulae. This problem is exacerbated in the case of part-time learners for whom less detailed records are maintained. It has only in recent years (and again mostly because of funding) become the practice to raise more systematically with part-time students questions regarding their reasons for joining a course, the uses they have in mind for the learning they will gain from the course and their longer term intentions regarding further study. When researching the reasons why students leave any course (and also to gain, for example, student satisfaction data for marketing or funding purposes), it has been a much more difficult task to track part-time learners, whose whereabouts are likely to be unknown to the provider. The mismatch between the, usually, high level of commitment and participation shown by part-time learners, and data collected about them, remains a fruitful area for future research.

The value and benefits of previous learning

A majority of student responses see a value and relevance for their previous learning. It provides them with broad experiences and benefits (63 per cent), it is progressive and forms a foundation for further learning (26 per cent). For a smaller group (12 per cent) it provides them with practical outcomes and enables them to acquire specific skills, such as study skills, the skills of judgement, how to work within a learning group, how to take criticism, and how to be reflective and critical learners (Jarvis *et al.* 1998). A further 19 per cent stated that their previous learning had no connection to current learning and was of no particular use in relation to what they were currently studying (Tables 7.8 and A5.5).

Students also value the freedom to work at their own pace, and regard each learning episode as part of a valuable cumulative process. Some students (approximately one third of this sample) seem to approach each new learning episode as if it had no relationship with previous learning experiences. They seem not to recognize the full extent of their learning and this may imply that little learning is taking place because they regard such measurements as relating to outcome-testing. This comment is speculative, because that particular question was not asked in this survey, but the language used by about one third of respondents in my sample suggests that these students focus more on the enjoyment of their course (important as that undoubtedly is), rather than the precise learning that is taking place. This accords with Lovell's point cited above. Not all students may wish to become active learners, of course, and it may be that for some the demands would be too taxing and not allow them to enjoy the comfort of a course. I also believe, as indicated earlier, that many students underestimate both their ability to learn and the extent of their learning. These views have implications for local and national policy, and further research into these questions could be fruitful.

This is not to imply a criticism of the students or their tutors, but it does have potential implications, for example, for inspections under the CIF, as indicated in Chapter 2, and a point I take up again below. This is because one criterion of the CIF questions the degree to which students are encouraged to recognize the extent of their learning progress, and to gain the skills to enable them to become independent learners. Tutors in this sample generally show themselves to be caring of their students, but the generally paternalistic attitude they show does not seem to encourage independence in their students, nor does it encourage self-reliance amongst learners. For some students who may not recognize the full extent of their learning, nor perhaps understand the assessment systems being employed by their tutor, careful preparation will be needed to enable them to meet the requirements of the CIF. More particularly, they will need more encouragement to gain a full appreciation of what they are actually learning and its value to them and their future learning goals (see below and my references to the CIF in Chapter 2). A small number of learners (about 9 per cent) show different views from most of their peers towards their involvement as learners. The benefits of participating in a range of ways, cited by the majority of students, seem not to be recognized by this small group. In general, students are reluctant to complain and are particularly reluctant to criticize their tutor. Most do not see themselves, for example, as customers who have paid a fee for a service and who should expect high-quality provision at all times, but rather show themselves grateful for the effort made by tutors on their behalf and seem to regard their learning as a privilege rather than a right and an opportunity for which they have paid.

Curriculum and gender factors

Chapters 7 and 8 have shown that, generally speaking, when considered by curriculum choice, these research data show limited examples of differences, and less than one might have anticipated. Those instances where differences emerged have been explained in Chapter 9, and I shall not repeat them here. Responses analysed by gender show few variations from the 3:1 ratio of women to men that reflects the balance of adult education students. I suggest that further research into this aspect of adult learning is needed to examine whether gender or curriculum do have measurable effects on attitudes to learning. The few examples where age appears to be an influencing factor in responses have been discussed within the text.

The pleasure of learning

A general sense of well-being permeates students' descriptions of their learning and they describe high levels of enjoyment and make several references to a sense of fulfilment. The encouragement and support they receive from their peers and their tutor gives added impetus to learning. Adult learning is enjoyed by many students for its human contact, and a sharing in the mutual pleasure of learning during lessons and outside the classroom often leads to lasting friendships. This accords with Green and Preston's statement (Green and Preston 2000), cited in Chapter 1, that different forms of learning can have a positive effect on people's lives, including the enhancing of self-esteem. The adult learning experience is seen as an enjoyable contribution to the lives of individuals, whatever the nature of their learning and whether or not it leads to an accredited outcome. This is in contrast to the findings of an earlier survey (McGivney 1992) and to the government's policy of placing the attainment of qualifications high on their criteria for public funding. It is further evidence that a qualification is not seen as the only valid outcome of a learning experience, and 'raises the question of whether the gap between the values and priorities of policy-makers and those of learners can be bridged' (McGivney 2002: v).

From the data I have gathered it appears that large numbers of adults (79 per cent) follow learning programmes purely for the process and for the pleasure they gain from learning, and without any apparent consideration of accreditation, qualification or work-related goal (see Appendix 4). As Tom Schuller reminds us, adults learn for many reasons:

> ... the work/pleasure divide did not cover the whole spectrum of students' motives, which were complex. For instance, some people studied neither for qualifications nor for pleasure but to enable them to play a bigger role in their communities. (Schuller, cited in Kingston 2002: 41)

And as Alan Tuckett has pointed out in the same article by Kingston,

> there was a tendency for people to give reasons for learning which matched the prevailing messages they were getting from government and institutions. And in recent years these were all focused on qualifications. (Tuckett, cited in Kingston 2002: 41)

Learning as an adult, whatever the activity, is a confidence-building and life-enhancing experience that is greatly valued by its participants for bringing educational, physical, psychological and social benefits.

Reassessing the value of adult education and its curriculum

As discussed in Chapter 5, one significance of adulthood, however defined, is that adult learners bring with them more extensive experiences of learning and life which will affect their approaches to current learning, although views differ, as we have seen, on the extent to which these experiences are recognized by individual learners. Adults are not grown-up children, and their educational requirements are different. Adult education, therefore 'ceases to be simply any kind of education which contingently happens to be open to adults, and becomes instead something specifically and uniquely related to adulthood in terms of what is taught, how it is taught, and how it is organised' (Lawson 1975: 106). For Tennant, however, the weakness of this argument is the belief that 'the identity of adult education is premised on the identity of the adult', and thus may be seen to offer 'the promise of a distinct and coherent theory of adult learning' (Tennant 1997: 36). As discussion on andragogy in Chapter 5 showed, a fully coherent theory to satisfy this belief is lacking.

It has been suggested that when attempting to define the word 'adult' we find that it is a societal-based term and that each nation will use its own criteria for deciding when a person becomes an adult (see Chapter 5). Similarly, in our present-day world, what constitutes 'education' is determined by each country, and although there is at present a large measure of similarity between many countries, it was not always so. Over the centuries, during, for example, the times of Plato, the Roman Empire or the sixteenth century, different views were held over what constituted the fundamental studies for successful citizenship and the balances between disciplines were different. Music and astronomy, for example, received a much higher place in the hierarchy of disciplines in the time of Plato than they do today. But at all times, the school curriculum was determined as a society-specific series of activities which were morally acceptable and within the laws of that society (Peters 1967).

When we speak of an 'educated person' we generally refer to much more than that which the individual acquired during his/her schooling. We include learning and cultural experiences that were gained outside school or after the initial period of schooling, whether of a formal or experiential nature, and indeed we imply almost by definition that to have become 'educated' the individual must have gained much more than 'just' fundamental school-based learning because the term implies some degree of maturity. What form, then, might that education take? Firstly, and most simply, it might include further and/or higher education, or specialist training, all experienced as an adult. These aspects of our education system are widely recognized as forming a route through which individuals can gain skills and qualifications that carry some 'currency' in terms of future employment, as well as forming part of a general education. It might also include part-time liberal education (perhaps the study of local history or drama, a language or a craft, and it might include self-directed cultural learning (e.g. a study of art or participation in musical activities). All these experiences contribute to the educated person's portfolio of knowledge and, if they are fortunate enough to include significant periods of time travelling to see other nations and cultures, these would be regarded as valuable additions to their 'education'.

What then is 'adult education'? One answer is 'it depends when the question is asked, and of whom'. To offer comments (not actually definitions) on adult education from a period of over 80 years gives some indication of the changing emphases in this sector of education over that period. From the statement in the Ministry of Reconstruction Report (1919: 5) that adult education should be universal and lifelong (quoted in Chapter 2), there followed:

> Adult education is all responsibly organised opportunities to enable men and women to enlarge and interpret their own living experience.
> (Hutchinson 1963: 232–3)

> Adult education is the process by which men and women (alone, in groups or in institutional settings) seek to improve themselves or their society by increasing their skills, knowledge or sensitiveness; or it is any process by which individuals, groups or institutions try to help men and women improve in these ways. (Houle 1972: 32)

> Adult education ... consists of all those forms of education that treat the student participants as adults – capable, experienced, responsible, mature and balanced people. (Rogers 1986: 17)

> Community, adult and family learning will be essential ... It will help improve skills, encourage economic regeneration and individual prosperity, build active citizenship, and inspire self-help and local development.
> (DfEE 1998: 48)

What is significant in changing terminology over the decades is both the move from using the term 'education' to that of 'learning', but also the reluctance of writers (especially governments) to offer adult education the recognition it received in earlier times. By reaffirming its place in 'further education' (*Further and Higher Education Act*, 1992) or by referring to it as 'adult community learning' (*Learning and Skills Act*, 2000) successive governments have continued to deny it a proper recognition in its own right. This is particularly ironical at a time when current rhetoric, as mentioned previously, is about the value of *all* learning (my emphasis), 'suitable to the requirements' of individual need (DfES 2000: Chapter 21, Part 1, Section 3a). During the period between the 1950s and the 1980s distinctions were clearer than they are today. Higher education stood most easily identified, although the then 'binary divide' maintained a dual provision of universities and polytechnics. Further Education was largely catering for 'vocational' education for 16–19 year olds, with some adults being permitted to join in with younger students on courses still focused on the needs of the younger people, and some 'non-vocational' courses. Alongside higher and further education stood 'adult education' – largely provided by local education authorities, the Workers' Education Association and university extra-mural departments – 'the responsible bodies' – together with national organizations such as the National Federation of Women's Institutes. In some parts of the country there was no separate adult education service and all part-time and full-time adult learning courses, other than higher education and voluntary activities, were provided by the local further education or technical college (Fieldhouse, *et al.* 1996).

> People as learners do not easily differentiate between what is vocational and what is non-vocational. These are terms used by politicians, funders and some providers. The breadth of people's interests is clear and it cuts across such boundaries.   (Sargant 1991: 20)

Adult educators offer strong arguments that what Nell Keddie calls the distinctive nature of adult education should be safeguarded and the focus of the lifelong learning agenda may now mean that all learning will move closer to becoming the seamless robe of learning opportunity that many have long sought. Post-compulsory teaching is now increasingly student-focused, but only in terms of its delivery, providers being required to follow established curricula or to produce trained and educated workers. Adult education enjoys the position of being learner-centred, not just in its delivery but in its planning, its assessment and its whole *raison d'être*. If, as suggested above, the term 'adult education' today is used to refer to any institutionalized learning undertaken by adults, it may be argued by some that this is an improvement; that there are fewer barriers between the different providers, and less confusion in the minds of the general public; and greater progress towards the establishing of a 'seamless robe' of learning. Others might argue, however, that one result has been to diminish even further the status of liberal adult education. Despite the terminology of the 1944 Education Act (HMSO 1944), which refers to 'further education for adults', the culture of liberal part-time adult education continued in most parts of the country to operate alongside further education colleges and in some areas such services have attracted a larger number of students than their local full-time further education college. Although some distinctions between various aspects of post-compulsory education were breaking down as late as the 1980s, the 1992 *Education Act* produced an even more marked separation of types of adult learning, as I have stated previously by, in essence, creating a culture in which work-related ('vocational') adult learning was regarded as being of importance (which, of course, it is) – and thus worthy of funding – whilst liberal ('non-vocational') adult learning was not. This distinction manifested itself in the funding regimes established by the Further Education Funding Council, which under the Act was to fund only those courses regarded as 'vocational', i.e. those leading to an accredited certificated outcome, including Basic Skills and Welsh in Wales (see 'Schedule 2' of the Act).

Adult educators have long argued the distinctive nature of adult education, and Alan Rogers points out that 'any concept of education based on the view that initial education can provide all the learning needed for life, in any of its aspects (individual growth, occupation or social roles), is inadequate' (Rogers 1986: 8). Normal use of the word 'learning' refers to that process of change and adaptation which we all engage in all the time; it is not just a formal, structured provision made available to us by others. Since learning is an ongoing process throughout life it is reasonable to argue that it is the experience of the adult learner which is a significantly identifiable difference that distinguishes him/her from a child learner. And Jones (1990) argues that, however defined, adult *part-time* education certainly deserves equal treatment with full-time provision (my emphasis).

Implications for policy and practice

The research findings described in Chapters 7, 8 and 9 have implications for policy-makers and practitioners at local and national levels. They can be used to inform current practice and to help in raising awareness, standards and quality in adult learning. The findings also suggest improvements which, if embraced within new policy, could further improve and develop the experience and opportunities for adult learners. My findings show that, for many students, adult education is as much a process as an outcome-oriented activity. The process of learning, with its individual-focused approach and its social aspects, is as important – for some individuals, more important – as any accredited outcome that may be available. At a time when measurable and instrumental gains from learning are given high priority, the alternative benefits of a learning experience that are recognized and enjoyed by many adult learners must be acknowledged and given due credence.

The local level
At an immediate local level, the findings from this research can be used to inform staff and students in colleges, and local authority officers, of the

perceptions of those involved in adult education courses. The collected data from their colleges include useful evidence of the need for tutor training, and student awareness-raising, particularly in relation to the requirements of the CIF. Data in Chapter 8 shows that many tutors seem unaware of the way in which their teaching style and what they expect from students seem almost contrary to the expectations of the CIF.

On a wider local level, data can be adapted to be used for tutor training courses across the country, and also for the training of senior managers and college governors, particularly in relation to their responsibilities for the leadership and management elements of the CIF (see next section). They can also assist students' organizations in clarifying their role in a partnership approach to teaching and learning. I have offered criticisms of the CIF in Chapter 2, but it provides a helpful set of criteria against which to measure the performance of providers and learners, before and after inspection. The inspections carried out by Ofsted and the ALI have a considerable effect on adult learning, its participants and its providers (see below), and it is important that their requirements are widely understood. Improvements to quality in learning are not undertaken, of course, simply in order to gain a high inspection grade, but to improve adult teaching and learning. Tutors, in partnership with their students, need to develop an increased awareness of learning objectives and outcomes, of the ways in which both parties contribute to the learning process to raise quality and how to prepare for and adapt to meet the needs of each learner.

The national level
Results of this study can inform and assist users and providers of adult learning beyond the geographical boundaries of my research. In addition, there are a number of issues that have implications at national level, both for policy and for practice. In terms of policy, I have indicated throughout this book that I believe part-time adult learning to be an important part of the lifelong learning agenda, and I have cited data from this study to indicate that the learners and tutors involved support this viewpoint. In some ways, adult education has been contributing towards that end for a very long time, but it lacks the recognition by politicians and some practitioners that would afford it the status I believe is justified in creating a genuinely learning society. A small sign of encouragement appeared in recent years when the results of an enquiry into further education and training (*Success for All*, DfES 2002) was published.

> The [FE] sector should be at the cutting edge of our aspiration to enshrine lifelong learning into the daily lives of our citizens, and the culture of our

country. ... It must also ensure that adult learners have greater access to excellent provision for basic skills, training for work and learning for personal development.   (DfES 2002: Foreword)

The same document goes on to state:

Adult and Community Learning forms a vital part of the Government's drive to support social inclusion, to widen participation in learning, to build communities' self-confidence and capacity and to promote good citizenship and personal development.   (Ibid.: 25)

These are helpful signs, but too often previously government rhetoric has not been followed by the practical improvements described and proposed, and the effects of funding cuts continue to have serious implications for much adult learning. Evidence from this study shows the commitment that many adults have for their learning and the many ways in which they use their learning to enhance their lives. One of these is the way adult education is used by so many as a foundation for, and a gateway into, further learning of different types, including accredited and 'vocational' learning that is high on the government's agenda. If lifelong learning is to encourage the development of learning and skills it would, I believe, be a lost opportunity not to develop and exploit links between adult education and other fields of learning to enable individuals to extend their learning in whatever direction is appropriate for them. Adults have wide interests and extensive learning needs, and a curriculum needs to be devised that is at all times relevant to these. As Tuckett suggests:

Adults bring such a diversity of experience to their studies, and have such a wide range of goals, that they will never have the full range of their learning needs captured by a national curriculum put together at speed, and with the schools' model in mind.   (Tuckett 2002: 34)

Our ageing society means that increasing numbers of adults will be undertaking 'formal', but not necessarily accredited, learning and I would expect governments to take more seriously the contributions made by all learning to the lifelong learning agenda. My research has shown that, for many students, the benefits of adult learning are as much in the process as in the outcomes, and in the stimulation of social interaction. If we are to avoid creating 'inner cities of the mind, depriving the poorest especially of the hobbies and learning which bring joy, fun, self-esteem and opportunity' (Fatchett and Smith 1991: 86) then we must ensure that the value of learning of all types, relevant to individual need and at all ages, is recognized by all. The most effective learning will be directly relevant to the individual's need at a given time in his/her life, whether or not it leads to a qualification.

> Adult learners, whether in certificated or un-certificated programmes, frequently place most value on 'soft' outcomes such as increased confidence and feelings of self-worth.   (McGivney 2002: v)

Whatever its nature and wherever provided, learning opportunity must be inclusive and genuinely lifelong. The recent census shows that there are already more people over 60 than under 16 in Britain (Tuckett 2002: 34), and the learning needs of an increasing older population must be given serious attention and practical support, not only to meet the needs of individuals, but also to recognize the contribution they can make to the learning society. There are pragmatic as well as humanitarian reasons for encouraging adults to continue to learn – 'learning is cheaper than visits from the doctor or the social worker' (ibid.: 34). Adults need not only to gain new skills and develop existing abilities, they need to understand and be confident in what they are doing, know how well they are progressing and what they need to do to improve (ALI and Ofsted 2001). These research data show the willingness and commitment by adults to their learning.

Implications for the CIF
Several references have been made within this book to the power of the LSC and to the requirements of inspections. I have indicated, also, that in my view the CIF, as presently formulated, does not meet the needs of all adults learners in ensuring the best and highest-quality learning opportunities for them, regardless of the planned outcomes of their learning. This is because it is designed to cater for a very wide range of adult education and training and, like so many other government documents, is strongly influenced by accreditation and vocationalism. But it does offer a helpful set of criteria by which to assess provision and practices for adult learning, and it is at present the means by which judgements are made by inspectors that will affect all post-compulsory learning provision other than higher education. If, therefore, the criteria that the CIF offers are to be used to test current systems and practices, and to stimulate improvement and development, all learners and tutors will need to be more involved in that process. The following four aspects of adult education, to which I have referred, have implications for learners, tutors and providers in terms of the published criteria of the CIF:

1. *Active and passive learners*: the positive aspects of active learners, as described in this study, need to be encouraged. Much of what is described by some learners meets the requirements of the CIF and should be more widely encouraged and facilitated to enhance learning for students and for tutors. Such positive approaches to learning, in any case, are likely to enhance quality of the process quite apart from inspection or accreditation requirements. Passive learners can be helped to become more aware of their learning and how they can aid its process and quality by becoming more actively involved participants. To be able to understand and explain their learning will help passive learners to become clearer about their achievements and their learning goals.

2. *Tutors' attitudes towards students' attendance and the completion of homework*: I have indicated that, for many tutors in this study, students' punctual attendance at classes and completion of homework is considered to be the extent of their contribution towards learning quality. This is in such contrast to those tutors who speak of the positive and stimulating results of active participatory learners. Some tutors, I believe, need to be persuaded to encourage a greater degree of participation by their students, producing beneficial results for both learners and tutors. If the degree of preparation and caring for their students shown by tutors was balanced by an equal effort to assist them to become independent, critically reflective learners, students and tutors would benefit considerably.

3. *Responsibility for learning quality*: my data show that tutors either regard the quality of learning as their responsibility (48 per cent), or something they share with others (40 per cent), although a tiny minority consider that they have no responsibility for it at all (2 per cent). The research data do not suggest that tutors in the third category are any less prepared or caring about their students' learning, but for any tutor to suggest that they bear no responsibility for the quality of their students' learning must be of concern, as also is the uncertainty shown by many tutors as to where the responsibility for quality lies. These findings have serious implications for adult learning and imply the need for further tutor training, particularly with regard to the requirements of the CIF.

4. *Focus on teaching rather than learning*: most tutors in my sample, however caring and hard-working they show themselves to be (and are seen to be by their students), focus principally on their performance as tutors and not on facilitating their students' achievements as learners. With the main emphasis of the CIF placed on the progress

and achievement of each individual learner, this reveals a serious imbalance within the adult learning partnership. This paternalistic approach by tutors militates against the enabling of students to become more self-directed self-reliant critical learners.

Wider implications for adult learning

The insights into adult learning and teaching that this study has provided have wider implications than the more immediate requirements of the CIF. If the findings of this research are representative of adult learners and tutors across the country, then much remains to be accomplished if we are to ensure that our students gain the maximum benefit from their learning.

Students need to be helped to gain additional confidence in their role as learners, and enhanced self-esteem will assist them in better understanding and appreciating their current learning. This can be brought about by acknowledging the integrity of their curriculum choice, and developing an approach to adult learning provision by government that is more inclusive and less judgmental. Students should be helped to discover how previous learning can positively contribute to enhancing the current learning process, and to use the knowledge and skills it provides to make full use of current and future opportunities. Gaining a better understanding of the need for assessment of progress and achievement, and how it is carried out, should reduce the undoubted anxiety expressed by many students in this research towards what they see as unwelcome examinations. Increased confidence, and better knowledge of purpose and process will increase their ability to learn, and help to ensure that they gain the greatest benefit from their learning. A learning society has to be more than a credentialized society, and adult education helping people to acquire the skills referred to above makes an important contribution to this. The developments of research by the Learning and Skills Development Agency into ways of measuring the benefits and outcomes of non-accredited learning will assist in such learning gaining wider recognition for its contribution.

Possible future research

Most research leaves questions unanswered or avenues unexplored. The publication of a set of research findings in any form can at most represent a picture of those research questions or problems that have been investigated and what outcomes have been discovered up to the time of publication, and within the parameters of the research design. This book has stated the research questions that were formulated; it has explained the methodology followed and the research questions employed; and it has set these against a background of relevant published literature. Data have been analysed and the findings summarized, producing a set of conclusions and recommendations. There will, nevertheless, be areas of research related to this study that could build upon its findings and develop additional information about the quality of adult learning and teaching.

Findings from research data have demonstrated the importance of learning to many adults and their varying views about the role they play in its process. The data also show that some students acknowledge the lessons learnt from previous learning and have the ability to apply those lessons to new learning. But other students did not indicate they do so in responses to my questions, and this has significance both for the requirements of the CIF and also for the effectiveness of current practice. The same data show that, so far as this sample is concerned, gender and curriculum choice make little difference to respondents' views, and that the physical environment seems to be much less important to students than it does to tutors. All these aspects relating to adult learning are important in their different ways and the results of further research could provide more information on each of them. A project that explored further the views of adults on quality in learning, both before and following a course of study, would be valuable. This would enable comparisons to be made of perceptions at different stages in the learning process, and assist in measuring the effectiveness of a particular learning episode.

Men remain under-represented in adult education across the country and some effort has been made to attract more of them on to courses. It may be that the lower participation rates by men reflect the current curriculum offer, or that the timing of some courses is not convenient to some men, but some data in this study suggest that perhaps there are circumstances when gender differences will produce a perceptual difference in learning. This factor should be explored further both to help in raising attendance levels by men and to ascertain whether there are any significant gender differences in ways in which individuals approach learning.

Relatively 'active' and 'passive' learners have been identified in this research, and I acknowledge that, especially in the case of passive learners, it has not been possible to quantify the extent to which they are learning, despite the language they employ to describe their involvement. Further research to gain data from active and passive learners would enable useful comparisons to be made of the extent to which high degrees of active participation by students do, or do not, coincide with higher levels of learning. My data suggest that at least some students are not gaining the most from their learning experience because they do not believe it is their place to question or challenge their tutor. And tutors, by adopting the paternalistic approach that I have described, may not be encouraging their students to be reflective or critical learners.

Tutors need to be made more aware of how to cater for the needs of each individual learner. The findings from this research that tutors focus more on their teaching than on their students' learning, is of concern, and tutors need to be helped to support students in becoming independent learners who value their learning experience and to develop skills of critical judgement of its processes and outcomes. Together, these two influences are likely to result in a less fulfilling learning experience for some students, and suggest a lower degree of encouragement than all learners should expect. One has to acknowledge that part-time tutors do not receive the level of support and encouragement that they deserve. Rates of pay, support facilities and training opportunities all need to be improved, but I believe tutors themselves could do much more to argue their own case, as well as to argue for better facilities for their work in adult education.

Research regarding what impact the physical environment has on learning, on the ways in which various forms of assessment are received and understood by learners, and research on the retention of students on courses, as distinct from the recruitment of students, would each assist in our understanding of these different aspect of adult learning.

Concluding remarks

One research question identified in Chapter 1 asked whether those students who recognize and draw upon the value of their previous learning may be acknowledged as arbiters of quality in their own learning. What is clear from these data is that some active learners consciously apply to new learning the lessons of their previous learning. Some claim that as a result they know more about how to choose courses, what are the attributes of a good tutor, how to approach their studies systematically and effectively and what action to take if they are not satisfied. This group of learners, approximately one third of the sample in this study, show themselves, therefore, in my view to be competent to be acknowledged as arbiters in the quality of their learning. They show themselves to be self-reliant and motivated, moving towards becoming self-directed in their learning and developing the skills of working independently. These students may be seen as good consumers of learning as they appear to make the most of those opportunities made available to them.

Some students are less active than others during the learning process, but nevertheless demonstrate that they have a clear perception of their learning needs and are able to draw positively on their previous learning experiences, recognising a logical link with new learning.

In an age of lifelong learning, no government should ignore the importance of non-accredited learning (whether undertaken part-time or full-time), both as a means to achieve the stated goal of a fully inclusive learning society, and as an immensely important element in the lives of so many citizens. The use of part-time learning experiences, such as those described here, as a means of returning to learning, as a gateway into further learning and as a means of personal development that produces more active, creative and interested people, means that the benefits to society of this type of learning must not be ignored. This contribution to the lifelong learning agenda has been under-recognized and undervalued by governments for far too long. Adult education is not simply a way of keeping people occupied, but adult educators have not generally been known as effective lobbyists. Despite the origins of adult education, which included critical engagement with social order and a quest for social justice, adult educators today generally seem less inclined to undertake political action to support their arguments. Students also, despite undoubted commitment to their learning, and tenacity in overcoming many obstacles to continue learning, are seldom inclined to exercise their political freedom in the form of protests. Rather, when confronted with financial cutbacks, or reduced learning provision, they are more likely passively to accept the results.

Some of the demographic changes that are affecting our society have been referred to earlier, and it is tempting to speculate that the increase in the number of citizens over 60 years of age may be accompanied by increased political awareness of the voting power that, collectively, they possess.

Learning is more than an economic necessity

This study has recorded the various perceptions of participants of quality in learning. It has shown the commitment students and tutors bring to adult education and has also revealed areas which, I have suggested, need attention and action. I have witnessed over many years the important effects that learning has had on the lives of individuals. Its life-enhancing experiences have been demonstrated in the data, as have the contributions adult education is making to the policies of lifelong learning. The value and importance of learning must not be confined to economic advantages because 'people require the provision of adult education classes to help them in their work, in their leisure and, indeed, in enriching the whole of their lives' (Jarvis 1995a: 7). Kennedy concluded after two years of studying further education provision that learning is vital to personal and national prosperity:

> Our work over the last two years has confirmed our conviction that learning is central to both economic prosperity and the health of society. We believe that the achievement of economic goals and social cohesion are intertwined.
>
> (Kennedy 1997, cited in Jarvis 2001: 12)

Governments must realize that learning cannot be 'limited by the straightjacket of predictable outcomes' and that 'completing tick boxes of generic skills undermines the enthusiasm and passion of intellectual work. Intelligence and intellectual struggle cannot be reduced to predictable outcomes, however politically and administratively convenient that might be.' (Rowland 2001, cited in McGivney 2002: 31).

I posed, above, the question 'Does it matter ?' I believe it does. I believe it matters that adult learners do not receive the recognition and support for the learning that means so much to them. I believe it matters that the work of their tutors is under-recognized (except by the students themselves). I believe it matters that the valuable contribution made by adult education to the professed goals of lifelong learning is undervalued by the very government that promotes lifelong learning high on its political agenda.

As a nation, I believe we must support and encourage adult education, whether part-time or full-time, accredited or non-accredited, as well as all other forms of learning opportunity. We have a long way to go before adult lifelong learning is recognized as a natural, fully inclusive and widely acknowledged contribution to the lives of individuals, and to the culture of our society.

Appendix 1   Summary of Curriculum Groups used for Data Coding

Group	Courses within the group
A	Visual Arts (includes Interior Design)
B	Basic Skills
C	Business and Office Skills
D	Computing and Mathematics
E	Crafts Group 1 – Light crafts (includes Lacemaking and Needlecrafts)
F	Crafts Group 2 – Heavy crafts (includes Woodwork, Wood Carving, Upholstery)
G	Dance and Movement (includes RSA Exercise to Music, Tap and Yoga)
H	(Not used)
I	Domestic and Family Skills (includes Cookery, Flower Arranging, Sugar Crafts)
J	English and Communication (includes Counselling)
K	Historical topics
L	Languages (includes ESOL, BSL, EFL)
M	Music
N	(Not used)
O	Sports (includes Swimming)
P	General Interest (includes Accounting, Antiques, Aromatherapy, Astronomy/Space History, Bridge, Classical Civilization, Countryside and Wildlife, Discovering Essex, First Aid, Garden Design, Gift for Healing, Homeopathy, Human Physiology and Health, Law, Life Skills, Massage, Meditation, Photography, PLA courses, Politics, Psychology, Reflexology, RYA courses, St John's Ambulance, Self-hypnosis, Sociology, Travel and Tourism, Walking, Wine, Women Returners).

Appendix 2   Student Questionnaire

ISSUES OF QUALITY IN PART-TIME ADULT LEARNING
STUDENT AND TUTOR PERSPECTIVES

This questionnaire is part of a three-year research project, which investigates issues of quality in part-time adult learning from the perspectives of students and tutors.

The process of successful adult teaching and learning is a transaction; a partnership between students and tutors. Each brings to that transaction individual values and views on what constitutes quality, and each draws on previous learning experiences, often gained over many years and in a variety of settings.

This project attempts to discover the value of those previous experiences for the individual learner, how they influence the quality of current learning and how the experienced learner can ensure a higher quality of learning in the future.

ISSUES OF QUALITY IN PART-TIME ADULT LEARNING (Student questionnaire)

STUDENT AND TUTOR PERSPECTIVES

Thank you for agreeing to take part in this survey. Data collected will provide valuable information as part of my Doctoral research project and I really do appreciate your time.

The information gained will also add generally to our better understanding of adult teaching and learning.

- Please answer all questions as fully as possible. It is suggested that you use key words or phrases to save time, but please write as much as you wish.
- You will see that you need not be identified from the questionnaire, but if you wish to be further involved with this survey, please complete the details at question 18.

Q1   Please enter the details of this course:

   College/ Venue: _____   Course title: _____

   Course ref (if known): _____   Day of week: _____

   Time: _____

Q2   Why did you choose *this* course? _____

_____

Q3   Do you have a specific use in mind for the knowledge or skills gained from this course?

_____

Q4   For how many years have you been an *adult* student? _____

Q5   Please describe your learning experiences as an adult:

_____

_____

Q6   Is your current course a course of quality? (Please tick)

   YES ☐ *(Please go to question 7)*   NO ☐ *(Please go to question 8)*

Q7   What is it that makes this a course of quality? (Please use key words or phrases)

_____

_____ *(Please go to question 9)*

Q8   Why is this *not* a course of quality? (Please use key words or phrases)

_____

_____

Q9   Who is responsible for ensuring and maintaining the quality of your course?

_____

Q10 Who is responsible for ensuring quality in all aspects of the work of this college?

_____

Q11 Do you, as a student, have a part to play in ensuring a quality learning experience for yourself and your fellow students? (Please tick)

YES ☐ *(Please go to question 12)*

NO ☐ *(Please go to question 13)*

Q12 How do you, as a student, contribute to a quality learning experience for yourself and your fellow students?

_____

_____

_____ *(Please go to question 14)*

Q13 Why is the quality of this course *not* your concern?

_____

_____

Q14 How and why do you value your learning as an adult?

_____

_____

Q15 How do you think your previous experiences as an adult learner affect your current learning?

_____

_____

_____

Q16 Please add here any other comments you wish.

_____

_____

_____

Q17 And finally ...

The following personal details are requested solely for statistical purposes. Please complete as appropriate:

Are you FEMALE? ☐   Are you MALE? ☐

Just one more page ...

Into which age group do you fall?

Under 21 ☐   21–30 ☐   31–40 ☐

41–50 ☐   51–60 ☐   Over 60 ☐

How many courses do you plan to attend this year? _____

Q18 If you wish to be kept in touch with this survey and its progress, please complete the details below, as appropriate.

Name: _____ Telephone: _____ Fax: _____

Address: _____

_____

_____

_____ Email: _____

Thank you again for your valuable help. Peter Boshier

(If you wish to contact me: Telephone: 01279 876343, Fax: 01279 876843, Email: 101363.535@Compuserve.com)

| PLEASE RETURN THIS QUESTIONNAIRE BY PLACING IT IN ONE OF THE BOXES PROVIDED AT YOUR COLLEGE |

OR if you prefer, send it direct to:

Peter Boshier Coopers Dunmow Road Beauchamp

Roding ONGAR CM5 0PF

Appendix 3   Tutor Questionnaire

ISSUES OF QUALITY IN PART-TIME ADULT LEARNING
STUDENT AND TUTOR PERSPECTIVES

This questionnaire is part of a three-year research project, which investigates issues of quality in part-time adult learning from the perspectives of students and tutors.

The process of successful adult teaching and learning is a transaction; a partnership between students and tutors. Each brings to that transaction individual values and views on what constitutes quality, and each draws on previous learning experiences, often gained over many years and in a variety of settings.

This project attempts to discover the value of those previous experiences for the individual learner, how they influence the quality of current learning and how the experienced learner can ensure a higher quality of learning in the future.

ISSUES OF QUALITY IN PART-TIME ADULT LEARNING (Tutor questionnaire)

STUDENT AND TUTOR PERSPECTIVES

Thank you for agreeing to take part in this survey. Data collected will provide valuable information as part of my Doctoral research project and I really do appreciate your time.

The information gained will also add generally to our better understanding of adult teaching and learning.

- Please answer all questions as fully as possible. It is suggested that you use key words or phrases to save time, but please write as much as you wish.
- You will see that you need not be identified from the questionnaire, but if you wish to be further involved with this survey, please complete the details at question 19.

Q1   Please enter the details of this course:

College/ Venue: _____ Course title: _____

Course ref: _____ Day of week: _____ Time: _____

Q2   Do you teach other subjects as well? If so, please list them:

_____

Q3   For how many years have you been a tutor of *adults*? _____

Q4   Do you also teach, or have you taught elsewhere? (Please tick, as appropriate)

YES ☐ in Higher Education ☐ in Further Education ☐ in Adult Education ☐ in Schools ☐ in Voluntary Sector ☐

NO, I do not, nor have I taught elsewhere ☐

Q5   Is this a course of quality? (Please tick)

YES ☐ (*Please go to question 6*) NO ☐ (*Please go to question 7*)

Q6   What is it that makes this a course of quality? (Please use key words or phrases)

a) within your control as tutor:

_____

_____

b) within the control of others:

_____ (*Please go to question 8*)

Q7   Why is this not a course of quality?

_____

Q8   How do you as a tutor ensure a quality learning experience for all your students?

_____

_____

Q9   What does 'quality' mean to you in your teaching? (Please use key words or phrases)

_____

_____

Q10 Who is responsible for ensuring and maintaining the quality of your course?

_____

Q11 Who is responsible for ensuring quality in all aspects of the work of this college?

_____

Q12 Do your students have any responsibility for the quality of their own learning?

YES ☐ *(Please go to question 13)* NO ☐ *(Please go to question 14)*

Q13 How can, and do, students contribute to the quality of their learning experiences?

_____

_____

_____ *(Please go to question 15)*

Q14 Why do you consider that students *do not* have any responsibility for the quality of their learning?

_____

Q15 What benefits or challenges for you, as tutor, are evident when students become more involved in the quality of their own learning?

_____

_____

_____

Q16 How do you adapt your teaching to ensure that your students' needs for a quality learning experience are met?

_____

_____

_____

Just one more page ...

Q17 Please add here any other comments you wish.

_____

_____

_____

Q18 And finally ...
The following personal details are requested solely for statistical purposes. Please complete as appropriate:
Are you FEMALE? ☐ Are you MALE? ☐
Into which age group do you fall?
Under 21 ☐   21–30 ☐   31–40 ☐
41–50 ☐   51–60 ☐   Over 60 ☐
How many courses do you expect to teach this year? _____

Q19 If you wish to be kept in touch with this survey and its progress, please compete the details below, as appropriate.
Name: _____ Telephone: _____ Fax: _____

Address: _____ Email: _____

Thank you again for your valuable help. Peter Boshier
(If you wish to contact me: Telephone: 01279 876343, Fax: 01279 876843, Email: 101363.535@Compuserve.com)

PLEASE RETURN THIS QUESTIONNAIRE BY PLACING IT
IN ONE OF THE BOXES PROVIDED AT YOUR COLLEGE

OR if you prefer, send it direct to:
Peter Boshier Coopers Dunmow Road Beauchamp
Roding ONGAR CM5 0PF

Appendix 4   Accredited and Non-accredited Courses

A summary of accredited and non-accredited courses attended, or taught by, survey respondents.

STUDENTS

ACCREDITED			NON-ACCREDITED			GRAND TOTAL
Female	Male	Total	Female	Male	Total	
297	78	375 (21%)	1,064	345	1,409 (79%)	1,784

TUTORS

ACCREDITED			NON-ACCREDITED			GRAND TOTAL
Female	Male	Total	Female	Male	Total	
49	16	65 (26%)	141	45	186 (74%)	251

Appendix 5   Supplementary Tables

Tables A5.1–A5.14 on the following pages provide data taken from earlier tables in the book, cross-referenced by response group and curriculum group, as indicated on each table.

Table A5.1: Data from Table 7.1 cross-tabulated by response group and curriculum group

Students' responses to the question 'What is it that makes this a course of quality?'													
Response group	A: The tutor, lecturer or instructor and pedagogy		B: Learning outcomes – examination, knowledge or skill		C: Adult learning atmosphere – stimulating and supportive		D: Meeting personal needs		E: Course content and materials		F: Physical environment facilities equipment, group size		Totals	
Curriculum Group	F	M	F	M	F	M	F	M	F	M	F	M	F	M
A	76	31	12	0	12	6	13	2	9	3	1	0	123	42
B	9	5	3	3	1	3	1	0	0	0	0	0	14	11
C	12	4	11	2	0	0	3	1	2	0	1	0	29	7
D	48	24	21	13	5	2	4	0	14	7	7	2	99	48
E	73	1	13	4	9	0	7	2	2	0	0	0	104	7
F	27	16	6	3	2	2	5	2	1	3	1	0	42	26
G	139	15	12	0	20	1	19	0	0	1	0	0	190	17
I	42	7	10	0	4	1	5	0	4	0	0	0	65	8
J	22	8	12	3	9	2	6	2	5	1	0	0	54	16
K	43	16	5	5	5	0	1	0	6	1	1	0	61	22
L	162	98	35	7	22	12	14	8	24	12	7	2	264	139
M	12	5	2	1	0	2	1	0	2	0	0	0	17	8
O	17	3	0	0	0	0	0	0	0	0	0	0	17	3
P	97	25	47	4	22	7	16	4	25	6	0	1	207	47
Totals with % of gender response	779 61%	258 64%	189 15%	45 11%	111 9%	38 9%	95 7%	21 5%	94 7%	34 8%	18 1%	5 1%	1,286	401

Curriculum groups
A: Visual Arts (includes Interior Design)
B: Basic Skills
C: Business and Office Skills
D: Computing and Mathematics
E: Crafts Group 1 – Light crafts
     (includes Lacemaking and Needlecrafts)
F: Crafts Group 2 – Heavy crafts
     (includes Woodwork, Wood Carving, Upholstery)
G: Dance and Movement (includes RSA
     Exercise to Music, Tap Dance and Yoga)

H: (Not used)
I: Domestic and Family Skills (includes Cookery,
     Flower Arranging, Sugar Crafts)
J: English and Communication (includes Counselling)
K: Historical subjects
L: Languages (includes ESOL, BSL, EFL)
M: Music
N: (Not used)
O: Sports (includes Swimming)
P: General Interest (see Appendix 1)

Table A5.2: Data from Table 7.4 cross-tabulated by response group and curriculum group

Students' responses to the question 'Who is responsible for ensuring and maintaining the quality of your course?'

Response Group →	A		B		C		D		E		F		G		H		I		J		Other		Totals	
Curriculum Groups ↓	F	M	F	M	F	M	F	M	F	M	F	M	F	M	F	M	F	M	F	M	F	M	F	M
A	80	31	18	2	3	2	2	3	0	0	2	0	0	0	0	0	6	0	1	0	1	0	122	39
B	10	7	1	2	1	0	0	0	0	0	0	0	0	0	0	0	0	0	0	0	0	0	12	9
C	22	7	2	2	3	0	0	0	0	0	1	0	0	0	0	0	0	0	0	0	1	0	29	9
D	54	27	12	4	6	4	11	5	4	2	1	0	6	0	1	2	1	1	0	0	3	1	100	45
E	65	4	9	1	11	0	10	2	2	0	4	0	0	0	1	0	0	0	0	0	1	0	103	7
F	31	14	4	7	5	2	4	0	0	0	0	1	0	1	0	1	0	0	0	0	0	0	45	25
G	132	14	22	1	9	1	7	2	3	0	2	0	1	3	1	0	0	0	0	0	0	0	179	19
I	40	6	9	0	6	1	2	0	0	0	3	0	0	0	0	0	2	0	0	0	0	0	62	7
J	32	8	10	4	7	1	3	1	0	1	2	2	1	1	0	0	0	1	1	0	1	0	59	18
K	31	9	6	1	5	2	13	4	0	0	0	0	1	1	0	0	0	0	2	0	0	1	58	18
L	137	70	50	23	25	12	17	6	2	4	5	2	6	4	2	2	0	0	0	0	1	1	245	121
M	7	6	4	3	1	0	1	0	1	0	0	0	2	0	1	0	0	0	0	0	0	0	17	9
O	11	2	2	0	0	0	2	0	1	0	1	0	0	0	0	0	0	0	0	0	0	0	17	2
P	103	20	41	8	6	2	9	2	14	5	12	2	5	2	2	0	2	0	12	0	5	0	211	41
Totals and	755	225	190	58	88	27	81	28	27	10	33	6	25	9	10	5	11	1	16	0	13	3	1,249	372
% of gender responses	60%	60%	15%	16%	7%	7%	6%	8%	3%	3%	3%	2%	2%	2%	1%	1%	1%	–	1%	–	1%	1%		

Response groups

A: Tutor, teacher, lecturer, instructor
B: Tutor and students
C: Tutor and college (i.e. excluding the students)
D: The college only
E: An external agency only
F: Tutor and external agency (i.e. excluding students and the college
G: Tutor, students and college
H: The students alone
I: Tutor, college and external agency (i.e. excluding students)
J: The college and external agency (i.e. excluding tutor and students)
K: Other groupings

Curriculum groups

A: Visual Arts (includes Interior Design)
B: Basic Skills
C: Business and Office Skills
D: Computing and Mathematics
E: Crafts Group 1 – Light crafts
F: Crafts Group 2 – Heavy crafts
G: Dance, Movement and Yoga
H: (Not used)
I: Domestic and Family Skills
J: English and Communication
K: Historical subjects
L: Languages (includes ESOL, BSL, EFL)
M: Music
N: (Not used)
O: Sports (includes Swimming)
P: General Interest

Table A5.3: Data from Table 7.6 cross-tabulated by response group and curriculum group

Students' responses to the question 'How do you, as a student, contribute to quality learning experience for yourself and your fellow students?'

Response Group	A: Active participation		B: Completing homework/ working outside class hours		C: Attendance and punctuality		D: Passive participation		E: Social interaction and mutual support		F: A 'detached' attitude		Totals	
Curriculum Groups	F	M	F	M	F	M	F	M	F	M	F	M	F	M
A	64	35	12	2	11	0	11	3	6	2	3	0	107	42
B	6	4	1	3	0	1	2	0	1	0	0	1	10	9
C	11	4	6	3	4	1	2	0	3	0	1	1	27	9
D	42	20	6	3	13	7	12	9	12	3	9	4	94	46
E	62	4	8	0	1	0	17	0	9	2	4	1	101	7
F	21	19	0	1	5	0	4	3	6	1	4	1	40	25
G	102	11	4	1	30	3	18	0	6	1	11	0	171	16
I	30	2	6	0	7	1	8	2	6	1	0	0	57	6
J	41	12	6	3	3	1	1	1	2	0	3	0	56	17
K	41	14	5	1	4	0	1	0	1	0	5	4	57	19
L	154	93	50	16	28	7	16	7	11	4	7	3	266	130
M	10	5	2	1	1	0	0	2	2	0	1	0	16	8
O	11	2	0	1	1	0	2	0	2	0	0	0	16	3
P	156	32	9	2	18	3	15	1	4	0	9	2	211	40
Totals and % of gender responses	751 61%	257 68%	115 9%	37 10%	126 10%	24 6%	109 9%	28 7%	71 6%	14 4%	57 5%	17 5%	1,229	377

Curriculum groups

A: Visual Arts
B: Basic Skills
C: Business and Office Skills
D: Computing and Mathematics
E: Crafts Group 1 – Light crafts
F: Crafts Group 2 – Heavy crafts
G: Dance, Movement and Yoga
H: (Not used)

I: Domestic and Family Skills
J: English and Communication
K: Historical subjects
L: Languages (includes ESOL, BSL, EFL)
M: Music
N: (Not used)
O: Sports (includes Swimming)
P: General Interest

Table A5.4: Data from Table 7.7 cross-tabulated by response group and curriculum group

Students' responses to the question 'How and why do you value your learning as an adult?'							
Response Group	A: Broad benefits of learning		B: Second chance or new opportunity		C: Specific purpose or benefit		Totals	
Curriculum Groups	F	M	F	M	F	M	F	M
A	104	44	17	2	4	0	125	46
B	7	5	3	3	2	4	12	12
C	24	8	3	0	2	0	29	8
D	91	40	5	4	8	4	104	48
E	90	7	8	0	0	0	98	7
F	38	23	1	0	0	0	39	23
G	166	14	9	0	3	0	178	14
I	52	6	6	1	1	0	59	7
J	44	13	8	2	3	0	55	15
K	60	21	6	1	0	1	66	23
L	228	116	19	8	17	7	264	131
M	15	7	1	0	0	0	16	7
O	17	3	1	0	0	0	18	3
P	181	31	19	1	8	1	208	33
Totals and % of gender response	1,117 88%	338 90%	106 8%	22 6%	48 4%	17 4%	1,271	377

Curriculum groups
A: Visual Arts
B: Basic Skills
C: Business and Office Skills
D: Computing and Mathematics
E: Crafts Group 1 – Light crafts
F: Crafts Group 2 – Heavy crafts
G: Dance, Movement and Yoga
H: (Not used)

I: Domestic and Family Skills
J: English and Communication
K: Historical subjects
L: Languages (includes ESOL, BSL, EFL)
M: Music
N: (Not used)
O: Sports (includes Swimming)
P: General Interest

Table A5.5: Data from Table 7.8 cross-tabulated by response group and curriculum group

Students' responses to the question 'How do you think your previous learning experiences as an adult affect your current learning?'								
Response groups	**A: Broad experiences and benefits**		**B: Foundation for further learning; progressive**		**C: Practical outcomes and benefits**		**Totals**	
Curriculum Group	**F**	**M**	**F**	**M**	**F**	**M**	**F**	**M**
A	60	17	18	10	4	1	82	28
B	4	4	0	2	0	0	4	6
C	5	4	4	0	4	0	13	4
D	38	22	14	4	3	2	55	28
E	38	4	21	1	4	0	63	5
F	16	10	6	4	1	6	23	20
G	66	4	21	2	16	2	103	8
I	18	3	7	1	4	1	29	5
J	20	7	10	3	4	1	34	11
K	28	7	7	7	7	4	42	18
L	95	45	53	30	17	19	165	94
M	6	2	3	1	3	3	12	6
O	9	1	1	0	2	0	12	1
P	79	16	25	4	8	1	112	21
Totals and % of gender response	482 64%	146 57%	190 23%	69 27%	77 10%	40 16%	749	255

Curriculum groups
A: Visual Arts
B: Basic Skills
C: Business and Office Skills
D: Computing and Mathematics
E: Crafts Group 1 – Light crafts
F: Crafts Group 2 – Heavy crafts
G: Dance, Movement and Yoga
H: (Not used)

I: Domestic and Family Skills
J: English and Communication
K: Historical subjects
L: Languages (includes ESOL, BSL, EFL)
M: Music
N: (Not used)
O: Sports (includes Swimming)
P: General Interest

Table A5.6: Total student respondents by curriculum group, age group
and gender

Total respondents: 1,784 (1,364 women, 420 men)						
Age groups	**Under 30**		**30–50**		**Over 50**		**Totals**
Curriculum groups	**F**	**M**	**F**	**M**	**F**	**M**	
A: Visual Arts	11	1	31	5	88	39	175
B: Basic Skills	4	2	7	4	5	3	25
C: Business & Office Skills	10	2	20	5	3	10	50
D: Computing & Mathematics	22	14	65	19	23	19	162
E: Light Crafts	4		21	3	82	13	123
F: Heavy Crafts	7		13	6	30	16	72
G: Dance, Movement & Yoga	7	1	49	4	137	14	212
I: Domestic & Family Skills	10		19	5	38	3	75
J: English & Communication	14	2	21	9	24	6	76
K: Historical subjects	2	1	7	4	52	21	87
L: Languages	47	12	115	40	122	98	434
M: Music	1		2		5	2	10
O: Sports	1		5	1	13	2	22
P: General Interest	55	4	125	15	47	15	261
Totals	195	39	500	120	669	261	1,784

Table A5.7: Data from Table 8.1 cross-tabulated by response group and curriculum group

Tutors' responses to the question 'What is it that makes this a course of quality – within your control as tutor?											
Response Category	A: Me – my preparation, skills, qualifications, pedagogy, being up to date		B: The course content, materials and structure		C: Assessment, outcomes, examination		D: Student interaction and social aspects		E: 'Detached approach'		Totals	
Curriculum Group	F	M	F	M	F	M	F	M	F	M	F	M
A	15	4	3	0	0	0	0	0	0	0	18	4
B	7	4	1	0	1	0	0	0	0	0	9	4
C	3	2	1	1	1	0	0	0	0	0	5	3
D	13	4	1	1	6	0	0	0	0	0	20	5
E	12	0	2	0	1	0	0	0	0	0	15	0
F	3	3	0	3	0	0	0	0	0	0	3	6
G	23	3	3	0	0	0	1	0	0	0	27	3
I	6	0	1	0	0	0	0	0	1	0	8	0
J	6	0	2	0	0	0	0	0	0	0	8	0
K	4	3	0	2	0	0	1	0	0	0	5	5
L	28	11	3	1	2	1	1	0	0	0	34	13
M	2	3	1	1	0	0	0	0	0	0	3	4
O	0	0	0	0	0	0	0	0	0	0	0	0
P	21	8	3	3	4	1	1	0	0	1	29	13
Totals and % of gender responses	143 78%	45 75%	21 11%	12 20%	15 8%	2 3%	4 2%	0 –	1 1%	1 2%	184	60

Curriculum groups

A:	Visual Arts	I:	Domestic and Family Skills
B:	Basic Skills	J:	English and Communication
C:	Business and Office Skills	K:	Historical subjects
D:	Computing and Mathematics	L:	Languages (includes ESOL, BSL, EFL)
E:	Crafts Group 1 – light crafts	M:	Music
F:	Crafts Group 2 – heavy crafts	N:	(Not used)
G:	Dance, Movement and Yoga	O:	Sports (includes Swimming)
H:	(Not used)	P:	General Interest

Table A5.8: Data from Table 8.2 cross-tabulated by response group and curriculum group

Tutors' responses to the question 'What is it that makes this a course of quality – within the control of others?'

Response group	A: Professional support, college systems and training opportunities		B: Students' attendance, their effort and homework		C: Equipment and facilities, teaching and learning environment		D: Accredited course, examination boards, curriculum		Totals	
Curriculum Group	F	M	F	M	F	M	F	M	F	M
A	6	0	2	3	3	0	0	0	11	3
B	5	2	1	1	1	0	0	1	7	4
C	1	1	1	0	1	0	2	1	5	2
D	3	1	3	0	10	0	1	3	17	4
E	3	1	2	0	5	0	3	0	13	1
F	0	1	0	3	2	2	0	0	2	6
G	5	0	8	1	4	2	2	0	19	3
I	2	0	1	0	2	0	1	0	6	0
J	2	1	2	0	2	0	0	0	6	1
K	2	0	1	2	1	1	0	2	4	5
L	8	1	9	2	7	0	6	3	30	6
M	0	0	0	1	2	1	0	0	2	2
O	0	0	0	0	0	0	0	0	0	0
P	8	4	5	3	3	0	9	3	25	10
Totals and % of gender response	45 31%	12 26%	35 24%	16 34%	43 29%	6 13%	24 16%	13 28%	147	47

Curriculum groups

A:	Visual Arts	I:	Domestic and Family Skills
B:	Basic Skills	J:	English and Communication
C:	Business and Office Skills	K:	Historical subjects
D:	Computing and Mathematics	L:	Languages (includes ESOL, BSL, EFL)
E:	Crafts Group 1 – light crafts	M:	Music
F:	Crafts Group 2 – heavy crafts	N:	(Not used)
G:	Dance, Movement and Yoga	O:	Sports (includes Swimming)
H:	(Not used)	P:	General Interest

Table A5.9: Data from Table 8.3 cross-tabulated by response group and curriculum group

Tutors' responses to the question 'Who is responsible for ensuring and maintaining the quality of your course?'

Response group	A		B		C		D		E		F		G		H		I		J		Totals	
Curriculum Group	F	M	F	M	F	M	F	M	F	M	F	M	F	M	F	M	F	M	F	M	F	M
A	8	3	4	1	3	0	1	0	0	0	0	0	0	0	1	0	0	0	0	0	17	4
B	3	0	4	2	0	1	1	0	0	0	0	0	0	0	0	0	1	0	0	0	9	3
C	3	0	1	1	0	1	1	0	0	0	0	0	0	0	0	0	0	0	0	0	5	2
D	7	1	7	2	2	0	2	1	0	0	1	0	1	0	0	0	0	0	0	0	20	4
E	6	0	2	0	0	1	1	0	4	0	1	0	0	0	1	0	0	0	0	0	15	1
F	1	7	1	2	1	0	0	0	0	0	0	0	0	0	0	0	0	0	0	0	3	9
G	16	1	4	1	2	1	2	0	0	0	1	0	2	0	0	0	1	0	0	0	28	3
I	4	0	2	0	0	0	1	0	0	0	1	0	0	0	0	0	0	0	0	1	8	1
J	2	1	4	0	1	0	0	0	1	0	0	0	0	0	0	1	0	0	1	0	9	2
K	0	2	2	1	0	1	1	1	0	0	0	0	0	0	1	0	0	0	0	1	4	6
L	16	7	9	0	2	4	3	0	3	1	0	0	2	0	0	0	0	0	0	0	35	12
M	3	1	0	0	0	0	0	1	0	0	0	0	0	0	0	0	0	0	0	0	3	2
O	0	0	0	0	0	0	0	0	0	0	0	0	0	0	0	0	0	0	0	0	0	0
P	12	5	8	1	5	3	0	1	0	0	2	0	1	0	0	0	2	0	1	1	31	11
Totals and % of gender response	81 43%	28 47%	48 26%	11 18%	16 9%	12 20%	13 7%	4 7%	8 4%	1 2%	6 3%	0 —	6 3%	0 —	3 2%	1 2%	4 2%	0 —	2 1%	3 5%	187	60

Table A5.10: Data from Table 8.4 cross-tabulated by response group and curriculum group

Tutors' responses to the question 'How can, and do, students contribute to the quality of their learning experience?'									
Response group	A: 'Active' participation		B: Completing 'homework' and bringing materials		C: Attendance and punctuality		D: 'Passive' participation		Totals and % of total responses	
Curriculum group (see below)	F	M	F	M	F	M	F	M	F	M
A	8	2	5	1	2	0	1	1	16	4
B	4	1	0	0	1	1	1	2	6	4
C	1	1	1	0	1	0	2	1	5	2
D	6	1	4	2	6	0	3	1	19	4
E	7	1	7	0	1	0	1	0	16	1
F	1	4	2	4	0	1	1	1	4	10
G	11	1	8	2	2	0	4	1	25	4
I	3	0	4	0	1	0	0	0	8	0
J	6	1	2	0	0	0	0	0	8	1
K	2	2	2	3	0	1	0	0	4	6
L	11	7	11	3	10	0	2	1	34	11
M	0	1	2	1	2	0	1	0	5	2
O	0	0	0	0	0	0	0	0	0	0
P	10	6	9	3	7	0	4	0	30	9
Totals and % of gender responses	70 39%	28 48%	57 32%	19 33%	33 18%	3 5%	20 11%	8 14%	180	58

Curriculum groups

A:	Visual Arts	I:	Domestic and Family Skills
B:	Basic Skills	J:	English and Communication
C:	Business and Office Skills	K:	Historical subjects
D:	Computing and Mathematics	L:	Languages (includes ESOL, BSL, EFL)
E:	Crafts Group 1 – light crafts M: Music	M:	Music
F:	Crafts Group 2 -heavy crafts	N:	(Not used)
G:	Dance, Movement and Yoga	O:	Sports (includes Swimming)
H:	(Not used)	P:	General Interest

Table A5.11: Data from Table 8.5 cross-tabulated by response group and curriculum group

Tutors' responses to the question 'What does quality mean to you in your teaching?'							
Response group	**A:** My performance as tutor; my knowledge, preparation and assessment, with clear objectives		**B:** Students – high standards, attendance, learning progress, results, enjoyment		**C:** Facilities and equipment		**Totals**	
Curriculum group	**F**	**M**	**F**	**M**	**F**	**M**	**F**	**M**
A	13	2	5	1	0	0	18	3
B	5	3	2	1	0	0	7	4
C	2	1	3	1	0	0	5	2
D	15	2	5	2	0	0	20	4
E	11	1	5	0	0	0	16	1
F	1	4	1	7	1	0	3	11
G	17	4	9	0	0	0	26	4
I	4	0	4	0	0	0	8	0
J	7	2	2	0	0	0	9	2
K	3	5	1	1	0	0	4	6
L	23	4	10	4	1	0	34	8
M	2	1	0	1	0	0	2	2
O	0	0	0	0	0	0	0	0
P	28	8	3	3	0	1	31	12
Totals and % of gender response	131 72%	37 63%	50 27%	21 36%	2 1%	1 2%	183	59

Curriculum groups

A:	Visual Arts	I:	Domestic and Family Skills
B:	Basic Skills	J:	English and Communication
C:	Business and Office Skills	K:	Historical subjects
D:	Computing and Mathematics	L:	Languages (includes ESOL, BSL, EFL)
E:	Crafts Group 1 – light crafts	M:	Music
F:	Crafts Group 2 -heavy crafts	N:	(Not used)
G:	Dance, Movement and Yoga	O:	Sports (includes Swimming)
H:	(Not used)	P:	General Interest

Table A5.12: Data from Table 8.6 cross-tabulated by response group and curriculum group

Tutors' responses to the question 'How do you, as a tutor, ensure a quality learning experience for all your students?'								
Response group	A: Preparation, keeping up to date, pedagogy		B: Knowing students' needs, individually focused teaching		C: Regular assessment		Totals	
Curriculum Group	F	M	F	M	F	M	F	M
A	10	5	6	0	1	0	17	5
B	5	2	3	1	2	1	10	4
C	4	1	1	0	0	1	5	2
D	11	2	3	2	3	0	17	4
E	11	0	5	1	0	0	16	1
F	1	7	2	3	0	0	3	10
G	21	3	4	1	3	0	28	4
I	5	0	2	0	1	0	8	0
J	7	1	0	0	1	1	8	2
K	3	6	1	0	0	0	4	6
L	22	10	7	2	4	0	33	12
M	1	1	1	0	1	0	3	1
O	0	0	0	0	0	0	0	0
P	21	10	8	1	3	1	32	12
Totals and % of gender response	122 66%	48 76%	43 23%	11 17%	19 10%	4 6%	184	63

Curriculum groups

A: Visual Arts
B: Basic Skills
C: Business and Office Skills
D: Computing and Mathematics
E: Crafts Group 1 – light crafts
F: Crafts Group 2 -heavy crafts
G: Dance, Movement and Yoga
H: (Not used)

I: Domestic and Family Skills
J: English and Communication
K: Historical subjects
L: Languages (includes ESOL, BSL, EFL)
M: Music
N: (Not used)
O: Sports (includes Swimming)
P: General Interest

Table A5.13: Data from Table 8.7 cross-tabulated by response group and curriculum group

Tutors' responses to question 'How do you adapt your teaching to ensure that your students' needs for a quality learning experience are met?						
Response group	**A:** Reassess and listen, alter pace, change content, replan, ensure flexibility		**B:** Cater for individual needs		**Totals**	
Curriculum Group	F	M	F	M	F	M
A	14	4	3	0	17	4
B	6	2	3	2	9	4
C	5	1	0	1	5	2
D	16	3	3	0	19	3
E	11	1	4	0	15	1
F	1	5	1	3	2	8
G	23	3	2	1	25	4
I	6	0	2	0	8	0
J	7	1	1	0	8	1
K	4	3	0	1	4	4
L	29	8	4	1	33	9
M	3	2	0	0	3	2
O	0	0	0	0	0	0
P	29	11	2	1	31	12
Totals and % of gender response	154 86%	44 81%	25 14%	10 19%	179	54

Curriculum groups

A:	Visual Arts	I:	Domestic and Family Skills
B:	Basic Skills	J:	English and Communication
C:	Business and Office Skills	K:	Historical subjects
D:	Computing and Mathematics	L:	Languages (includes ESOL, BSL, EFL)
E:	Crafts Group 1 – light crafts	M:	Music
F:	Crafts Group 2 -heavy crafts	N:	(Not used)
G:	Dance, Movement and Yoga	O:	Sports (includes Swimming)
H:	(Not used)	P:	General Interest

Table A5.14: Data from Table 8.8 cross-tabulated by response group and curriculum group

Tutors' responses to the question 'What benefits or challenges for you, as tutor, are evident when students become more involved in the quality of their own learning?'								
Response group	A: Makes my job and course more motivating, interesting and stimulating		B: More work for me, challenges me		C: More student progress, more confidence		Totals	
Curriculum Group	F	M	F	M	F	M	F	M
A	8	2	5	1	3	1	16	4
B	2	1	4	2	3	1	9	4
C	3	0	1	0	1	1	5	1
D	4	1	7	2	9	1	20	4
E	6	1	7	0	2	0	15	1
F	1	6	2	2	0	0	3	8
G	13	2	10	1	5	0	28	3
I	4	0	3	0	2	0	9	0
J	2	0	4	0	2	1	8	1
K	1	5	2	1	1	0	4	6
L	11	5	7	1	13	2	31	8
M	1	0	0	1	2	1	3	2
O	0	0	0	0	0	0	0	0
P	12	6	13	4	6	2	31	12
Totals and % of gender response	68 37%	29 54%	65 36%	15 28%	49 27%	10 19%	182	54

Curriculum groups

A:	Visual Arts	I:	Domestic and Family Skills
B:	Basic Skills	J:	English and Communication
C:	Business and Office Skills	K:	Historical subjects
D:	Computing and Mathematics	L:	Languages (includes ESOL, BSL, EFL)
E:	Crafts Group 1 – light crafts	M:	Music
F:	Crafts Group 2 – heavy crafts	N:	(Not used)
G:	Dance, Movement and Yoga	O:	Sports (includes Swimming)
H:	(Not used)	P:	General Interest

References

Adult Learning Inspectorate/Office for Standards in Education (2001), *The Common Inspection Framework for Inspecting Post-16 Education and Training*. Coventry and Coventry: ALI/Ofsted.

Advisory Council for Adult Continuing Education (ACACE) (1982), *Adults: Their Educational Experience and Needs*. Leicester: ACACE.

Allport, G. (1961), *Pattern and Growth in Personality*. New York: Holt, Rinehart & Winston.

Armstrong, P. F. (1989), 'Right for the wrong reasons: a critique of sociology in professional adult education', in B. P. Bright, *Theory and Practice in the Study of Adult Education: The Epistemological Debate*. London: Routledge.

Ashworth, A. and Harvey, R. (1994), *Assessing Quality in Further and Higher Education*. Bristol: Kingsley.

Association of Metropolitan Authorities (AMA) (1999), *Lifetime Learning: Looking Towards 2000 – Partners in Building a Learning Society*. London: AMA.

Ball, C. (1985), 'What the hell is quality?', in D Urwin (ed.) *Fitness for Purpose – Essays in Higher Education by Christopher Ball*. London: SRHE/NFER-NELSON.

— (1990) *More Means Differ*. London: Royal Society of Arts.

Ball, C. and Coffield, F. (1999), 'Our Learning Society', *Royal Society of Arts Journal*, 21 April. London: Society for Research into Higher Education/NFER-Nelson.

Barnett, R. (1990), *The Idea of Higher Education*. Buckingham: SRHE/Open University Press.

— (1992), *Improving Higher Education: Total Quality Care*. Buckingham: SRHE/Open University Press.

Barnett, R. and Griffin, A. (eds) (1997), *The End of Knowledge in Higher Education*. London: Cassell.

Beckett, F. (1991), 'Learning tainted with leisure', *The Times Educational Supplement*, 1 October. London: Times Newspapers.

Blair, A. (1999), Speech on the occasion of the 10th anniversary of the Institute for Public Policy Research. London: 10 Downing Street Press Office, cited in Hodgson and Spours (1999).

Boshier, R. (1980), *Towards a Learning Society*. Vancouver: Learning Press.

Boud, D. (1989), 'Some competing traditions', in S. W. Weil & I. McGill (eds), *Making Sense of Experiential Learning*. Buckingham: SRHE/ Open University Press.

Boud D, Cohen, R. and Walker, D. (1993a), Introduction: understanding learning for experience', in D. Boud, R. Cohen and D. Walker (eds) (1993b), *Using Experience for Learning*. Milton Keynes: SRHE/Open University Press.

Boud, D., Cohen, R. and Walker, D. (eds) (1993b), *Using Experience for Learning*. Milton Keynes: SRHE/Open University Press.

Boydell, T. (1976), *Experiential Learning* (Manchester Monographs No. 5). Manchester: Department of Adult Education, University of Manchester.

Brannen, J. (ed.) (1992), *Mixing Methods: Qualitative and Quantitative Research*. Aldershot: Avebury.

Bright, B. P. (1989), *Theory and Practice in the Study of Adult Education: The Epistemological Debate*. London: Routledge.

Brookfield, S. D. (1986), *Understanding and Facilitating Adult Learning*. Milton Keynes: Open University Press.

Brown, A. and Dowling, P. (1998), *Doing Research/Reading Research: A Mode of Interrogation in Education*. London: RoutledgeFalmer.

Bryman, A. (1988), *Quality and Quantity in Social Research*. London: Unwin Hyman.

Calder, J. (1993), *Disaffection and Diversity*. London: Falmer Press.

Cara, S. (1991), 'Learning tainted with leisure', *The Times Educational Supplement*, 1 November. London: Times Newspapers.

Coare, P. and Thomson, A. (1996), *Through the Joy of Learning: Diary of 1,000 Adult Learners*. Leicester: NIACE.

Coffield, F. (1997a), *Can the UK Become a Learning Society?* London: King's College.

Coffield, F. (ed.) (1997b), *A National Strategy for Lifelong Learning*. Papers presented at Close House, University of Newcastle. Newcastle: University of Newcastle.

Coffield, F. (1999), 'Breaking the consensus: lifelong learning as social control', *British Educational Research Journal*, 25, (4).

Coffield, F. (ed.) (2001), *What Progress are We Making with Lifelong Learning?: The Evidence from Research*. Newcastle: Department of Education, University of Newcastle.

Coffield, F. and Williamson, B. (1997), *Repositioning Higher Education*. Buckingham: SRHE/Open University Press.

Cohen, L. and Manion, L. (1994), *Research Methods in Education* (4th edn). London: Routledge.

Commission on Adult Education (Ireland) (1985), *Lifelong Learning*. Dublin: The Stationery Office.

Courtney, S. (1992), *Why Adults Learn: Towards a Theory of Participation in Adult Education*. London: Routledge.

Cousin, G. (1990), 'Women in liberal adult education', *Adults Learning*, 2, (2).

Cropley, A. (1980), 'Lifelong learning and systems of education: an overview', in A. Cropley (ed.), *Towards a System of Lifelong Education: Some Practical Considerations*. Oxford: Pergammon Press, p. 1, cited in J. Field and M. Leicester (2000), *Lifelong Learning: Education across the Lifespan*. London: RoutledgeFalmer.

Cropley, A. (ed.) (1980), *Towards a System of Lifelong Education: Some Practical Considerations*. Oxford: Pergammon Press.

Cullen, J. (2001), 'Informal learning and widening participation', in F. Coffield (ed.), *What Progress are We Making with Lifelong Learning?: The Evidence From Research*. Newcastle: Department of Education, University of Newcastle.

Daines, J. (1994), 'Learning outcomes in the WEA', in *Adult Learning*, September. Leicester: NIACE.

Daines, J., Daines, C. and Graham, B. (1993), *Adult Learning: Adult Teaching* (3rd edn). Nottingham: Department of Adult Education, University of Nottingham.

Davenport, J. (1993), 'Is there any way out of the andragogy morass?', in M. Thorpe, R. Edwards and A. Hanson (eds), *Culture and Processes of Adult Learning*. London: Routledge/Open University Press.

Denzin, N. K. (1989), *The Research Act*. New Jersey: Prentice Hall.

Department for Education (DfE) (1995a), *Value-added in Education: A Briefing Paper*. London: DfE.

Department for Education (DfE) (1995b), *Lifetime Learning*. Sheffield: DfE.

Department for Education and Employment (DfEE) (1998), *The Learning Age: A Renaissance for a New Britain*. London: The Stationery Office.

Department for Education and Employment (DfEE) (1999), *Learning to Succeed* (A White Paper). London: The Stationery Office.

Department for Education and Science (DES) (1991), *Education for Adults*. London: HMSO.

Department for Education and Science (DES) (1992), *Further and Higher Education Act*. London: HMSO.

Department for Education and Skills (DfES) (2000), *Learning and Skills Act*. London: The Stationery Office.

Department for Education and Skills (DfES) (2002), *Success for All*. London: DfES.

Department of Trade and Industry (DTI) (1991a), *Managing into the '90s: The Route Ahead*. London: DTI.

Department of Trade and Industry (DTI) (1991b), *Leadership and Quality Management*. London: DTI.

De Wit, P. (1992), *Quality Assurance in University Continuing Vocational Education*. London: HMSO.

Education Act (1944). London: HMSO.

Elliott, G. (1999), *Lifelong Learning: The Politics of the New Learning Environment*. London: Kingsley.

Entwistle, N. (1993), *Teaching and the Quality of Learning*. London: Committee of Vice Chancellors and Principals/SRHE.

Evans, N. (1994) *Experiential Learning For All*. London: Cassell.

Fatchett, D. and Smith, S. (1991) cited in *Education Journal*, 2 August.

Feigenbaum, A. V. (1991), 'Total quality control' (4th rev. edn), cited in E. Sallis (1995), *The Industrial and Philosophical Origins of Quality Assurance* (Mendip Papers No. 75). Bristol: The Staff College.

Field, J. (1990), 'Creating leisure', in *Adults Learning*, 2, (2). Leicester: NIACE.

— (2000), *Lifelong Learning and the New Educational Order*. Stoke on Trent: Trentham Books.

— (2001), 'Lifelong learning and social inclusion: engaging the hard to reach', in F. Coffield (ed.) (2001), *What Progress Are We Making with Lifelong Leaning?: The Evidence from Research*. Newcastle: Department of Education, University of Newcastle.

Field, J. and Leicester, M. (2000), *Lifelong Learning: Education across the Lifespan*. London: Routledge Falmer.

Fieldhouse, R., Baynes, P., Benn, R., Drews, W., Field, J., Groombridge, B., Hamilton, M., Mcllroy, J., Marks, H., Martin, I. and Sergant, N. (1996), *A History of Modern British Adult Education*. Leicester: NIACE.

'Flowers of the realm' (1991) *The Times*, Leader, 9 August. London: Times Newspapers.

Fowler, F. J. (1993), *Survey Research Methods* (2nd edn). London: Sage.

Freire, P. (1972), *Pedadogy of the Oppressed*. Harmondsworth: Penguin Books.

Further Education Unit (FEU) (1991), *Quality Matters*. London: FEU.

Gagne, R. M. (1972), 'Domains of Learning', *Interchange* 3, (1), cited in A. Rogers (1986) *Teaching Adults*. Milton Keynes: Open University Press.

Giddens, A. (1998), *The Third Way*. Cambridge: Polity Press.

Green, A. and Lucas, N. (1999), *Further Education and Lifelong Leaning: Realigning the Sector for the Twenty-first Century*. London: Institute of Education.

Green, A. and Preston, J. (2000), 'Finding the glue that can fix cracks in our society', (Centre for Research on the Wider Benefits of Learning). *The Times Higher Education Supplement*, 22 June. London: Times Newspapers.

Green, D. (1994), 'What is quality in higher education? Concepts, policy and practice', in Green, D. (ed.) (1994), *What is Quality in Higher Education?* Buckingham: Open University Press, p. 12, cited in M. Tight (1996), *Key Concepts in Adult Education and Training*. London: Routledge.

Griffin, C. (1983), *Curriculum Theory in Adult and Lifelong Education*. London: Croom Helm.

— 'Didacticism: lectures and lecturing', in P. Jarvis (ed.), *The Theory and Practice of Teaching*. London: Kogan Page.

Groombridge, B. (1983) 'Adult education and the education of adults', in M. Tight (ed.), *Education for Adults, Vol. 1: Adult Learning and Education*. London: Croom Helm.

Group of 8 (1999), (Köln Charter) *Aims and Ambitions for Lifelong Learning*. Cologne: G8 Summit.

Halliday, J. (ed.) (1998), *Values in Further Education*. Stoke-on-Trent: Threntham.

Harris, T. A. (1973), *I'm OK – You're OK*. London: Pan Books.

Harrison, R. (1993), 'Disaffection and access', in J. Calder (ed.), *Diversity and Disaffection*. London: Falmer Press, cited in Uden, T. (1994), *The Will to Learn*. Leicester: NIACE.

Harvey, L., Burrows, A. and Green, D. (1992), *Criteria of Quality: a Summary Paper*, Quality in Higher Education Project. Birmingham: University of Central England, Birmingham.

Havighurst, R. J. (1972), *Developmental Tasks in Education* (3rd edn). New York: McKay.

Hodgson, A. (1997), 'Building institutional capability for national education reform: the case of the formative value-added system' in A. Hodgson and K. Spours (eds), *Dearing and Beyond: 14–19 Qualifications, Frameworks and Systems*. London: Kogan Page.

Hodgson, A. (ed.) (2000), *Policies, Politics and the Future of Lifelong Learning*. London: Kogan Page.

Hodgson, A. and Spours, K. (1997), *Value-added and Attainment Research and Development Newsletter*, No. 5. London: Institute of Education.

— (1999), *New Labour's Educational Agenda: Issues and Policies for Education and Training from 14+*. London: Kogan Page.

Hodgson, A. and Spours, K. (eds) (1997), *Dearing and Beyond: 14–19 Qualifications, Frameworks and Systems*. London: Kogan Page.

Hoggart, R. (1995), *The Way We Live Now*. London: Pimlico.

Hostler, J. (1982), 'The art of teaching adult studies', *Adult Education*, 14. Leicester: NIACE.

Houle, C. O. (1961), *The Enquiring Mind*. Madison, WI: University Press, cited in A. Rogers (1986), *Teaching Adults*. Milton Keynes: Open University Press.

— (1972), *The Design of Education*. San Francisco: Jossey Bass.

— (1984), *Patterns of Learning*. San Francisco: Jossey Bass.

Hutchins, R. M. (1968), *The Learning Society*. London: Britannica.

Hutchinson, E. (1963), 'Introduction' to *Adult Education*, 35, (5). Leicester: NIACE.

James, W. B. (1983), 'An analysis of perceptions of the practices of the adult educators from five different settings', *Proceedings of the Adult Education Research Conference, no. 24*. Montreal: Concordia University/University of Montreal.

Jarvis, P. (1984), 'Andragogy: a sign of the times', *Studies in the Education of Adults*, 16, (32).

— (1995a), *Adult & Continuing Education: Theory and Practice* (2nd edn). London: Routledge.

— (1995b), 'Teachers and learners in adult education: transaction or moral interaction?', *Studies in the Education of Adults*, 27, (1).

— (1997), *Ethics and Education for Adults in a Late Modern Society*. Leicester: NIACE.

— (1999a), *The Practitioner/Researcher: Developing Theory from Practice*. San Francisco: Jossey-Bass.

— (1999b), 'A strategic research agenda for lifelong learning in learning societies', in A. Tuijnman and T. Schuller (eds) (1999), *Lifelong Learning Policy and Research*. London: Portland Press.

— (2001), *The Age of Learning: Education and the Knowledge Society*. London: Kogan Page.

Jarvis, P. (ed.) (2002), *The Theory and Practice of Teaching*. London: Kogan Page.

Jarvis, P., Holford, J. and Griffin, C. (1998), *The Theory and Practice of Learning*. London: Kogan Page.

Jones, L. (1990), 'Part-time education: a case for equal treatment', *Adults Learning* 1, (6). Leicester: NIACE.

Keddie, N. (1980), 'Adult education: an ideology of individualism', in J. C. Thompson (ed.), *Education for a Change*. London: Hutchinson.

Kelly, T. (1970), *A History of Adult Education in Great Britain* (2nd edn). Liverpool: Liverpool University Press.

Kennedy, H. (1997), *Learning Works: Widening Participation in Further Education* (The Kennedy Report). Coventry: Further Education Funding Council.

Kerlinger, F. N. (1970), *Foundations of Behavioural Research*. New York: Holt, Rinehart & Winston.

Kershaw, N. F. (1979), *Active Learning: A Guide to Current Practice in Experiential and Participatory Learning*. London: Further Education Unit.

Kidd, J. R. (1973), *How Adults Learn*. New York: Association Press.

Kingston, P. (2002), 'More work, less play', *The Guardian Education*. London: Guardian Newspapers.

Knapper, C. K. and Cropley, A. J. (1991), *Lifelong Learning and Higher Education* (2nd edn). London: Kogan Page.

Knowles, M. (1980), *The Modern Practice of Adult Education* (2nd edn). Chicago: Association Press.

— (1990), *The Adult Leaner: A Neglected Species*. Houston, TX: Golf.

Labour Party (1997), *Lifelong Learning*. London: The Labour Party.

Lavender, P. (1999), 'Qualifications are not the only learning outcomes', *Adults Learning*, 11, (4). Leicester: NIACE.

Lawson, K. H. (1975), *Philosophical Concepts and Values*. Nottingham: Department of Adult Education, University of Nottingham.

— (1996), 'From citizen to self' in J. Wallis (ed.), *Liberal Adult Education: The End of an Era?* Nottingham: Continuing Education Press, University of Nottingham.

— (1998) *Philosophical Issues in the Education of Adults*. Nottingham: Continuing Education Press, University of Nottingham.

Layer, G. (2002), 'Horses for courses', *The Times Higher Education Supplement*, 25 January. London: Times Newspapers.

Longworth, N. (1999), *Making Lifelong Learning Work: Learning Cities for a Learning Century*. London: Kogan Page.

Longworth, N. and Davies, W. K. (1996), *Lifelong Learning*. London: Kogan Page, p. 8, cited in P. Oliver (ed.), *Lifelong Learning and Continuing Education: What is a Learning Society?* Aldershot: Ashgate Arena.

References 215

Lovell, R. B. (1980), *Adult Learning*. London: Croom Helm.

McGivney, V. (1992), *Tracking Adult Learning Routes*. Leicester: NIACE.

— (2002), *A Question of Value: Achievement and Progress in Adult Learning*. Leicester: NIACE and DfES.

McNair, S. (1997), 'Is there a crisis? Does it matter?', in R. Barnett and A. Griffin (eds), *The End of Knowledge in High Education*. London: Cassell.

Marsh, C. (1982), *The Survey Method*. London: Allen & Unwin.

Martin, I. (2001), 'Lifelong learning – for earning, yawning and yearning', *Adults Learning*, 13, (2). Leicester: NIACE.

Maskell, D. (2001), 'Standard swindles', *The Times Higher Education Supplement*, 23 March. London: Times Newspapers.

Maslow, A. H. (1968), *Towards a Psychology of Being*. Princeton, NJ: Van Nostrand.

Melia, T. (2001), 'Quality assurance in education and training: its recent history', *College Research*, 4, (2). London: Learning and Skills Development Agency.

Meziro, J. (1998), 'Cognitive processes: contemporary paradigms of learning', in P. Sutherland (ed.), *Adult Education: A Reader*. London: Kogan Page.

Ministry of Reconstruction (1918), *Committee on Adult Education Interim Report*. London: HMSO, p. 5, cited in P. Jarvis (2001), *The Age of Learning*. London: Kogan Page.

— (1919), *Adult Education Committee, Final Report*. London: HMSO, p. 5, cited in P. Jarvis (2001), *The Age of Learning*. London: Kogan Page.

Nagel, T. (1982), 'Libertarianism without foundation', in P. Jeffrey (ed.), *Reading Nozick*. Oxford: Blackwell.

National Advisory Group for Continuing Education and Lifelong Learning (NAGCELL) (1997), *Learning for the Twenty-First Century* (NAGCELL First Report). London: NAGCELL.

— (1999), *Creating Learning Cultures: Next Steps in Achieving the Learning Age*. (NAGCELL Second Report). London: NAGCELL.

National Association for Teachers in Further and Higher Education (NATFHE) (1992), *A Question of Quality*. London: NATFHE.

Newman, M. (1979), *The Poor Cousin: A Study of Adult Education*. London: George Allen & Unwin.

Norris, C. (1985), 'Towards a theory of participation in adult education', *Adult Education*, 58, (2). Leicester: NIACE.

Office for Standards in Education (Ofsted) (1995), *Inspecting Youth Work: Inspecting Adult Education*. London: Ofsted.

Office of the Deputy Prime Minister (ODPM) (2002), *The Learning Curve: Developing Skills and Knowledge for Neighbourhood Renewal.* London: Neighbourhood Renewal Unit, ODPM.

Oliver, P. (ed.) (1996), *Lifelong Learning and Continuing Education: What is a Learning Society?* Aldershot: Ashgate Arena.

Paterson, R. W. K. (1979), *Values, Education and the Adult.* Boston: Routledge and Kegan Paul.

— (1989), 'Philosophy and adult education' in B. P. Bright, *Theory and Practice in the Study of Adult Education: The Epistemological Debate.* London: Routledge.

Pedler, M. (ed.) (1983), *Action Learning in Practice.* Aldershot, Gower.

Peters, R. S. (1967), *The Concept of Education.* London: Routledge & Kegan Paul.

Phillips, E. M. and Pugh, D. S. (1987), *How to Get a PhD.* Milton Keynes: Open University Press.

Powell, B. (1991), *Measuring Performance in the Education of Adults.* Leicester: UDACE.

Preston, J. & Hammond, C. (2002), *The Wide Benefits of FE: Practitioner Views.* London: Centre for Research on the Wider Benefits of Learning.

Pring, R. A. (1995), *Closing the Gap.* London: Hodder & Stoughton.

Purdey, M. and Gale, P. (1988), *The Adult Education and Training Manual, Vol. 1,* Lancaster: Framework Press.

Ranson, S. (1994), *Towards the Learning Society.* London: Cassell.

Revans, R. (1983), 'Action learning: its origins and nature', in M. Pedler (ed.), *Action Learning in Practice.* Aldershot: Gower.

Riddell, S., Baron, S. and Wilson, A. (2001), *The Learning Society and People with Learning Difficulties.* Bristol: Policy Press.

Rogers, A. (1986), *Teaching Adults.* Milton Keynes: Open University Press.

Rogers, C. (1974), *Freedom to Learn.* Westerville, Ohio: Merrill.

Rogers, J. (1971), *Adults Learning.* Harmondsworth: Penguin Books.

Rowland, S. (2001), Extract from inaugural lecture, University College, London, cited in *The Times Higher Educational Supplement*, December 21–28. London: Times Newspapers.

Russell, L. (1973), *Adult Education: A Plan for Development* (The Russell Report). London: HMSO.

Sallis, E. (1990), *The National Quality Survey* (Mendip Papers 009). Bristol: The Staff College.

— (1995), *The Industrial and Philosophical Origins of Quality Assurance* (Mendip Papers 075). Bristol: The Staff College.

Sargant, N. (1991), *Learning and 'Leisure'.* Leicester: NIACE.

Sargant, N. with Field, J., Francis, H., Schuller, T. and Tuckett, A. (1997), *The Learning Divide*. Leicester: NIACE.

Scarlett, C. and Winner, A. (1995), 'Quality issues in informal women's education in the voluntary sector', *Adults Learning*, 7, (3). Leicester: NIACE.

Schuller, T., Byner, J., Green, A., Blackwell, L., Hammond, C., Preston, J. and Gough, M. (2001), *Modelling and Measuring the Wider Benefits of Learning: A Synthesis* (Wider Benefits of Learning Papers No. 1). London: Institute of Education and Birkbeck College, Centre for Research on the Wider Benefits of Learning.

Scott, D. and Usher, R. (1996), *Understanding Educational Research*. London: Routledge.

Simpson, E. L. (1980), 'Adult learning theory: a state of the art', in H. Lasker, J. Moore and E. L. Simpson (eds), *Adult Development and Approaches to Learning*. Washington, DC: National Institute of Education.

Skinner, B. F. (1971), *Beyond Freedom and Dignity*. New York: Knopf.

Small, N. (ed.) (1992), *The Learning Society: Political Rhetoric and Electoral Reality for Lifelong Learning*. (Papers by Fowler, G., Molyneaux, F. and Taylor, J.) Nottingham: Association for Lifelong Learning.

Smith, J. and Spurling, A. (2001), *Understanding Motivation for Lifelong Learning*. London: Campaign for Learning.

Spours, K. (ed.) (1996), *Value-added Strategies for Raising Attainment and Achievement*. London: Institute of Education Post-16 Education Centre.

Squires, G. (1981), *Cognitive Styles and Adult Learning*. Nottingham: University of Nottingham.

Stuart, M. and Thompson, A. (eds) (1995), *Engaging With Difference: The 'Other' in Adult Education*. Leicester: NIACE.

Sutherland, P. (ed.) (1998), *Adult Education: A Reader*. London: Kogan Page.

Taylor, R. (1996), 'Preserving the liberal tradition in "New times"', in J. Wallis (ed.), *Liberal Adult Education: the End of an Era?* Nottingham: Continuing Education Press, University of Nottingham.

Tennant, M. (1997) *Psychology and Adult Learning* (2nd edn). London: Routledge.

The Times (1991), 'Flowers of the realm' (leader). 9 August. London: Times Newspapers.

Thompson, J. C. (ed.) (1980), *Education for a Change*. London: Hutchinson.

Thorndike, E. L. (1928), *Adult Learning*. London: Macmillan.

Thorpe, M., Edwards, R. and Hanson, A. (eds) (1993), *Cultures and Processes of Adult Learning*. London: Routledge/Open University Press.

Tight, M. (1983), *Education for Adults, Vol. 1 Adult Learning and Education*. London: Croom Helm.

— (1991), *Higher Education: A Part-time Perspective*. Buckingham: SRHE/Open University Press.

— (1996), *Key Concepts in Adult Education and Training*. London: Routledge.

Titmus, C. J. (ed.) (1989), *Lifelong Learning for Adults: An International Handbook*. Oxford: Pergammon.

Tough, A. T. (1971), *The Adult's Learning Projects*. Toronto: Ontario Institute for Studies in Education.

Training and Enterprise National Council (TEC) (1997), *A Lifetime of Learning, a Lifetime of Work: Developing a Learning Society*. London: TEC.

Tuckett, A. (1997), *Lifelong Learning in England and Wales: An Overview and Guide to Issues Arising from the European Year of Lifelong Learning*. Leicester: NIACE.

— (2002), 'Look out for the smaller fish in the big pond', *The Times Educational Supplement*, 25 October. London: Times Newspapers.

Tuckman, B. W. (1972), *Conducting Educational Research*. New York: Harcourt Brace Javanovich.

Tuckman, B. W. and Jensen, M. (1977), 'Stages of small group development', *Groups and Organisational Studies*, 2, (4).

Tuijnman, A. and Schuller, T. (eds) (1999), *Lifelong Learning Policy and Research*. London: Portland Press.

Uden, T. (1994), *The Will to Learn: Individual Commitment to Adult Learning*. Leicester: NIACE.

Uden, T. (1996), *Widening Participation: Routes to a Learning Society*. Leicester: NIACE.

UNESCO (1999), *Learning: the Treasure Within* (Report to UNESCO International Commission on Education for the Twenty-first Century). Paris: UNESCO Publishing.

Unit for the Development of Adult Continuing Education (UDACE), (1989) *Performance Indicators and the Education of Adults*. Leicester: NIACE.

Urwin, D. (ed.) (1985), *Fitness for Purpose – Essays in Higher Education by Christopher Ball*. London: SRHE/NFER-NELSON.

Usher, R. and Edwards, R. (1996), 'Liberal adult education and the postmodern movement', in J. Wallis (ed) *Liberal Adult Education:*

the End of an Era? Nottingham: Continuing Education Press, University of Nottingham.

Usher, R., Bryant, I. and Johnson, R. (1997), *Adult Education and the Postmodern Challenge.* London: Routledge.

Verner, C. (1964) 'Definitions of terms', in G. Jensen, A. Liverwright and W. C. Hillerbeck (eds), *Adult Education: Outcomes of Emerging Field of University Study.* Washington, DC: Adult Education Association of the USA.

Wagner, L. (1998), *The Radical Implications of Lifelong Learning* (Philip Jones Memorial Lecture, 12 March). Leicester: NIACE.

Wallis, J. (ed.) (1996), *Liberal Adult Education: The End of an Era?* Nottingham: Continuing Education Press, University of Nottingham.

Weil, S. and McGill, I. (eds) (1989), *Making Sense of Experiential Learning.* London: Routledge.

Williams, G. L. (1978), *Towards Lifelong Education: A New Role for Higher Education Institutions.* Paris: UNESCO.

Williamson, B. (1998), *Lifeworlds and Learning: Essays in the Theory, Philosophy and Practice of Lifelong Learning.* Leicester: NIACE.

Wiltshire, H. (1956), 'The great tradition in university adult education', *Adult Education,* 29. London: NIAE.

— (1980), 'On being an adult educator', *Studies in Adult Education,* 12, (1). Leicester: NIACE.

Young, M. (2000), 'Bringing knowledge back in: towards a curriculum for lifelong learning', in A. Hodgson (ed.), *Policies, Politics and the Future of Lifelong Learning.* London: Kogan Page.

Index

Lightning Source UK Ltd.
Milton Keynes UK
UKOW030614250412

191417UK00002B/7/P